COMPUTER SECURITY MANAGEMENT

COMPUTER
SECURITY
MANAGEMENT

DENNIS VAN TASSEL

University of California
Santa Cruz, California

PRENTICE-HALL, INC.
Englewood Cliffs, New Jersey

Library of Congress Cataloging in Publication Data

Van Tassel, Dennis
    Computer security management.

    (Prentice-Hall series in automatic computation)
    Bibliography: p. 192-212
    1. Electronic data processing departments
    —Security measures. I. Title.
HR5548.2V33   658.7'7   70-39392
ISBN 0-13-165464-0

Printed in the United States of America

Prentice-Hall International, Inc., London
Prentice-Hall of Australia, Pty. Ltd., Sydney
Prentice-Hall of Canada, Ltd., Toronto
Prentice-Hall of India Private Limited, New Delhi
Prentice-Hall of Japan, Inc., Tokyo

To
Eric and Sonia

PREFACE

This book is written for those interested in computer security. Computer security is not just a one-man job. If a computer center is to maintain a desired level of security, all the staff must be aware of the special security needs of a computer center. Managers, system analysts, programmers, auditors, operators, and clerical personnel—all have a part to play in computer security.

As computers grow in their importance in organizations the need to protect against sabotage, fire, flood, and fraud increases. Recent years have disclosed multi-million-dollar frauds and disasters in computer centers. Some organizations have been ruined after computer-center irregularities. Other organizations have recovered only with great difficulty.

Computer security is a type of insurance. Needs must be evaluated. The amount and type of risk to be assumed must be intellectually arrived at after careful study of the risks involved. This book provides the information necessary to evaluate and provide security for your computer center.

The first chapter will help motivate the reader by illustrating many of the computer-related crimes that have been committed in the past. Each of the following chapters has a checklist that can be used to evaluate your present security level and needs. These checklists also provide a summary of the major points covered in each chapter.

The book covers the subject of past crimes and disasters, company security, embezzlement, EDP controls, auditability, program security, cryptographic techniques, disaster protection, insurance, service bureau relations, and time-sharing security.

The author has attempted to treat the management of computer security as thoroughly and accurately as possible. But I am sure I have overlooked some problem areas and solutions. For that reason, I would be very happy to hear from any readers who would like to suggest improvements for later editions.

Dennis Van Tassel

University of California
Santa Cruz, California

CONTENTS

COMPUTER SECURITY MANAGEMENT

COMPUTER CRIME

One very positive sign in man's existence comes from an unlikely source, that is, his ability to commit criminal acts no matter how difficult the circumstances. He escapes from escape-proof prisons, tampers with tamper-proof devices, and burglarizes burglar-proof establishments. No level of technology has found itself above the ingenuity of a clever, albeit dishonest, mind, not even the computer.

These examples of larceny under difficult circumstances illustrate Dansiger's basic rule: "Whenever something is invented, someone, somewhere, immediately begins trying to figure out a method to beat the invention." Computerized larceny has several advantages over regular old style larceny. Actually, the plain and obvious fact is that computerized larceny is seldom discovered and usually difficult to prosecute even if it is discovered. And since the details are not yet common knowledge perhaps it is worth reconstructing them here, to establish a broad pattern of its development. To start with, address customer files are copied

*Reprinted from AFIPS Conference Proceedings, 1970.

usually with the help of the owner's computer, thus adding insult to injury. Once they are copied the files are sold to a competitor, and if the competitor uses the files discreetly no one is the wiser, except maybe the sales manager who notices that one company has suddenly become quite aggressive.

Many thefts are simply a by-product of a computer. An example is the computer operator who steals a hundred checks, prints them on a computer on Friday night, cashes them during the weekend, and skips town on Monday. This is not really computerized stealing since the fault lies in the safety of the checks and not the computer. But the crime is usually still blamed on the computer even though a manual check-writing machine could have been used just as well.

There are several mythical examples of computer crime. I call them mythical because they actually did happen, but the victim of the crime was usually so embarrassed to admit he had been taken so easily, that rather than suffer humiliation, he would prefer to hush up the crime. The first mythical example supposedly took place in a large bank when computers were first being used. An alert programmer noticed that the interest is calculated to the nearest cent and then truncated. That is, if the interest is calculated out to be 2.3333 . . . it is simply left at 2.33—thus contributing nicely to the bank profits. The programmer simply fixed the computer to add some of the truncated portion to his account and in a short while ended up with a very sizable bank account. All the time the customer accounts stayed in balance. Eventually he was caught by bank auditors who noticed he was withdrawing large sums and not making similar deposits.

Another enterprising young man who received his first set of bank depositors' slips with magnetically imprinted account numbers on the bottom, correctly surmised that the new computer system probably only checked the magnetically imprinted account numbers on the bottom of the checks. So he promptly went to his bank and carefully dispersed his full supply of imprinted slips among the neat stacks at the bank desk. Not too surprisingly, the slips were used all day by customers making deposits, and even less surprisingly, the man stopped in the following morning and closed his account, which had mushroomed to over $50,000, and has not been seen since. Needless to say, this scheme no longer works.

Crime, like any other business, offers the highest rewards to those who are first to try out a new method.

One of the more interesting aspects of this case is the fact that even though the fault was the improper design of the computer system, the computer was the scapegoat. Using the computer as a scapegoat is a common present-day phenomenon. Election returns are miscalculated and the computer is blamed when it is really the fault of the programmer. The next time a businessman blames the computer for an error, ask him if he doesn't have people telling the computer what to do. It is safe to assume that if the computer is unreliable, so is the rest of the business, especially today when most businesses depend so heavily on computers.

Since the computer cannot defend itself, nor prove the accuser at fault, it is safer to blame the computer than another person. This common acceptance of the computer as a "giant uncontrollable brain" has led to at least one very successful embezzlement. Three employees (an account executive, a margin clerk, and a cashier) of the Beaumont, Texas, office of E. F. Hutton & Co., a major New York securities firm, allegedly used the computer as a scapegoat while they were milking customer accounts for more than half a million dollars over a period of several years. They were finally caught in 1968.

This enterprising trio skimmed funds from customer accounts. Every time a client noticed that his accounts were incorrect, the customer was allegedly told that the "dumb computer" had made a mistake, a fable which received instant credibility. The computer all the time was giving the correct results, but the excuse covered up the fraud.

Nine years earlier, between 1951 and 1959, another broker-age firm, Walston & Co., was electronically siphoned of $250,000. By the time the theft was uncovered, the thief had become vice-president. Frank, a manager of a back-office operation, programmed Walston's data processing system to transfer money from a company account to two customer accounts—his and his wife's.

Even though his scheme was extremely simple it nevertheless rates a niche in the history of data processing crime. He simply went into the office on a Sunday morning and punched up cards to transfer money from a company account to two customers'—his own and his wife's accounts. The system was further programmed to show the money had gone to purchase stock for the two accounts. Next, he sold the supposedly purchased stock, pocketed the cash, and transferred some more money.

The only reason he got caught was because he withdrew a huge sum of money right before the end of the year, thus cheating himself out of the interest. The company was suspicious and examined his accounts. Obviously, they found major irregularities, but they were unable to figure out the embezzling system, mainly because Frank hadn't stolen any money from customers' accounts. "What he did was absolutely undetectable without internal auditing," said William D. Fleming, Walston president. "Before it happened no one dreamed such a thing could be done, and if he hadn't explained how he did it, we probably still wouldn't know."

Like most people, Frank took pride in his work and he showed the auditors how he managed this smooth embezzlement. The embezzler had been with the company for years and had the most thorough knowledge of the data processing system in the firm. Embezzlers who can repay the stolen money seldom go to jail, and since Frank couldn't repay the money he served a year in Sing Sing prison.

At the same time Walston & Company was learning a few things about data processing that computer salesmen usually overlook, another brokerage firm, Carlisle & Jacqueline, was being bilked out of $81,000. Richard D., data processing manager of Carlisle & Jacqueline, instructed the computer to write checks to fictitious persons and send them to his home address. Again a little bad luck stopped this scheme. The post office accidently returned one of the checks to the firm and the clerk who received it blew the whistle. George Muller, a managing partner of Carlisle and Jacqueline, refused to discuss the case. "We'd have to be crazy to give out all the details now so that anyone who wanted to could do it again," says Mr. Muller. The embezzler was convicted, repaid the money, and received a suspended sentence.

In this more recent example it was again only an accident that the computer embezzlement was discovered. In the following case lady fortune smiled with favor on a programmer, Milo, and frowned on the National City Bank of Minneapolis. Milo had a very bad credit rating and occasionally wrote checks on an empty account, but the data processing service center where Milo worked had just been hired to computerize the check-handling system at the bank where he had his account. While writing programs to warn the bank of customers with empty accounts and incoming checks he simply programmed the computer to not report his personal checks any time his accounts had insufficient funds to cover them. The program allowed each of his bad checks to clear the bank.

The only reason the scheme was discovered was because the computer broke down and the bank was forced to process the checks by hand, and without warning in came one of Milo's checks. The check bounced and the scheme was discovered. The check-bouncing programmer pleaded guilty in 1966, repaid the money, and received a suspended sentence.

Most criminal uses of computers are by individuals, but organized crime has not overlooked the possibility of large profits through the use of computerized embezzlement. There are already at least two cases of large-scale criminal use. In 1968, a Diners' Club credit card fraud resulted in at least a $1,000,000 loss to the credit card company. A computer printout of real Diners' Club customers was used by the gang to make up phony credit cards having real names and account numbers on blank Diners' Club cards. According to the police, the computer listing was stolen in 1967 by Alfonse in New York. At the same time 3,000 credit cards disappeared. After the crime was discovered Alfonse was rubbed out in a gangland-style murder.

The forged credit cards were sold along with other forged identification documents for $85 to $150 per ID package to persons engaged in motor vehicle thefts. Federal agents said that the forged cards were often used to finance a leisurely trip to Atlanta, Georgia, with a stolen car, followed by an air trip home, by way of Miami, Florida.

The most interesting aspect of this case is the sophisticated level of organization. The gang found out that the club's computers were programmed to reject only false names and/or numbers, so the first indication of fraud often didn't come until the real customer received his bill and complained. Thus, ID packages would be completely safe for thirty to sixty days with almost no risk to the user.

Federal agents said that Las Vegas casinos may have been

bilked out of hundreds of thousands of dollars after granting credit on the basis of forged Diners' Club credit cards. However, federal agents also said that if any hotel wanted to cooperate in underworld "skimming" of profits, this could be a method of operations since bad credit losses are tax deductible.

In another case a computer was used by a crime organization to embezzle over $1,000,000 in Salinas, California, before the owner was caught in 1968. A service bureau owner, Robert, used his computer to budget embezzlements so smoothly that he was able to take a quarter of a million dollars within a year from a fruit and vegetable firm without the loss being noticed.

Robert was an accountant and he noticed that the fruit company had no complete audit operation. His method included having the computer calculate just how much should be embezzled during a specific period. He did this by using false and real data in different computer runs and by comparing the results on the cost of produce, and this way was able to keep all operation costs and profits in balance. The only reason he was caught was because a small-time bank became suspicious of the size of a check made out to a labor organization. Robert was sentenced to from one to ten years for grand theft and forgery.

Banks have traditionally been cautious when protecting their money from embezzlement, so it is not surprising that there have been few examples of computer-related crime, but a recent example shows that they also can be victims. In 1970 it was discovered that a total of $900,000 was taken from the National Bank of North America and a branch of Bankers Trust Company in New York.

The scheme involved five men, including three brothers, a bank vice-president and an assistant branch manager.

The brothers were allegedly able to manipulate bank funds without the banks' computers detecting them by making out deposit slips for cash transactions when they were actually depositing checks, according to the district attorney's office.

Since cash transactions are recorded as immediate deposits, checks subsequently drawn were covered by the false cash deposits.

If the deposits were made as checks, the computers would not credit the money to the account immediately. When checks were drawn, the computer would indicate insufficent funds with an uncollected check on deposit, a spokesman for the district attorney's office said.

Two companies were involved in the operation of the scheme, according to the district attorney's office. Bay Auto Sales had an account at the National Bank of North America, and Baywood Stables had an account at the Bankers Trust, both in Jamaica, Queens.

The brothers were members of both companies. The scheme was uncovered when a bank messenger failed to deliver a bundle of checks to the clearing house, leaving $440,000 worth of checks uncovered. According to authorities the scheme had been going on for four years.

As the three previous examples show, organized crime has already discovered the possibilities available in criminal use of computers but so far no really big embezzlements have been discovered. Yet several very ripe possibilities exist. One of the most obvious is in the area of large payrolls in companies as in the old story about the bar that was losing money. When a check was run, it was noticed that the bartender rang up each sale on one of four registers. Of course, when it was discovered the owner had only three registers, the problem was solved.

Similar schemes have been used with payrolls. Either friends or fictitious people are paid extra amounts each week. This is especially easy if there is a high turnover of help, or lots of overtime, or piece work pay. Another payroll trick is to deduct extra amounts for tax or other payroll deductions each week and transfer the money to your account. Then at the end of the year calculate everyone's deductions correctly for income tax purposes. The only way someone could catch this is to save all your weekly payroll stubs and see if the deductions add up correctly at the end of the year. People have a tendency to believe the veracity of a computer printout, but careful observation shows that computer programmers and auditors usually sit down each week and calculate their pay to see if it is actually correct. Just a couple of years ago an engineer of an aerospace firm calculated his own interest on his bank account and noticed that it was incorrectly calculated by the bank—in the bank's favor. After several letters the bank decided to humor the guy and check out his account and sure enough the customer was correct. No one had thought to question the computer. When is the last time you calculated your bank interest or paycheck to see if it was correct?

Another area of computer crime which is especially vulnerable is in the area of payroll manipulation. This fact is known by most auditors so payrolls are usually audited rather closely. There was at least one case where a large payroll theft was committed. A group of young men manipulated the computers of the Human Resources Administration in New York City in order to divert over $2.7 million from the anti-poverty program budget. Over a period of nine months false pay checks were made out to 40,000 non-existent youth workers. It is estimated that up to 30 people may have been involved in the scheme.

We have already seen one example of a computer being used to calculate how much to embezzle in the Salinas, California, case. Police can expect to see more of this since organized crime has both the money and the know-how for computer usage. Some of the ways in which computers are used to prevent crime include the analysis of payrolls for excessive overtime pay, or the analysis of inventories for excessive breakage, or selection of any large change in price of items being purchased or sold. All these could be mistakes or legitimate changes, but they could also be an indication of embezzlement.

The use of breakage or tolerance allowances is another especially vulnerable area for computerized stealing. Most companies such as warehouses or department stores have a shrinkage allowance to cover items which are lost, broken, or the result of bookkeeping errors. But if a programmer modified the shrinkage allowance at the same time a large-scale theft was going on, the theft would probably not be noticed. Once the theft was completed the shrinkage allowance could be reset to its original level. The previous examples of crime have been just criminals modifying the old techniques for the field of crime. But computers have brought forth a new era of crime. This is already evident in the case when a computer was used to calculate how much to embezzle. But there are areas of crime which are unique to the computer field.

A June, 1968, Baltimore headline stated that "Computer Gambling" was taking place in the Social Security Administration. But an investigation showed that all that was happening was

80-column cards were being used in the passing of wagers in the numbers racket by a data processing operator. The possibility of computerized gambling is quite real because blackjack and roulette programs that work quite well are available. The only thing holding the computer back is most people prefer the friendly blackjack dealer or the spin of the roulette wheel.

There has always been a rather good market in hot computer gear such as cards, tapes, or disks but because of their size, stolen computers have not until recently entered the picture. In early 1969 a $2,500 Wang Computer disappeared from the Argonne National Laboratories. It was later traced to Iowa State University by the FBI. A student working in a training program of Argonne had fallen in love with his Wang computer and took it back to college to do his homework. However, as computers decrease in size we can expect to hear of more stolen computers.

Not only is there a good market in computer gear, but also many a computer hour has been quietly sold by a third-shift operator or a dishonest electronic data processing (EDP) manager. Quite often the buyer is even in direct competition to the establishment where the time is "stolen" since one's competitor would have the most suitable machine and software. In late 1967, the Chicago Board of Education accused five employees of its data processing bureau of setting up their own data processing firm while using the Board's equipment. These five, who have since resigned, allegedly were operating equipment during slow hours and had been doing business with many reputable firms in the city.

The state investigating office found itself in a legal quagmire when becoming involved in this case, since matters involving computer misuse, especially any unauthorized use, are so new there are very few precedents to guide lawyers as to whether something like this could be considered criminal.

In addition to answering the veracity of the accusation, the following questions must be answered. Does the use of an unmetered scanner—paid for but not in use—by those authorized to use it for the Board but who use it for non-Board business constitute a crime?

The most common theft in the computer business is in the area of software. Programs can be copied and sold and the copier is almost guaranteed immunity from any legal action since the original never disappears. Competitors sometimes hire programmers on the hope that even if the programmers won't bring any software with them they will at least bring all the software ideas with them to their new jobs. There is no way to estimate software thefts because they are so seldom discovered and quite often are not even of concern to the loser.

One rather large software theft case came to light on the British computer scene. The case involved the biggest commercial installation in progress in Europe, the state-financed airline BOAC. The programming projects involved $100 million programmed on 360/50's and 700 Ferranti terminal displays. The *London Times* in April, 1968, printed a short story which revealed that BOAC was investigating the circumstances in which some employees had expropriated information for consultative work.

The alleged plagiarism included a combination of IBM's PARS (Programmed Airline Reservation System) and the corporation's own $7 million investment in software.

Another software house was implicated as the receivers of the information. It has not been determined whether any legal action will be taken, but company disciplinary measures have already been taken against employees.

Another software theft which was discovered took place in Texas. In this case the man was prosecuted criminally for taking computer programs. He worked for a company that developed geophysical programs for oil companies. Each program had a value of about $50,000. He took programs home to work on them and kept copies of them. Within a short time he had 50 programs and convinced his roommate to approach a major oil company with the programs. The oil company acted like it was interested and cooperated with the police in accumulating evidence. Both the programmer and his roommate were tried and convicted and both received five-year prison sentences.

The Internal Revenue Service has long heralded their computers as devices to prevent income fraud so there was some poetic justice involved in the discovery in June, 1970, that these same computers had been used to embezzle money.

No programming frauds have been discovered, but clerical staff has been discovered manipulating input documents.

One would-be computer embezzler was an adjustment clerk

who came upon information that some tax credits were not being claimed, possibly because they had been misfiled.

Through data she prepared for the computer, she transferred the credits from one taxpayer's account to another. Each time the credit was recorded, she transferred it to another account. When she felt sure she had covered her trail enough, she credited the tax credit to a relative and refund checks for $1,500 were duly issued.

The embezzlement was uncovered when the IRS Inspection Service, pursuing its regular audit program, came across a complaint from a taxpayer who claimed he had never gotten credit for $1,500 he had paid.

Another misbehaving computer clerk was caught through a banker's alertness. This clerk had manipulated records and established a false tax credit from a true taxpayer for a relative. When the relative took the refund check to the local bank, the banker became suspicious about the size of the refund and alerted IRS.

Inspectors retraced the path of the check back to its source and found the document effecting the transfer to the relative.

Recently a news item reported that a spy had turned over to Communist East Germany business information on over 3,000 West German companies. A former data processing department employee made duplicates of tapes stored at his company's leased-time facility and passed these behind the Iron Curtain.

And last but not least, there was the young man who simply changed the program to accept the last card of the file as the final total. This was accepted by the company because no one had time to check out the computer totals. His only mistake was that he went skiing one weekend and broke his leg.

CONCLUSION

If better protection measures for computer information are not developed soon, the examples in this chapter will seem small in comparison to the new crimes that will take place. I have purposely skipped all examples of sabotage, accidents (man-made or natural), errors and information thefts that could occur with computers. The future holds a real gold mine for a criminal who specializes in manipulating or stealing computer information. One good computer raid could have an immense payoff. If there is any truth in the wise old saying that we should be able to learn from our mistakes, hopefully this short history of computer-related crime will alert us and help us to prevent crime in the future.

References

Aaron, W. "Embezzlement-detection and control," Speech before the National Retail Merchants Association EDP Conference, 1968.

Adelson, A. M. "Computer bandits", TRUE, February 1969, pp. 50, 74-77.

Adelson, A. M. "Whir, blink-jackpot!" WALL STREET JOURNAL, April 5, 1968, pp. 1, 15.

Allen, B. "Danger ahead, safeguard your computer", HARVARD BUSINESS REVIEW, November-December 1968, pp. 98-101.

"Calculated computer errors manipulate three banks' security; $1 million lost" COMPUTERWORLD March 25, 1970, p. 1.

"Computer takes rap in securities swindle", DATAMATION August 1968, p. 111.

Dansiger, J. "Embezzling primer", COMPUTERS AND AUTOMATION, November 1967, pp. 41-43.

"Diners club fraud involved printout", COMPUTERWORLD September 18, 1968, p. 1.

"Employee accused of illegal computer use", DATAMATION December 1967.

"FBI tracks wandering Wang", BUSINESS AUTOMATION April 1969, p. 38.

"Fortifying your business security" THE OFFICE August 1969, pp. 39-52.

"Individual responsibility", DATA SYSTEMS NEWS 10: 2, February 1969, p. 4.

Ottenberg, M. "Electronic tax fraud investigated at IRS," THE EVENING STAR Washington, DC, June 24, 1970, p. A-1.

"Program plagiarism alleged in UK case", DATAMATION June 1968, p. 91.

"$1 million embezzlement arranged by accountant", COMPUTERWORLD 1969.

COMPANY
SECURITY

Whether it is a gigantic complex such as one in Washington, D.C., or a small college computer center, computer security should be part of a total security program. If security just centers around the computer, any industrial thief can simply concentrate on undefended portions of the company such as non-computer files, computer input documents, dishonest employees, or waste documents. He will still get the information he wants. The same security program that protects computer integrity also prevents industrial espionage, sabotage, theft, vandalism, and pilferage.

Recent crime statistics show that 75% of crimes against persons were closed by arrest, but only 22% of crimes against property ended with an arrest. If we consider information thefts or manipulations, it is safe to assume the percentage of crimes even discovered is less than 22%. Illegal information manipulation includes snooping through personnel records on office rivals, modifying payroll records, or modifying a personal or a friend's credit record. While businesses are somewhat on guard against removal of physical objects, they are not usually aware of information thefts or manipulations and, consequently, do not think about it until something is missed.

BASIC SECURITY PRECAUTIONS*

A. Doors, door frames, and door locks
☐ 1. Solid core doors are preferable to panel doors or doors with glass pane.
☐ 2. Thin paneled or hollow cored doors should be lined with metal sheets.
☐ 3. Glass paneled doors should be covered with closely spaced steel bars or with strong mesh on the inside of the door.
☐ 4. If there is glass in the door, the unlocking of the door from the inside should require a key and not simply a turnpiece. In the jargon of locksmiths, the lock should be "keyed from within."
☐ 5. Exterior door hinges should have non-removable hinge pins.
☐ 6. If the door is sufficiently strong but the door frame is weak, a lock should be used whose security does not depend on the door frame for mounting.
☐ 7. Door locks should have a deadbolt feature and should be used in conjunction with pick resistant key cylinder.
☐ 8. Spring latches are not effective unless fitted with a dead locking feature.
☐ 9. If a padlock is used, it should be of a pick resistant quality and should have a hardened shackle. All identification numbers should be removed from the padlock before use.
☐ 10. Overhead doors should be locked either by electric power or slide bolts and/or a pick resistant cylinder lock.
☐ 11. Elevator doors opening directly into offices or unguarded areas should be equipped with key controlled locks.
☐ 12. Where it is necessary that "panic bars" be used on doors (like a movie theater fire door) the panic bar should have an alarm feature which will indicate when the door is opened during business hours.

B. Windows
☐ 1. All windows other than those providing access to fire escapes should be secured by ferry gates, bars, or mesh which cannot be removed from without or by key controlled inside locks.
☐ 2. Windows leading to fire escapes should be equipped with key controlled inside locks.
☐ 3. Outside hinged windows should have non-removable hinge pins.

C. Hatchways
☐ 1. Hatchways should be secured from the inside with barrel bolts, padlock and eye or heave hook and eye.

D. Transoms
☐ 1. Transoms should be covered with metal bars or mesh which cannot be removed from without or
☐ 2. Transoms should be secured from the inside with key controlled window locks.

E. Metal Gates
☐ 1. Accordion type gates should be equipped with top and bottom slide tracks and should be locked with a padlock which is pick resistant and which will resist the use of force. Padlocks should have identification numbers removed before use.
☐ 2. Outside hinges should have non-removable hinge pins.

F. Lighting
☐ 1. The interior of the premises should be illuminated throughout the night.
☐ 2. The safe should be well illuminated and easily visible from the street.
☐ 3. The cash register should be left open at night and should be visible from the street.
☐ 4. All outside access points, especially rear and side alley doors, should be well lighted.

G. Safes
☐ 1. When using a safe for a purpose other than the protection of records from fire, use a "chest type" safe. Such safes are designed to protect valuables against burglary.
☐ 2. If the safe is a movable type, remove the wheels and anchor the safe to the floor.

Also, as general practice:
Do not leave a written copy of the combination on the premises.

When an employee resigns or is discharged, change the combination.

On locking the safe spin the dial at least four times.

Make bank deposits as frequently as possible and try not to rely on a safe for the overnight protection of valuables.

H. Alarms
There are several types of alarms:
Central alarm systems which bring a direct response from the police and/or the alarm company are best. They are costly to install and carry a monthly rental.

Electronic alarms are available which telephone a tape recorded message to whomever you designate.

Local alarms ring a bell on the premises. If used the neighbors should be solicited to notify the police when the alarm is activated.

☐ 1. An alarm should not be designed to be deactivated from outside the premises. Use an alarm which employs a time delay feature and de-activization by key from within.

I. Keys
As general practice:
Keys should be possessed only by responsible personnel and by as few personnel as possible and reasonable.

Change the key cylinder whenever a key-holding employee is discharged or resigns, or when a key is lost.

Do not use a system of locks which is master keyed unless absolutely necessary.

Do not leave keys lying around during the day where some unauthorized person can take them and have copies made.

Use of a highly pick resistant key cylinder will generally make key duplication more difficult.

New York City Police Department issued this basic security checklist at an Office Equipment & Systems Group meeting.

*Reprinted from THE OFFICE, August 1969.

The first thing to consider when setting up any security program is who will head it. If a person of low stature is chosen, most employees will circumvent and ignore him, if not ridicule him. A responsible executive should be chosen; one sufficiently high in rank to get things done quickly. The person chosen should be granted decision-making responsibilities and be able to respond in an emergency without consulting others. Since most criminals are experts in their fields, an expert such as a security consultant should be called in to initially aid the company security officer and to determine areas of greatest weaknesses and to recommend the most effective type of safeguard for each situation.

ESTABLISH A SECURITY PROGRAM

Today's crook will steal or tamper with almost anything, including computer gear. Computer gear is a favorite target since it is compact, unserialized, and expensive, but the same safeguards that protect computer gear will also protect expensive office machines. This includes even tab supplies such as paper and data processing cards which are easy to sell and impossible to identify. Phony delivery men or repairmen are a favorite subterfuge for stealing equipment, information, or snooping.

The repairman simply comes to an office during the noon hour, says that he is there to repair a certain item, gives a secretary a phony receipt, and walks out of the building with the desired item. This can be a file cabinet or set of magnetic tapes "which are supposed to be moved." Electric typewriters, electric adding machines, and the new small compact desk computers are favorite targets. The security program should be set up so that all repairmen and delivery men are checked out and prior approval is necessary for removing any company property. If there is no security program, it is not fair to blame an employee for not challenging a bogus repairman. Closed-circuit TV cameras are a deterrent for after hours and out of the way places, but even a TV camera is occasionally stolen.

One of the most elementary areas of security involves intrusion prevention and detection. Among the intrusion preventors are fencing, lighting, locks, perimeter alarms, and guard systems. Detectors can be used to protect warehouse facilities or to protect vacant offices during closed hours. Uniformed guards add to the

INTRUSION PREVENTION

protection since their patrol itineraries can be randomized so as to keep an intruder off guard.

Physical security is the easiest and cheapest form of security if it is planned when a facility is built. But in many of today's research centers open perimeters are in style, giving little physical security.

The best perimeter protection involves walls or chain-link fences with proper lighting around the facility. Light is always one of the best protections against nighttime break-ins. Several types of lighting are available and the Illuminating Engineering Society publishes the AMERICAN STANDARD FOR PROTECTIVE LIGHTING which outlines boundary lighting standards.

In addition to standard perimeter precautions such as proper lighting, fences, and guards, an alarm system is often installed. One of these protective devices consists of a taut, nearly invisible wire strung along the top of a fence or wall and held at a scientifically calibrated tension. Pressure from an intruder or relaxation from being cut will set off either a silent or noisy alarm, notifying authorities of the intruder's presence.

A similar device is a line of plastic tubing concealed under a carpet. Stepping on the tubing causes an alarm to go off. This type of device is difficult to detect before activating it.

Guard Services

Uniformed guards can provide both preventive and follow-up protection. Well-trained professional guards can be hired by the individual company or hired from a recognized guard agency such as Pinkerton, Burns, or Global security systems. The advantage of company-owned guards is less expense and tighter control. But a private guard agency offers the advantages of better trained guards, less personnel worries, and also many auxiliary services such as pre-employment checks for job applicants, security investigations, undercover agents, and temporary additions in patrols during a crisis period.

Alarms and Locks

Today a large variety of alarms is available. They include photo-electric alarms that report any breakage of the light beam, motion detectors that detect any movement by either sound or light rays within the protected area, and premise alarms that go off when a door or window is opened after the alarm has been activated for the night. Other more complicated devices include automatic telephone dialers or complete vibration detection-systems. An expert consultant may recommend a special type of security system.

Alarms can be installed to notify the police, owner, or security guard of any intrusion or fire. Sound-producing alarms such as sirens simply scare away intruders when they go off and they are quite often ignored by most everyone.

One of the oldest and cheapest forms of protection is the old-fashioned, simple lock. Locks like any other protective devices are good only if they are used properly. If expensive security locks are installed but never locked, they are of little use. Or, if many copies of keys are available, little protection is gained. The best lock situation includes good pick-resistance locks allowing for keys to be under absolute control. This means purchasing locks which cannot have a key duplicated at the corner store. The keys and locks are purchased from a lock company with the guarantee that the key pattern is not available as a standard commerical key blank. Thus local locksmiths do not even have the blank keys to duplicate the keys. As an added precaution all keys are stamped with the phrase "Do Not Duplicate."

Locks also offer in-plant security. This means that if one section of the plant is used during weekends, such as the computer center, the rest of the plant can be locked to prevent employees wandering through the rest of the plant during night shifts or weekends.

A new type of lock which can be opened only by an identification card is now available. These locks are constructed so that a record is kept of who opens each door, and locks can be installed so certain ID cards will open only the doors necessary for his function.

Visible identification cards have several other uses, one being to discourage the wandering visitor. The wandering visitor is one of the most common intruders in any computer center. Even though most computer installations have an "Only Authorized Personnel Allowed" sign on the door of the computer room, the rule is seldom enforced because it is impossible to tell who is authorized.

THE WANDERING VISITOR

One of the easiest ways to enforce this rule is to demand that all visitors must be escorted and all employees must have an ID badge.

Personnel can then be encouraged to challenge anyone not wearing a proper badge or anyone with a visitor's badge who is unescorted. Several years ago when I was looking for a different job I used to make it a point to look over the actual computer room before the interview. I succeeded in almost every case, sometimes actually talking to the computer operator about the installation and getting all the shop gossip in the process. Only once was I questioned by a secretary. I just told her I was looking for a restroom; she directed me to it and I left.

Guided tours are good public relations, but they also offer an excellent chance for petty thievery or for an intruder to get an advance layout of a plant. The following situation illustrates what can happen if guided tours are not closely supervised. After a large company had a tour for a ladies' group to their computer center a rather confused lady called up and asked the public relations man if she had done anything wrong by taking a few data processing cards out of a box lying next to the computer during the tour. She said she wanted them for souvenirs, and since there were so many she didn't think it would make any difference. After she got home she had second thoughts and decided she had better give them back. In this case it would have caused only a few hours of research and rerunning to locate the missing cards, but it could have caused some serious trouble. This is only a suggestion of what a knowledgeable malicious wanderer could do.

Another example of how a security program can be circumvented is found in the storage of card files, magnetic tapes, and magnetic discs. Most computer installations usually have strict rules about checking in and out computer files and may have a "Keep Out" sign on the storage room door. But many times—due to pressure to "get things done"—anyone can walk in and take a magnetic tape out. This is especially true during the night shifts where there is less supervision and high danger of theft. Instead of having a clerk check out all tapes needed for the night shifts before going home, the tape storage door is usually just left propped open. This invites disaster from fire or employee dishonesty.

There are now small portable magnetic devices which can be

passed over a magnetic tape or disk which destroy all information stored, and there exists at least one case of its use.

One of man's new and significant security inventions is closed-circuit television (CCTV). There are several types. Some go on only when an alarm is tripped, others are on all the time, and still others are just dummy cameras used to bluff the potential intruder. Some cameras are monitored by a central guard station as in a large warehouse, while others as in banks simply take a film which can be played back either on a routine basis or in case of suspicion. Often there is employee objection to the installation of cameras so this factor must be considered.

Closed-Circuit Television

Other more intricate types of electronic devices include modern bugging equipment. Even though new federal and state laws prohibit the legal sale of the most effective bugs to all except police groups, the bugs are still readily available. Several firms in the U.S. and Mexico sell schematic diagrams for people who want to make their own. And, according to private detectives, the bugs are sometimes advertised and sold as toys.

Bugging Devices

Newspapers, security magazines, and executive-oriented publications regularly have ads displaying electronic surveillance equipment. Investigators Information Service, an electronics firm in Los Angeles, has a sales brochure that lists many bugs. Most of the bugs advertised, however, are sold only to the police.

Examination of this firm's catalog or any similar catalog will reveal a wide selection of bugging aids. One device which sells for $25 and is advertised in various magazines is about the size of a pack of cigarettes, and it will pick up private conversations up to 100 feet away. It transmits through any FM radio and is advertised as a baby sitter or a device to record "trilling bird songs." The advertising literature cautiously points out that surreptitious use is unlawful. This is reminiscent of the wine bricks that were sold during prohibition and were labeled: "This is a decorative wine brick, which if placed in water and warmed will turn into an alcoholic drink. It is against the law to do this."

Bumper beepers are used in spy stories on TV, but they are also easy to make and are presently used by private investigators to track cars. They can be attached to a car in seconds and broadcast a signal received by a matched receiver. Thus someone is able to track a car without keeping it in sight. These are advertised with the message that "they can be used to check the routes and whereabouts of delivery vehicles." It is obvious that they can also be used for many other purposes. A rundown of present bugging devices is best shown on some of the TV spy programs. These shows use presently available devices and are far from being *all* make-believe.

Another more interesting device consists of a long distance "shotgun microphone" which can zero in on a conversation from a distance. Still another device is a telephone mouthpiece identical in appearance to the normal telephone mouthpiece except that it contains a bug which will record all conversations in the room including those not on the telephone. Miniaturization of electronics now includes the famous martini olive bug, cigarette lighter bugs, and microphones almost pin size that can be installed anywhere in seconds. The only defense for a business which is likely to be bugged is to assume bugging is done, and periodically have office checks. Reading one of the books on how to prevent and discover bugs is also a good idea. Stopping bogus repairmen from entering a plant and guarding delicate conversations is only the first step.

Bugging has become so common that congress has passed strict laws against illegal eavesdropping. But even the government has been caught with its bugs down in very embarrassing circumstances. The attorney general's office of Alabama found a bug in his office, for example, and most new police stations have some cells and rooms with bugs in them so they can listen to a hot suspect's conversation with other inmates and occasionally even their lawyers. If this sounds risky, it is only meant to sound that way. Illegal use of bugging devices can result in $10,000 fine and/or five years in jail. But since an industrial spy can expect to get over $10,000 a month from one good client, the penalties are obviously ineffective and prosecution has been largely nonexistent.

Mosler Research Products, Incorporated, Danbury, Connecticut, sells bugging equipment only to federal, state, and municipal agencies, but their catalog lists a wide array of bugging devices and suggests what is available for the industrial spy. Kits are available for bugging and debugging. Debugging has now become a good business which gives some indication of the prevalence of bugging devices, if not the fear of them at least.

Some of the most elementary procedures of keeping industrial secrets include the company's relationship with its employees. Employees must be warned that certain information is confidential. In addition there must be procedures for keeping information secret. These procedures can include sectioning off departments where secrets might be exposed, and then making that area off limits to all but qualified personnel.

Drawings, designs, blueprints, formulas, specifications, or computer reports should carry a restrictive legend. This should state that the data is secret and cannot be reproduced in whole or part or in any form without written authorization.

Coding privileged information will also help prevent unauthorized use. Restrictive legends or codes will not prevent the strongly motivated thief, but they will make his job more difficult and remind the careless employee to be cautious. Also, if no precautions are taken, it is very difficult to have legal grounds for safeguarding trade secrets. The courts expect that reasonable care and precautions in safeguarding secrets be taken. The courts take the view that if you don't take any precautions to guard a secret, why should they!

If most of a company's confidential information is given away to the trade press, or in public relations releases, or papers presented at industry conventions, the right to a trade secret is forfeited. This is similar to the situation of publishing something without a copyright and consequently losing the right to copyright it later.

A very good book by Richard M. Greene, Jr., BUSINESS INTELLIGENCE AND ESPIONAGE (Dow Jones-Irwin, Inc.), gives detailed instructions for setting up and maintaining a perfectly legal business intelligence system. Salesmen, company procedures, government reports, and conventions always provide a wealth of information on business trends and advances. These sources are used by many governments, including our own, to gather economic and military information on friend and foe.

Other procedures besides classifying secrets and controlling press releases include the checking out of prospective employees. Often the most elementary background checking is skipped, even when an applicant is being considered for a sensitive position. Sometimes this is done because of cost or inexperience of the personnel officer, but this oversight is occasionally expensive. One applicant who had been released from jail after an embezzlement

EMPLOYEE SECURITY

conviction was hired in a position where she proceeded to embezzle funds again. Even the most elementary check of the employee's application would have showed that there was a three-year gap in the employment history while she was in prison for embezzlement. Ex-convicts are not necessarily a bad employment risk, but awareness of an employee's record in a security situation is understandably necessary.

With confidential information and normal procedures to protect the physical security of a business, steps should also be taken to protect it from any employee's misuse. This starts when you hire the employee. Ask him to sign a pledge that advises him he will have access to confidential information and that he is expected to keep it that way.

An employer must also be careful that he does not involve himself in a lawsuit. If he hires from a competitor, and puts the employee to work developing a product or some proprietary software similar to what he developed at the previous job, a lawsuit may result. In most cases this doesn't happen, but there have been several of these lawsuits in the computer industry recently.

It is understandably difficult to hire anyone who does not have a few trade secrets, and since the courts allow the employee complete freedom of changing jobs and using his skills, this type of lawsuit is not very common for most employers. Thus, a company lawyer can and should be used to point out any weak spots.

A more realistic problem is an employee who leaves and takes a new job. The departing employee may sign a pledge saying that he has no company property such as computer files, programs, drawings, research reports, or any other type of company property. For employers a signed agreement is the only protection from employees appropriating information or property not their own. This not only offers legal protection, but reminds the employee of his obligation to the company. In today's mobile professional market, an employee who stays over five years in one job is rare and in some professions, such as programmers or system analysts, employees often leave after a year or two.

Unhappy employees are a prime threat to company secrets. Industrial spies know that if they can find someone who has been passed over for promotion several times, or someone who is lowly paid in a sensitive position, or someone heavily in debt because of gambling losses, he is an obvious possibility for bribery, coercion, and even blackmail. This usually starts off innocently by someone asking for some information and paying well for it. Once the employee has done it, he can be blackmailed the second time if necessary. Considering that a good industrial spy may make $10,000 a month plus expenses, he has a lot of resources available to find employees' weak spots. One firm even hires an industrial spy to attempt to obtain their own information—offering a bonus if he can get it in a particular period—thus checking their own security program. This might make a jittery group of employees if they know about it.

Modern business lives on mountains of paper and computers provide additional mountains of paper. These mountains only add to the security problem, and since more and more information is processed today by computer, paper shredding of computer reports is an essential part of any security program. In most large cities the burning of paper trash is forbidden, so paper shredding is the only protection against misuse of discarded confidential files. Telephone listings, customer files, payroll files, research reports, and personnel files are some of the reports that should be destroyed when no longer needed.

BETTER SHRED THAN READ

Part of any security program must be the classification of confidential documents. Programs can be written so that confidential computer reports are labeled. Sometimes this is done so that each page has a confidential label and a destroy date. Labeling with a destroy date facilitates the destruction of the report and reduces expensive storage costs. Since computer centers are notorious for rerunning spoiled reports, a label can remind the computer center to route the bad report to a paper shredder instead of to a close-by waste basket where it can be salvaged by an industrial spy or snoopy employee. At least one company found that a maintenance man was selling material he found in the waste baskets to a competitor. In true dramatic TV form, the firm obtained some revenge by using the man to feed misleading information for awhile before firing him. A similar situation arose when one salvage company offered an extremely low bid for picking up the daily trash from an office. The company was a subsidiary of a competitor and, of course, the contract was turned down.

If your organization handles customer files or even just a list of current purchases, there is probably no surer way to lose a customer than to let one of his reports fall into the hands of someone who shouldn't have it. Paper shredders can be a selling point both to governmental agencies and regular customers. Appendix 2 indicates how long records must be kept before they can be destroyed.

A good disposal policy pays other dividends. Not only does it guarantee that confidential reports will be kept no longer than necessary, thus lowering the chance of misuse, but it also eliminates filing and storage expenses. It costs about $225 a year in floor space and personnel charges to maintain one 4-drawer file cabinet.

CONCLUSION A free manual called INDUSTRIAL SECURITY MANUAL FOR SAFEGUARDING CLASSIFIED INFORMATION, available from the Department of Defense (DOD 5220.22-M), lists many ways to safeguard confidential information. Some of the following points come from this manual:

1. Appoint a responsible individual to supervise and direct security measures.
2. Warn your employees that certain information is confidential and that they are expected to help maintain its confidentiality.
3. Conduct a continuing educational campaign pointing out the danger to jobs, profits, and security by losing trade secrets.
4. Give out only enough confidential information for each employee to function efficiently. Access to confidential information should not be by position but by need to know.
5. Become aware of an use conventional safeguards such as alarms, fencing, locks, proper lighting, and guards.
6. Establish procedures so salesmen, public relation releases, and technical papers do not disclose confidential information.
7. Check out new employees and inform employees when they leave that they are still obligated not to disclose confidential information.

8. Classify and label all confidential documents.
9. Be aware of the possibilities of modern bugging devices and professional industrial spies.
10. Establish proper procedures for destroying paper waste products so they do not fall into the wrong hands.
11. Establish an inventory of company equipment.

These safeguards may seem troublesome, time consuming, or expensive, but the loss of confidential company information can result in loss of contracts, a lawsuit, losing sales or a market, and even financial ruin.

AMERICAN STANDARD PRACTICE FOR PROTECTIVE LIGHTING. **References**
    Illuminating Engineering Society. 345 East 47th Street, New York,
    New York. 1957.
"Area Protection Lighting for Industry." ILLUMINATING ENGINEERING,
    May, 1951, 244-248.
"Fortifying Your Business Security." THE OFFICE, August, 1969, 39-52.
Greene, Richard M., Jr. BUSINESS INTELLIGENCE AND ESPIONAGE,
    Dow Jones-Irwin, Inc., 1966.
Hiles, Richard A. "Paper Shredders," MODERN OFFICE. February, 1963.
Hoover, J. Edgar. "The U.S. Businessman Faces the Soviet Spy," HARVARD
    BUSINESS REVIEW, January, 1964, 140-157.
Hoover, J. Edgar. "Why Reds Make Friends with Businessmen," NATION'S
    BUSINESS, May, 1962.
"How I Steal Company Secrets," BUSINESS MANAGEMENT, October,
    1965, 58-66.
"How Safe Are Your Business Secrets?" BUSINESS MANAGEMENT, March,
    1968, 44-48.
HOW TO AVOID ELECTRONIC EAVESDROPPING AND PRIVACY IN-
    VASION, Investigator's Information Service, 806 S. Robertson Boule-
    vard, Los Angeles, Calif., 1967.
"How Your Company Can Thwart a Spy," BUSINESS MANAGEMENT,
    October, 1965.
"INDUSTRIAL SECURITY MANUAL FOR SAFEGUARDING CLASSFIED
    INFORMATION" (DOD 5220.22-M), Department of Defense, Wash-
    ington, D.C.
Lachter, Lewis E. "Preventing Business-Secret Espionage," ADMINISTRA-
    TIVE MANAGEMENT, December, 1965, 16-19.
Queeny, Jack. "Computer Spies: New Worry for Business," CHICAGO'S
    AMERICAN, January 16, 1969.
Van Tassel, Dennie. "Information Security in a Computer Environment,"
    COMPUTERS AND AUTOMATION, July, 1969.

EMBEZZLEMENT: DETECTION AND CONTROL

Embezzlement is probably as old as the practice of hiring someone to work.

Herodotus tells us that the mason who built the stone treasury of Rameses III built a secret entrance through which he passed nightly to steal a portion of the royal treasury.

In St. Luke, the 16th chapter has a parable of a faithless servant who falsified records in favor of his employer's creditors because he was being fired.

Aristotle refers to the embezzlement of funds by road commissioners and other officials.

Several famous frauds have come from British history. The most famous involved the South Sea Company in 1720. The South Sea Company agreed to repay the public debt of the British government in return for some very favorable overseas trading concessions. By fraudulent means the shares of the company were driven up from 128 pounds to over 1,000 pounds, after which the directors of the company dumped 5,000 shares on unsuspecting buyers. At the same time the cashier absconded with 100,000 pounds. As a result of these chicaneries a parliamentary investigation was held, and Aislabie, Chancellor of the Exchequer, and several members of Parliament were expelled from the House.

More recent embezzlements include a $3,700,000 embezzlement from a bank in Long Beach, California in 1959, a $2,000,000 embezzlement from a bank in Sheldon, Iowa, in 1961 which caused the bank to close its doors, and a large West Coast paper company, in business for over 100 years, bankrupted by a $200,000 embezzlement by its bookkeeper.

Contrary to popular opinion, the government is not immune from embezzlements. The San Francisco mint lost thousands of dollars which five employees stole while pocketing newly minted halves and quarters. And even more recently, the service men's clubs in Vietnam were taken for over a million dollars in a case where no one was ever prosecuted.

Even areas of public trust are not immune to embezzlements. During 1967, an office employee of the Fresno United Crusade was accused of taking $21,000 from Crusade funds. Several union treasuries also have been raided, and a former bursar of the University of Manitoba, a "pillar of a local church," was convicted of a million-dollar embezzlement that halved the university endowment fund in 1933.

Even though embezzlements are commonly reported in news stories, comparatively few embezzlements get into public print. For example, embezzlements of small amounts by clerks, salespersons, and laborers are not sufficiently interesting to warrant publication, and most embezzlements by bonded employees are not published.

Some people attempt to blame the frequency of embezzlement on our capitalistic society, but the existence of embezzlement in countries such as Russia questions the credibility of this criticism. A Russian decree of August 7, 1932, calls for capital punishment for theft of public property. Embezzlement is linked with treason (enemies of the people) as to the seriousness of the offense. But it seems that Russia is not more successful in their prosecution or prevention of embezzlement, even though several embezzlers have actually had the death penalty imposed on them in Russia.

Computers have changed the typical embezzler. Previously the typical embezzler was in his early thirties, married, the father of two children, and stole for a three-year average before being caught. He was an individual with accounting and treasury responsibilities, or a major officer with his firm. His embezzlements usually involved disbursements, receipts, inventory, or payroll.

Today the embezzler is often a person in the computer center, quite often a person of fairly low status in the company. The computer center may even be said to decrease the amount embezzled by non-computer center employees while increasing the portion in the computer center.

Embezzlers are found in all strata of society, vocations, and professions. Embezzlers are seldom professional criminals and are usually older than most other criminals. Embezzlers are also much more successful than other criminals. Embezzlers obtain much more money than other criminals and are seldom caught or prosecuted. Several surety companies have reported that less than one in a hundred employers prosecute an embezzler. Prosecution takes place only where many thousands of dollars are concerned and the case is one of public knowledge.

As already stated, the most distinctive facts regarding embezzlement are the very high frequency of the offense and its incidence in all strata of society. The high frequency of embezzlement seems to indicate that in business there is always something to embezzle, and thus a very large portion of the population has embezzled some amount (usually small) at one time or another. While embezzlement is usually called white-collar crime because white-collar embezzlers usually obtain larger, more newsworthy sums, embezzlers are in fact represented by all classes and groups.

In the United States approximately one billion dollars a year is lost because of employee theft of goods, while another three billion is lost to embezzlement. Recent government hearings estimated that another five million is lost to industrial espionage. This last estimate is too low because a great deal of lost information has no price on it but still is valuable, and information thefts are seldom discovered. Because of the information explosion it is safe to assume that the monetary value of stolen information could soon exceed the value of both stolen goods and money. When goods or money are stolen they are usually insured, but lost information is not insured even though it is a very costly type of theft.

"Knowledge is power" is an old cliche, but it rings truer today than ever before. Examples of information which is valuable if used improperly before it becomes public knowledge include proposed freeway routes or airport sites, or plant or institution sites. Any of these will send land prices soaring. Merger negotiations, proposed stock splits, or law suits can also send stock prices up or down. Research findings, if sold to a competitor, can bring ruin to a company. Credit and legal files can and are used to smear a potential political candidate. Some governmental agencies have acquired power through using their large dossier files. Many of these dossier files are now being computerized.

While information thefts are already an expensive type of business loss they are also connected with the more traditional types of thievery. This is because illegal information manipulation can be used to cover up an embezzlement. Information thefts are valuable only if they can be turned to some advantage. The traditional goal is gaining some cash through embezzlement.

Several criteria indicate that the climate for embezzlement is usually good. The first and most obvious concerns the company itself: there must be something available to steal. The next criterion is that there must be possible opportunity to steal it. This criterion is met by degrees, but even the military establishment which has the tightest and most expensive controls possible has its share of troubles. Even though no security system is foolproof, loose or little control definitely encourages loss.

EMBEZZLEMENT CRITERIA

Some companies fail to use an independent audit. While this may save a little operating expense, it nevertheless opens the possibility for embezzlement. Most embezzlements or thefts take place in establishments that have weak controls. Just as closed circuit television helps prevent and catch bank robbers, good audit procedures help control, prevent, and uncover embezzlements. Since many embezzlements are casual acts with little premeditation, a little tighter control would help prevent this type of theft. Tight controls will also slow down the premeditated thief, making him realize the difficulty being encountered and the possibility of being caught. Unless they are pursuing an altruistic cause of some sort, few people will attempt to steal something if they know they will be caught.

EMBEZZLERS   There are several general types of white-collar embezzlers. The first is the weak individual. He is given the chance to embezzle or steal something simply because of weak management controls. This individual often steals without considering the possible consequences. After doing it once or twice it begins to look easy. This individual might do it only a few times and then stop. This type of dishonesty is common in many people, and if they do it only to a limited extent they usually are not caught. This person is simply a product of a weak personality and weak controls.

The next type of embezzler is the unhappy employee. He is the most common, the most dangerous, and usually the most expensive. If he is caught, it is usually because he has formed a habit and has become sloppy about it, not because it is an isolated event. He may be an executive who was demoted or passed over for promotion. He may be an employee to whom promises were made for a new title, raise in pay, or to improve his status in some other way. But the boss either forgets or changes his mind about the promises, or maybe business conditions or employee actions force a revision of former promises. Then the employee is able to feel that he has been cheated and what he steals is rightly his anyway.

The third type of white-collar thief is the employee who lives beyond his means. He may be a gambler, drug addict, alcoholic, not know how to handle credit, or keep expensive friends. This type is usually the easiest to spot since his personal problems often follow him to work in the form of creditors or he habitually is absent.

The fourth type of embezzler also has a weak personality and is manipulated by someone more powerful. Sometimes blackmail is used to force the victim to do as he is told. Other times the victim is forced to do some little act to pay off a debt, thus becoming more and more involved in petty thievery.

There are several safeguards used by financial institutions to prevent embezzlements that can also prevent embezzlement in a computer environment. The first is the segregation of duties among employees and departments to assure proper functioning of automatic checks and balances. Computer installations have a tendency to cause more and more of the checking and balancing to be done within the computer department itself. This tendency should be resisted; instead, a separate department—not unlike our own government's systems of check and balances—should be set up to do the balancing of payrolls, ledgers, and to handle all other reports.

Physical handling of assets, recording of transactions, and supervision are actions which should be independent of each other. This does not mean that the individuals or departments cannot cooperate or communicate with each other. It simply means that no single person should be permitted to handle all the important phases of a transaction without the intervention of some other person who provides a cross-check. Without adequate separation of duties, accounts may be manipulated so as to make discovery of errors very difficult, if not impossible. All this is just an extension of the old rule that no employee who handles cash should be allowed to balance the ledgers.

The next safeguard is fixing responsibility. If a system of control is to function properly, each employee must understand his duties and must be held responsible for them. In some larger organizations the definition of responsibility is included in a written company manual. This should be written so that some degree of latitude is allowed or revisions will be necessary from time to time. The writing of an organizational manual will have another benefit in that it will force management to evaluate the organizational structure and the controls needed.

If an employee has a clear understanding of his duties, his responsibility and relationships with other employees and departments, it helps him to complete his duties. For example, if one employee is given the duties of checking out any apparent discrepancies in the computer log, he knows this is his responsibility and others should not be allowed to gloss over any errors or misuse because it will reflect on his own ability and integrity. This situation offers the employee a clear goal and responsibility which is desirable.

Along with fixed responsibility goes limited authority. If one employee has unlimited authority, then he is allowed to do anything he wishes and no checks or balances exist on his actions.

Even unlimited authority on one type of asset, such as petty cash or a computer file, can often lead to misuse. No one, not even an executive officer, should be allowed to perform his work without being checked, nor should policy be modified simply by the decision of one individual.

Unchecked control over an asset has greater danger when computers are used. One discreet company tried to change its accounts receivable aging procedures at year end to improve its reported current position. Aging was done manually, and required about 300 people. To apply the new procedures, it was necessary to hold orientation meetings and give new instructions to everyone of the 300 people involved. It was, of course, impossible to keep this quiet and the change was discovered by the auditor.

But suppose the same company wanted to make the same change after the aging process was done by computer. No orientation meeting, no written instructions—just modify the program and no one would be the wiser.

Embezzlement often occurs because one individual has complete authority over an asset with no checks. A good organization plan will clearly establish limits on the authority of each position.

Dual control of important assets is a traditional safeguard against fraud or illegal manipulation. Examples of dual control include the situation where two combinations are needed to open a vault, dual signatures are needed to cash a check, double verification of a program is required, and dual authorization is necessary before changing the operating system of a computer. Since collusion between at least two employees is necessary when dual control is used, the opportunity for fraud is lessened.

Another simple and commonly used method of control is rotation of duties. This means that one employee is not allowed to always update the same file or always post the ledger accounts. Knowledge of the rotation of duties will not only discourage dishonesty but also usually helps uncover it once it has happened. Rotation of duties should be at unannounced intervals so no one can prepare for it in advance. Sufficient time should also be allowed once personnel are rotated so that at least one and preferably two cycles of the work load can be completed to insure safety.

In a computer installation where there are a considerable number of monthly reports, rotation should be for at least one month in length. With operating personnel this means that either jobs are scheduled so they are run on alternating shifts or the personnel are shifted so their work schedule and duties change.

This can go so far as shifting computer operating personnel into control sections or tape library positions. Usually rotation of duties is just the using of rotation shifts. The actual shifting of duties has other advantages such as teaching employees the problems of other positions, and giving the company a wide back-up of trained employees to help during sickness or terminations.

The last safeguard is compulsory vacation. This is standard procedure in banks and other financial institutions. Compulsory vacation provides protection similar to the shifting of duties. Most employees jump at the chance to take vacations, but a few tend never to take vacations for various reasons—occasionally, because they are afraid others will uncover irregularities in accounts.

All employees who hold sensitive positions should be required to take two consecutive weeks' annual vacation. This should be an uninterrupted vacation and the employee should be requested not to come to work at all during his vacation period. A written rule to this effect should be adopted, not only to protect the company but also the employee. If any employee is so indispensable that he cannot be given an uninterrupted vacation, bad management is at fault and should be corrected.

Vacations should be taken during the period that the books are balanced and not just before or after. Or vacations should be taken during the monthly process cycle. This uninterrupted vacation allows each person's work to be verified by his associates and provides training and testing of other employees for promotion, besides protecting the institution from work stoppages due to illness, resignations, or deaths. Many thefts have been disclosed while the thief was absent due to accidental absence or sudden illness.

1. Does segregation of duties to assure proper functioning of automatic checks and balances exist?
2. Are responsibilities clearly defined so there is no misunderstanding about who is responsible for care of assets?
3. Are dual controls instigated where necessary?
4. Are duties rotated to discourage dishonesty?

EMBEZZLEMENT CHECKLIST

5. Are uninterrupted vacations compulsory?
6. Are employees paid salaries that will enable them to live comfortably and respectably without stealing?
7. Are employees required to live within their means in order not to encourage stealing?
8. Are periodic audits conducted along with unexpected ones?
9. Are petty cash funds uniformly controlled and audited?
10. Has a security expert or insurance consultant checked your company for security measures to protect inventory?
11. Does your insurance adequately cover possible loss through embezzlement? Are employees bonded where necessary?
12. Has the problem of stolen information been considered and protective measures taken?

LOOK FOR THESE BUSINESS THEFT DANGER SIGNALS*

1. Employees constantly borrowing small amounts of money.

2. Placing in petty cash checks that are undated, post-dated, past-dated, or requesting fellow employees to "hold" checks.

3. The return of personal checks for irregular reasons.

4. Appearance of collectors or creditors of the place of business. Also excessive use of the telephone to "stall-off" creditors.

5. Inclination toward covering up inefficiencies or the occasional falsification of figures.

6. Gambling in any form which goes beyond the ability to cover the loss.

7. Excessive drinking , night clubbing, and association with questionable characters.

8. Buying, or acquiring through "business" channels, expensive automobiles and extravagant household furnishings.

9. Explaining that a high standard of living is possible because of money inherited from an estate. This often warrants a confidential investigation.

10. Refusing to leave custody of records during the day. Working overtime regularly, and being the first in and the last out each day.

11. Refusing to take vacations and shunning promotions. This can denote a fear of detection.

12. Constant association with, and entertainment by, a supplier.

13. Carrying an unusually large bank balance or being a heavy buyer of securities.

14. Extended personal illness or family illness, without a plan of debt liquidation.

15. Bragging about exploits and/or carrying an unusually large amount of money.

16. Rewriting records under the guise of neatness.

*Reprinted from the March, 1968 issue of MODERN OFFICE PROCEDURES and copyrighted 1968 by Industrial Publishing Company, Division Pittway Corporation.

MAKE SURE YOU TAKE THESE

MINIMUM PRECAUTIONS

AGAINST EMPLOYEE DISHONESTY

If you don't, you may be a patsy for the office thief.*

☐ Have periodic audits, with unexpected ones in between.

☐ Make surprise counts of cash, securities, and accounts. Make independent review of all invoices paid during a given period.

☐ Reconcile bank statements monthly. Compare cancelled checks with vouchers and check stubs.

☐ Maintain separate petty cash fund from other disbursement funds. Put it in charge of an employee separated from incoming cash handling. Require signed uniform vouchers.

☐ Countersign all checks by someone not involved in check preparation. Serially number blank checks, leave them unsigned and under lock and key when not in use. Don't mail or deliver checks by same person who prepared them.

☐ Separate purchasing from receiving responsibilities, supervised by someone not authorized to pay bills. Use prenumbered purchase orders, with duplicates to receiving and accounting. Periodically audit purchasing department procedures. Supervise cash or credits on returned goods or complaints by two persons.

☐ Sign payroll checks by a person who does not prepare the payroll. Review amounts of work done, rates paid, overtime and incentive payments at frequent intervals. Return undelivered payroll money or checks to cashier or someone other than paymaster.

☐ Endorse incoming checks "for deposit only" to your account. Don't let a bookkeeper open, receive, or distribute incoming mail. Restrict access to customer records and ledgers to someone who does not handle incoming cash and checks. Confirm customers' unpaid balances, at least annually, by independent or outside auditor.

☐ Consult with layout experts, security architects, insurance engineers, and other specialists about security and protective measures for your building, open stock, goods, supplies, and equipment. Make complete physical inventory at least annually by someone not responsible for keeping inventory records. Make surprise counts of inventory frequently.

☐ Don't allow removal of merchandise without a prenumbered duplicate itemizing merchandise or supplies ordered. Don't allow drivers and outside truckers access to storage or stockroom without supervision.

☐ Require all sales to be written up on prenumbered forms.

☐ Obtain written applications from all new employees and investigate their past ten-year employment record with former employers. Require passes to take anything off the premises. Notify payroll department immediately when an employee is terminated. Check excessive overtime.

☐ Bond employees. Check your insurance coverage for robbery, burglary, and embezzlement. Have proper accounting methods to establish amounts of loss when it does occur.

☐ Discuss a comprehensive internal security program with your CPA or independent auditor, your internal security or protective agency, your insurance or bonding company, or your business consultant.

☐ Set up some form of policy and procedures so that employees should know what precautions they are expected to take to prevent employee dishonesty. Systematically spot check procedures on a surprise basis throughout the year.

*Reprinted from the March, 1968 issue of MODERN OFFICE PROCEDURES and copyrighted 1968 by Industrial Publishing Company, Division Pittway Corporation.

References   Aaron, William. "Embezzlement—Detection and Control," speech before the National Retail Merchants Association EDP Conference, 1968.

Hall, Jerome. THEFT, LAW AND SOCIETY. The Bobbs-Merrill Company, Inc. 1952.

Hill, Jr., O.A. "The Role of the Auditor with Respect to Internal Control and Fraud," THE INTERNAL AUDITOR, May/June, 1968.

"How to Protect Against the Million Dollar Racket," MODERN OFFICE PROCEDURES, March, 1968.

McNew, Bennie B., and Charles L. Prather. FRAUD CONTROL FOR COMMERCIAL BANKS, Richard D. Irwin, Inc., 1962.

Pratt, Lester A. BANK FRAUDS: Their Detection and Prevention, The Ronald Press Company, 1965.

EDP CONTROLS

A computer file can be inadvertently altered by defective hardware, defective programs, or erroneous input data. Erroneous input data in turn can be caused by error or fraud. Many of the precautions that prevent the entry of incorrect data can also prevent the entry of fraudulent data. In a recent survey of EDP auditors it was discovered that the majority of EDP frauds were implemented by modifying input data.

Modifying input data requires very little knowledge. To even the most trained eye, fraudulent punched cards look the same as punched cards containing legitimate transaction; thus, there is little possibility of detecting a forgery. To punch a card requires very little specialized knowledge in comparison with the knowledge necessary for a programmer- or operator-caused fraud. Another reason that modifying input for the sake of fraud is so popular is that the input cards are often readily available to many people while the programs or computer are obtainable by fewer people.

Anyone with the proper motivation, such as a desire for more money, and access to computer files can do a punched card modification. In fact, it is not necessary for the defrauder to have access to most assets to commit a manipulative fraud. All he has to do is alter records so payments or credits will be made during normal processing.

SEPARATION OF DUTIES

Before the computer, internal controls were rooted mainly in numbers of people and separation of their functions so that one person checked another. The basic protection provided here is that several people will seldom agree to commit a fraud together. And the more people it takes to perpetrate a fraud the higher the risk of getting caught. The safest fraud, of course, involves a single person doing some isolated unchecked task. One can assume that some very successful frauds have never been discovered.

Since the advent of computers, however, there has been a tendency to delegate more and more of the traditional controls to the computer center. The centralization of records in an EDP system makes a manipulative fraud even more possible than in a manual system. In an EDP system all records are usually available in one place. This makes any supporting manipulation necessary to cover up a fraud relatively easy.

Often computer center staff check input documents, post balancing figures, run computer reports, balance the report, and correct errors. This trend is dangerous because there is no separation of duties. It becomes even more alarming when one notices another trend: the delegation of authority to computers. Computers check input data for reasonableness, or shrinkages in warehouses, write off delinquent accounts, approve invoices, reorder stock, and grant credit.

Without some outside controls, large manipulation frauds are almost inevitable. The ideal situation is where one department authorizes transactions and produces the source documents, another prepares the machine readable data, another balances all transactions, and still another processes the data. Separation of duties prevents one person or group of people from dominating one type of transaction to the point that losses from fraud or error are not detected.

By using tight programming controls, the computer can perform many routine procedural checks which are often omitted in manual operations because they slow up the processing. Limit checks can catch unintentional as well as intentional errors. A simple limit check is using the program to flag any payroll checks over a certain amount for verification. Another safeguard is to have a total limit. Anytime a payroll or similar report exceeds an upper bound, a message is sent to the operator to check to see if it is correct. If the total limit is exceeded, it could be either a mistake or fraud.

PROGRAMMING CONTROLS

Other types of checks cover large price changes, inventory shortages, unusual dates, or other unusual fluctuations. But again, if too much dependence is put on computer checking without any control or audit, the company is certainly vulnerable to computer-related fraud.

The generally agreed method of preventing EDP frauds is to set up an internal control department. The control department should be entirely separate from the computer department. To prevent tampering, files will usually be stored in the internal control department. One of the functions that can be assumed by the internal control department is the computer library. Some large installations will prefer to have a separate library. The control department should need no access to the computer.

INTERNAL CONTROL DEPARTMENT

When setting up a control section, special emphasis must be put on control procedures. Enough information must be supplied so that the control section understands how the totals are generated and how to cross-check totals. Proper programming and detailed instructions can help. If the control clerks do not know what they are doing, it will soon become obvious to the programmers, operators, and report users. The clerks will be forced to depend on other people's word that discrepancies are all right. The less the computer center knows about the balancing of the reports the better. In fact, there is no reason for the computer center to have any interest in balancing reports. The computer center should be considered mainly a service organization. By utilizing the computer center as a service function management prevents domination of the equipment by one user such as accounting or manufacturing.

The establishment of an internal control department does not exclude controls of the originating departments. The control department is responsible for assuring that received data is correctly and completely processed. But the originating department is still responsible for seeing that their own information is properly gathered and that computer reports provide the necessary information. The control department will probably want some controls (hash totals, document counts) that the user department is not particularly interested in.

Some of the duties that a control department can take care of are:

1. Personnel checking and recording of receipts which should be independent of the computer operation. The source should be checked to see if it is valid and has proper authorization. Input-output control of source documents should be established here.

2. Control totals should be built up independently of the computer *before* the computer run. After the computer run, totals should be checked by the control department. Control totals created after the computer run invite the control clerk to depend on the output totals.

3. Input controls should include the following:
   a. Document counts. Prenumbered documents will help exclude substitution of documents.
   b. Control totals for dollars, rates, hours, units, quantities, etc.
   c. Batch controls.
   d. Summary controls (daily, weekly, etc.)
   e. System summary totals to control the number of records, deletions, and transactions in the file.

4. The control department should handle all rejected data. Totals will need to be adjusted, rejected data corrected, and recycled.

5. The control department should have as many of the following output controls as possible:
   a. Columnar totals.

b. Hash totals, like totals of order numbers in a batch, to determine that original data is included and unauthorized data is not added.

c. Check on keypunch accuracy.

d. Cross-footing to check columnar totals.

e. Zero balance to prove accuracy of computations within a known total. Zero balances can provide accuracy tests of input.

f. Record counts (input, output), transactions, tape numbers. These totals can be used to check later processing and to verify that all data is processed once and only once.

6. Controls should facilitate the audit procedures. For this reason the internal auditor should help set up control procedures.

7. Changes to master records, whenever possible, should be made on serially prenumbered documents. These documents should be registered at point of origin and again recorded at the control department.

8. Clear records of updates must be kept for later confirmation. Without clearly established audit trails no later auditing of updated master files will be possible.

9. The control department should have records of movement of data as follows:

a. Receipt from source.

b. Issue to operations (computer).

c. Return from operations (computer).

d. Return to source.

e. Distribution of reports.

10. Finally, all source documents should be reconciled. That is, when a four part cash receipt document is used, are all four parts present and processed?

The control department should share the responsibility for deciding what files (including source documents) should be stored and what files can be destroyed. Current versions of a file should never be released until the file itself can be reconstructed if it should be found defective. Audit consideration should also be taken into account before destroying files.

EXAMPLES OF INADEQUATE CONTROLS

There are many good examples of bad controls or no controls in EDP frauds. One of the most widely publicized took place in a brokerage firm. The man was a vice-president for a computer operation and he conducted his scheme on weekends by altering input decks. These fraudulent change cards would credit his account with a cash receipt and debit a large company account with a like amount; thus, he kept the books in balance. The cash receipt document was a four-part typed form. Next, he typed a cash receipt form for the amount of the fraudulent entry, destroyed three of the copies and added the fourth copy to the other cash receipts which were checked by the margin department for credit to brokerage accounts. There was no final reconciliation of prenumbered cash receipt forms so the fraud was complete.

One case where the classic separation of duties would have helped avoid a fraud concerned a payroll. The computer department had custody of the blank checks, prepared the payroll, had custody of the signature plates, prepared the checks, signed them, and mailed them out. Not very surprisingly, a fraud was set up to pay an employee who had left the company.

The processing of reject input data offers an easy means of fraud. If control of rejects is weak, it is necessary only to cause a reject on the data one wishes to manipulate in order to initiate a fraud. Such an example took place in a bank when machine-sensible input in the form of checks was used. The manager inserted a "read" flaw on the checks he wished to apprehend. Consequently, the manipulated checks were rejected during the entry run and were held for manual processing. Then the manager was able to convert the checks to his own use. It was not necessary to modify the computer system in this case. As this case points out, the importance of tight controls on exceptions cannot be underestimated; otherwise all that is necessary for a fraud is the insertion of intentional errors into input documents. This type of maneuvering allows for the manipulation of a legitimate transaction or the substitution of a fraudulent transaction for a legitimate one.

CONCLUSION

Just recently it has been realized by management that there should be an independent control group—an executive in charge of information—separate from the computer center. The job descrip-

tion of the executive might be the following: He will be responsible for the integrity of computer files. His duties will include the
processing of all monetary and nonmonetary transactions, updating of master files, quality and distribution of printed reports,
and retention of data. That is a lot of responsibility, but the
integrity of computer data is essential if the computer investment
is to pay off.

References

Aaron, William. "Embezzlement—Detection and Control," Speech before the
    National Retail Merchants Association EDP Conference, 1969.
Carmichael, Dr. D. R. "Fraud in EDP Systems," THE INTERNAL AUDI-
    TOR, May/June 1969.
"Halting the Electronic Hijacker," MODERN OFFICE PROCEDURES, Sep-
    tember, 1968.
Jacobson, Robert V. "Providing Security Protection of Computer Files,"
    American Management Association Conference on Security and Catas-
    trophe Prevention Management of the Computer Complex, November,
    1969.
Mroz, Gene P. "Computer 'Bug' Control," JOURNAL OF DATA MANAGE-
    MENT, January, 1970.

AUDITING

Recently, in Daytona Beach, Florida, a local auditing firm filed the following disclaimer on the city's financial statement: "We don't know where we've been, and we don't know where we are. But we think we're headed in the right direction." They wrote this because their auditors could not trace all the money and verify all the figures. The confusion was caused by the aesthetic separation of computer programs and audit trails, which in turn was caused by the city's rush to computerization, and city officials' and auditors' apparent failure to coordinate the conversion.

Daytona Beach had just received a new computer and they tried to get the previous year on the computer by using parallel runs wherever they could to aid the conversion. As might be expected, personnel qualifications were not what the city had hoped for, and the city had experienced the usual start-up troubles.

The auditing firm, Robertson, May, Zima, and Co., did not have time to check out all results. As Donald Zima said: "A few thousand dollars difference when you are talking about an $8 or $10 million budget, doesn't make that much difference. It can't be distorted that much." Almost as if to justify their situation, City Clerk David Edwards pointed out that one-fifth of all municipal audits in this country have disclaimers on them. It would be interesting to know how many of these cities have computerized records.

The auditor no longer has piles of paper to paw through. The classical "paper trail" or "audit trail" is vanishing and is being replaced by invisible arrangements of molecules in an iron-oxide coating on plastic tape or on drums and disks. And just as the paper audit trails are disappearing, either the traditional auditor will also vanish or the auditor will adjust to the new world of computers.

THE VANISHING TRAIL

When punched card machines were first introduced, the auditor could obtain some input cards and compare the results of the output to determine that the records had been correctly processed. Not very much savvy was needed to understand the tab equipment. Even then this simple kind of approach would not check reports or summary information accumulated throughout the process. So it is possible to process a paycheck correctly, but to accumulate annual tax data incorrectly. But the main point is that traditional audit approaches would still work even if some-what haphazardly, and there were sufficient mountains of paper reports to check things out by hand.

With the advent of mass-storage devices and on-line real-time systems all traditional approaches are obsolete. They just won't work anymore. The mountains of paper reports are no longer available most of the time and hand checking does not provide very much information. Today the computer must be used to do the auditing. Not only should audit aids be provided by the processing programs, but the auditors themselves should have programs of their own with which to audit.

It is essential that auditors be involved in the early planning of computer systems. There are many computer checks which, if built in at the time of initial programming, can greatly aid the auditor and help prevent fraud and error. Auditing quite often is thought of only in terms of fraud, but auditors are also interested

EARLY PLANNING

in seeing that errors are avoided. Many checks that were not possible before computers are easy to add to a program. The significance of this is evident when consideration is given to the fact that errors are normally a bigger loss than fraud.

In order to properly audit it, the auditor must work with the computer. Generally there are two ways to do this. The first is to use the processing programs to provide information the auditor will need; and the second is to have special programs to check the computer results.

USING REGULAR PROGRAMS

There is a tendency to provide less and less paper output with computers. Auditors can demand more output but not only does this defeat the purpose of the computer, it does not assure the results desired since the reports can be "doctored" to provide results which are not there. Auditors in the past have depended on the management reports to do their auditing, but management reports do not always provide the information that the auditor desires. This will become more true as on-line systems are developed.

The first thing the auditor should do is ask for all the checks he desires in the program. This will include making sure that limit checks are provided, special totals are provided, limits on price changes, etc. Some of these totals and checks may be desired by management, but many may only be required by the auditor. The next request should include any extra printouts desired. Some printouts may only be needed on a "request" basis. The program can be designed so that a switch can be set so that these extra reports will be printed when needed.

It is essential that as many as possible of these requests are included at the time the original programs are written. Otherwise, if the auditor asks for special program changes after the system is all programmed, he will probably be told that the program change is impossible or will cost $15,000.

In one rather amusing but all too typical case auditors were checking out freight car records. The auditors noticed that a great deal of time was spent tracking and correcting errors before the records could be reconciled. It was obvious that if these erroneous input records could be caught before they entered the file it would improve the accuracy of the resulting reports. Very often checks of inputs are added to a program only after a particular error has caused a great deal of grief and embarrassment.

In this particular case the auditors decided to punch up a test deck that was particularly incorrect and see what would happen. They added incomplete data, off-punched cards, erroneous dates. Railroad interchanges that didn't exist were punched. Not very surprisingly, all the incorrect input was gobbled up. No validity or logic tests had been designed in the program. A car interchange with a date of May 53 was taken and 22 days extra per diem was charged. The solution was obvious but expensive because no initial planning had taken place. The job had to be reprogrammed in order to recognize and segregate the erroneous data before it intermingled with valid data.

A good auditor will want his own programs. These programs should, whenever possible, be written by someone responsible to the auditor instead of the same person who writes the processing programs. The use of the auditors' own programmer or a service bureau would be desirable, albeit more expensive. Nevertheless, if this approach is taken the company programmer would not know both the processing and auditing programs. Thus an inside programming fraud is more difficult.

SPECIAL PROGRAMS

The use of programs to check data is more important with the advent of on-line time-sharing systems. Printed reports are usually kept to a minimum and input is often at widely scattered terminals. It is of course possible to print out large reports for the auditor to check but not only is this time consuming for both the auditor and the computer, it ignores the main characteristic of the computer. If the auditor can define what he wants to check, a program can be designed to do the checking and the auditor will have to analyze only the resulting printout. Some of the programs desired by the auditor might be the following:

1. A program that would take two copies of master files and printout all differences. Then the auditor could take a copy of all the updated transactions and check to see that the master files were properly updated. A program could be designed to do the checking too.
2. The auditor should keep a copy of current processing

programs. Then a program can be easily written to compare the auditor's copy with the program being used for processing. The auditor could audit the programs on a periodic basis or go in during a processing cycle unexpectedly, and demand the program and then check to make sure that his version matches the version being used.

3. The auditor can also go in on a surprise basis with his program and rerun a job. By taking the original computer run and his run he can compare the two runs to make sure they are identical.

4. Programs can be designed to check every Nth element in a file. These Nth elements can be examined at a desk or checked by the program.

5. A better system is to review every account and extract only those accounts not meeting certain logic tests. This way the program separates the wheat from the chaff and the auditor can spend his time analyzing only those accounts needing attention instead of the thousands that don't.

6. A program can be written to check all calculations. On a monthly payroll the auditor could at the end of the year develop a program to read in the 12 monthly payroll tapes and calculate all taxes and deductions, using his program to check for accuracy and correctness. Since it would be necessary to print out only discrepancies, very little printout should occur and the job would run very quickly. This way the whole year's payroll could be checked.

One example of a successful use of a program to do checking was on a payroll master file. In this case a program was used to compare persons on the payroll at the end of the period with persons on the payroll at the beginning of the period. Changes in personnel were compared with authorizations issued by the personnel department. Both additions and terminations were checked. In addition all changes in rates and other status were completely checked out by the computer. The program belonged to the auditor and not the data processing department. This application is a small example of what is possible by using the computer as an audit tool.

On-line inventory files offer another auditing problem. Files are changed by operators at terminals as orders are processed and new merchandise is received. These files are similar to the familiar airplane seat reservation systems. In order to audit this type of file it is essential that a transaction file be kept. The transaction file would contain detailed information, including type of transaction, time of day, and operator and terminal numbers. The difference between the inventory file (or any other similar on-line file) is: At the end of two successive days it should equal the total of the transactions for the day. Programs can be written to verify this. Daily transactions files are usually kept in case the computer system goes down. They also can provide a convenient audit tool with a little advance planning.

If no transaction files are kept, on-line files can be altered without a trace and the auditor will not be able to determine if the change was a program error, legitimate change, or the result of a fraud. Today it is possible to strengthen controls by recording and maintaining information previously found uneconomical to compile or store by other means. It is relatively cheap to retain on magnetic tape the history of all transactions as long as management and the auditor desire.

In a large department store a programmer decided his girl friend did not have to pay for purchases from the store that employed him. He simply inserted a routine in the billing program to transfer all charges of his friend's account to a suspense account. He also arranged the program so that when the trial balance was printed, the suspense account did not appear in detail, but it was included in the total—which thus tied in with the general ledger control. This fraud continued until the auditor, using programs of his own, ran a report that indicated the unexplained account. This type of fraud is very difficult to uncover without using audit programs or comparing original reports with a "clean" audit copy.

The internal auditor should have some control of programs. He must have a copy of all necessary programs and receive information on program changes. Auditor copies of programs will discourage unauthorized program changes. Necessary authorization and documentation of all program changes will also help control unauthorized program changes.

CONTROL OF PROGRAMS

Some have suggested that auditors should sit down and check out the program listing. This is nonsense because on a large complicated program it is difficult for the original programmer to determine exactly what the program does by its program listing. Program changes can be made after the listing is given to the auditor, or by an operator at the computer console; likewise, analysis of flowcharts is not very rewarding. First, there is no assurance that the hand-drawn flowchart will have in it the information desired. Machine-drawn flowcharts are usually rather unwieldy but can be of some use when checking out a particular routine.

MINI-COMPANY   Instead of trying to hand-check the program, the mini-company offers a greater reward because it uses the computer to do the checking.

The concept of the mini-company involves creating a special set of records and transactions for the auditor. These transactions are processed with normal processing but are used only by the auditor. The idea is that he can insert any type of transaction in this group and it will be processed with the regular flow of work.

This allows the auditor to use predetermined tests to make sure everything is still being processed correctly. Transactions can be constructed so that all program checks and limits are violated and to make sure the edits and checks are working properly. Transactions can be inserted with illegal dates, incorrect account numbers, incomplete data, out-of-sequence files, out-of-balance batches, edit violations, and data larger than field sizes.

This approach is especially useful after a major program change since controls often get dropped or modified unknowingly. A mini-company can be included along with a major computer conversion process to make sure everything is converted properly.

Reject transactions should show up and the auditor can check to see how they are handled. Accepted transactions can be checked to see if they are processed correctly.

It is important for the auditor to be able to make up test decks. While test decks may imply data processing cards, some test decks will be terminal input, tape files, or disk files. Technical help will be needed in constructing this type of file, but the auditor should be able to design the test.

In a case of fraud the mini-company is not always fool proof. A fraudulent program change could be designed to skip the mini-company. But use of the mini-company along with the auditor's own programs should provide good preventive measures.

The mini-company concept was explained by Joseph J. Wasserman in an excellent article in the HARVARD BUSINESS REVIEW, September-October, 1969. In this article Wasserman points out that this concept is particularly advantageous because it permits continuous testing of the system on a live basis. Old-style testing through the computer was forced to use all fictitious data or worry about disturbing real data. The mini-company is set up so it is by itself and can be separated from the real data easily without disturbing the other data. An example would be to establish a mini-company with all account numbers above any legitimate account. Then this mini-company could be easily separated from the other processing. Auditors can use the mini-company for periodic system reviews and quality controls too.

CONTROL OF FILES

The auditor will be quite interested in control of history files. First he must have a say in which files should be saved and for how long. Normally history files are maintained only a short period of time. In addition the auditor may want special history files kept for his own use. Without proper control of files no audit trails are possible. The auditor will be the only one interested in some history files.

For example, on an on-line time-sharing system the auditor would want a file of the daily transactions saved. This file would indicate what, where, and by whom each transaction was entered.

CONCLUSION

Early results indicate that computers are not beyond the possibility of use for embezzlement. Instead, not only are many old embezzlement schemes still useful, but many new schemes are also possible. Very powerful and sophisticated embezzlements are possible, such as stealing very small amounts from many people. If the auditor is not able to use the computer to do the auditing, then he is at quite a disadvantage with an embezzler who will surely use the computer. Increased sophistication and speeds of the computer will tend to favor the embezzler rather than the auditor unless the auditor understands the computer.

**AUDITING
CHECKLIST**

1. Are your auditors familiar enough with the computer operation?
2. Is the auditor involved in the early planning of computer programs?
3. Does the auditor suggest checks which should be in the regular programs?
4. Does the auditor have his own programs to double-check files?
5. Is the auditor dependent on the same programmers who write the original programs for his auditing programs? If so, this is undesirable.
6. Are files audited on a surprise basis?
7. Is the auditor promptly informed of program changes?

References

Aaron, William. "Embezzlement—Detection and Control," Speech before the National Retail Merchants Association EDP Conference, 1968.

"Audit Trails Lost in Computerization," COMPUTERWORLD, April 29, 1970.

Boni, Gregory M. "Impact of Electronic Data Processing on Auditing," THE JOURNAL OF ACCOUNTANCY, September, 1963.

Boutell, Wayne S. AUDITING WITH THE COMPUTER, University of California Press, 1965.

Brown, Harry L. EDP FOR AUDITORS, John Wiley and Sons, Inc., 1968.

Carmichael, Dr. D. R. "Fraud in EDP Systems," THE INTERNAL AUDITOR, May/June, 1969.

Freed, Roy N. "Computer Fraud—A Management Trap," BUSINESS HORIZONS, June, 1969.

Garland, Robert F. "Computer Programs—Control and Security," MANAGEMENT ACCOUNTING, December, 1966.

Goodman, John V. "Auditing Magnetic Tape Systems," THE COMPUTER JOURNAL, July, 1964.

Jacobson, Robert V. "Providing Security Protection of Computer Files," American Management Association Conference on Security and Catastrophe Prevention Management of the Computer Complex, November, 1969.

John, Richard C., and Thomas J. Nisse. "Evaluating Internal Control in EDP Audits." THE JOURNAL OF ACCOUNTANCY, February, 1970

Mroz, Gene P. "Computer 'Bug' Control," JOURNAL OF DATA MANAGEMENT, January, 1970.

Palmer, R. R., and W. J. Duma. "Auditing with Computers," BANKERS MONTHLY MAGAZINE, January 15, 1969.

Pauley, Charles A. "Audit Responsibilities in the Design of Computerized Systems," THE INTERNAL AUDITOR, July/August, 1969.

Wasserman, Joseph J. "Plugging the Leaks in Computer Security," HAR-
    VARD BUSINESS REVIEW, September-October, 1969.
Wasserman, Joseph J. "The Vanishing Trail," BELL TELEPHONE MAGA-
    ZINE, July/August, 1968.

PROGRAM
ERROR

Without a doubt the most common, embarrrassing, and expensive software loss is program error. Program errors are so common they have created a regular mythology of program error (often attributed to the computer instead of the program). Jokes, cartoons, and irate customers contribute to this mythology. The humorous treatment of computer errors even exists in some computer centers where you see the slogan "to err is human, but to really screw things up you need a computer."

Program errors or "bugs" often do not show up until some rare combination of circumstances reveals them. Program bugs originate because of errors in system design, errors in logic, errors in coding, errors in problem definition, or sometimes just incomplete definitions. There is a pessimistic school of thought which maintains, probably correctly, that all large programs have bugs and it is just a matter of time until they show up.

The WALL STREET JOURNAL reported the Borden Company had announced a $2.8 million "deficiency resulting from what appeared to be an error in switching part of the company accounting system over to computerization two years ago."

At Cape Kennedy a space launching failed because of a program error. The computer symbol equivalent to a comma was inadvertently left out of the program. The omission caused the rocket to go far off course and it had to be destroyed.

While these two program errors are larger than most, they illustrate the possible magnitude of the problem. Elimination of program error is primarily dependent on proper test program procedures. If a program blows up or gives nonsense results it becomes obvious that the program is not working. The real danger lies in the situation when the program almost works; that is, it runs and provides sensible answers, but still the answers are incorrect.

The first test step is for the programmer to check over his program logic and the keypunching himself. Once he is satisfied with that he should make up a test deck of fictitious data designed to test the programs logic. The test deck should test all the following:

1. Does the program contain the following routines and do they all work correctly: label checks, record counts, reel counts, transaction counts, sequence checks, consecutive number checks, hash totals, total fields, and cross footing?
2. Does the program check for reasonableness of input data? Most data values in real life problems have an acceptable range; it is a necessary part of the program to edit check the data reasonableness. Here are some fields that should be checked: date fields, account numbers, transaction amounts, and code fields.
3. Does the program still operate under extreme cases? If not, it is probable there are other situations where it will not operate correctly. Some examples are: Try processing one transaction only; will the program still run if the first or last transaction is invalid; will the program process a zero or minus transaction correctly?

Any of the above could indicate major program logic error that could go undetected for months or even years. More than once when a company adopted a new system they have discovered a major error in the old program system.

Programs should be tested out with data where the correct answers are known. This means figure out the expected results *before* running. Do not just check to see if results are correct.

Standard programming aids should be provided to help the programmer test his program. They include: file print routines, core dumps, trace routines, file copies, and record replacement routines. If these aids are not available it becomes difficult, if not impossible, to test a program properly.

Once the program is tested with test data the next step is to test the program by using actual data. Actual data often uncovers many errors that test data can't. One of the most common errors uncovered is that original information was incorrect or misunderstood and program revisions are necessary.

Since many new program systems are simply new systems (because of new hardware or extensive revisions and updating of old systems) parallel runs should be used as much as possible. Parallel runs consist of running the job under the old system and the new system and comparing the results. The minimum amount of parallel runs should be three cycles. This allows for testing of updated files and the using of actual data for testing.

"I understand how it juggled the books, but what did it do with the money."

From MODERN DATA, April 1970. Used with permission.

Parallel runs offer another advantage. That is, copies of the test runs can be and should be sent to the departments that will be using the computer reports to see if they meet proper specifications and provide the information desired. Very often, after the program is all checked out, a report is sent to the requesting department where they state the information is incorrect or change is desired. It is better to include the requesting department in the early testing in order to avoid this situation.

Recently, parallel testing was used by a telephone company operation involving rating and billing of toll messages. After the new system was completely tested out, the programming staff extracted 300,000 toll messages that had been run under the old system. The 300,000 messages were set up so they could be processed by the new system.

The results of the parallel runs were then sent to the audit department where they were carefully compared for exceptions. Any toll messages that created exceptions not encountered in the old system were traced by the systems design staff to discover the cause of discrepancy, and corrective action was taken before the new system was introduced.

PROGRAM REVISIONS

This essential discussion of new programs also applies to revisions of old programs. After test data are created they should not be thrown away as normally, but should be stored with the program documentation. Then, when a program revision is completed, the old test data should be used to make sure something hasn't been modified that shouldn't have been.

With program revisions it is usually possible to use actual data and parallel runs since all the necessary input is usually available. On any major program change at least one parallel run is desirable.

Many of the most troublesome kinds of program errors are introduced into programs as a result of routine program changes. Program changes are often quite difficult, even for the programmer who originally wrote the program. If the original programmer is not available, then the possibility of error is even greater.

Since it is quite difficult to test programs it is important that time be alloted for this function. If old test data or current data are available, they will help test the program changes. There is a great temptation to skip testing program changes, so it is a good idea to make testing of all program changes a formal requirement.

In order to facilitate the making of program changes and thus avoid errors it is also a good idea to encourage good program design and coding practice. Simple-minded, straight-line programming should be encouraged. Thus programming "tricks" should be discouraged. Programs should be designed in a modular fashion. It is obvious that programmers and their resulting programs known for their abstruseness only invite errors when modified.

The advisability of requiring flowcharts is a hotly debated subject. One school of thought considers anyone modifying a program insane to look at a hand-drawn flowchart because they feel it is probably incorrect and will thus mislead the programmer.

I personally consider at least a general flowchart helpful since it tells the programmer approximately what the program does. Machine-drawn flowcharts are usually too big and detailed, but they should be available for those who want to use them.

Two final conditions should be established to avoid program bugs. Program changes should be formalized. That is, records and authorization should be required before any program changes are made. If program changes are a rather casual process, the computer center is not only inviting error but also fraud. If no records are kept of program changes no one can know with certainty what version of a program was used to run the monthly billing.

The final condition is to provide time for program testing. This also results in formal program testing. Some computer installations have established their best and most experienced programmers in a separate department for testing all programs. Program testing should be given enough time and should not be assumed to be part of the writing of the program. The establishment of programming schedules where man-hours are alloted to system design, programming, and testing is desirable. As soon as each step is completed the step should be signed. This formal set-up establishes in both the programming and management view that all three steps are necessary and time should be allotted.

CHECKPOINT RECOVERY PROCEDURES   Checkpoint recovery procedures for long jobs should be considered as necessary as proper program testing. But the penalty for not thoroughly testing out a program system is incorrect results, whereas the penalty for not using checkpoint recovery procedures is only rerunning long jobs. If sufficient computer time is normally available, then this is not very serious; but if the computer shop is running on a fairly tight schedule, checkpoint recovery procedures should be seriously considered.

What is checkpoint recovery? Periodically, during processing, a "snapshot" is taken of the collection of data that truly represents the status at a given time of a program and its peripheral activities. Checkpoints are traditionally taken at some known time such at the end of a reel or every 2,000 records or at each Nth iteration of a matrix problem.

If the checkpoint truly represents the program, the job can be restarted at a point other than the beginning of the program. There are two reasons for using checkpoints. If there is a hardware failure or other type of error condition at some point during a long job, the job can be restarted after the hardware is repaired without going back to the beginning. All one must do is go back to one of the checkpoints. The second reason for using checkpoints is that it allows computer centers to interrupt long jobs to process a high priority job without losing all the work done.

The computer manufacturer normally supplies each computer center with checkpoint recovery routines. It is up to the installation to establish guidelines for using it. Checkpoint routines cost central processing unit (CPU) time during run time and usually involve some testing by the programmer. Therefore if checkpoints are used very often they will eventually cost more than they save.

What rules should be established for checkpoint use? First, it is obvious they should be used only for longer jobs. The second fact is they should not be taken very frequently since they require CPU time to execute. Several guidelines have been suggested. Some service bureaus require a checkpoint for every job that takes over 15 minutes. They enforce this by not being responsible for any machine or operator error which causes over 15 minutes of rerun time.

But in a nonservice bureau environment a checkpoint on a 20-minute job may not be desirable. In an article in the October, 1969, issue of SOFTWARE AGE, David P. Jasper develops some guidelines for checkpoint recovery procedures.

Jasper calculates on moderate to large-scale machines checkpoints represent an overhead between 0.18% and 1.7% of CPU time. He suggests that if the checkpoint is equal to or greater than 2.5 seconds, and if the entire system can be relied upon for not more than one failure in each 100-hour period, the time of a given run can exceed an hour before checkpoints should be considered.

PROGRAM ERROR CHECKLIST

1. Does the programmer check his program for keypunch errors?
2. Does the program provide bookkeeping records such as sequence checking, card counts, record counts, etc.?
3. Does the program check for reasonableness of data?
4. Does the program work for extreme conditions such as 1 transaction?
5. Is separate time provided for testing the program?
6. Are both test and actual data used for testing the program?
7. Are parallel runs used on program revisions?
8. Is there a formal policy established for program changes?
9. Are there standards for documentation and programs?
10. Are programs tested by someone besides the person who wrote the program?
11. Are programmers encouraged to write simple easy-to-understand programs and avoid tricks or obtuse coding?
12. Is patching of programs forbidden?
13. Is checkpoint recovery used in long programs?

References

Allan, Brandt. "Danger Ahead! Safeguard Your Computer," HARVARD BUSINESS REVIEW, November-December, 1968.

Gruenberger, Fred. "Program Testing and Validating," DATAMATION, July, 1968.

Harrison, William L. "Program Testing," JOURNAL OF DATA MANAGEMENT, December, 1969.

Jasper, David P. "A Discussion of Checkpoint/Restart," SOFTWARE AGE, October, 1969.

Wasserman, Joseph J. "Plugging the Leaks in Computer Security," HARVARD BUSINESS REVIEW, September-October, 1969.

Whelan, Thomas. "Software Security," talk before the American Management Association Conference on Security and Catastrophe Prevention Management of the Computer Complex, November, 1969.

OPERATOR
ERROR

Operator error is the second largest software loss. Programming error holds first place because it has the computer to help. Since most operator errors can be eliminated or discovered by tight programming controls, it is correct to include operator errors with software loss. From this alone a basic programming rule can be drawn: Don't leave anything for the computer operator that the program can do. The same rule applies to the clerical staff since programs once programmed correctly always perform correctly.

If crossfooting of totals has to be done, the program should do the crossfooting and provide an error message if the report does not crossfoot. Other necessary bookkeeping and checks are:

1. Record counts, paper counts, tape counts, number of new (old) transactions.
2. Time required for running the report. Large discrepancies can indicate something wrong.
3. Programs should print out any unusual changes; i.e., price changes of over 10 percent. This could indicate keypunch errors, fraud, or incorrect input decks.

4. The error routines should be strong enough so the operator can't just ignore the error. Serious errors should cause the job to abort or be corrected with no error override possible.
5. Programs should print out all serious errors on the computer console and the printer.
6. Programs should print out "END OF JOB" at the completion of all jobs. This means the operator, control clerks, and users do not just have to assume that they have all the report, but can verify it.

Here are a few examples of computer errors that could have been prevented by program checks and tight controls. A large New England manufacturing company came very close to losing one of its prime assets, a customer name and address file containing all billing, re-order, and inventory data. Like most companies, this firm keeps three copies—commonly called son, father, and grandfather. Keeping only three copies is a big risk. Periodically an extra file off-premise should be saved.

An inexperienced operator lost two-thirds of each copy of the file two weeks in a row. Unexpectedly, the third week the job was delayed and pushed into the day shift where an experienced operator recognized that the job was being processed too fast. He notified his supervisor and the error was discovered. Obviously there were very few program controls on this job and no desk checking was done of output. The loss of this file might have bankrupted the company. Record counts would have indicated something was wrong.

In another case a manager of a large airline noticed that records were occasionally being lost. The cause of the lost records could not be located. During a late night visit to the computer center he noticed that the operators were "speeding up" processing by bypassing an automatic safety device on the tape drives during rewind. The operators normally got by with this, but occasionally they snapped a tape and lost records reconstructing the tape. Close inspection of records counts and tape numbers should have pointed out the error source.

In another case the operator mounted the wrong day's tape. The program recognized the error and printed out a message saying so, but the operator ignored the message and pushed the restart button. This error was not discovered until month-end processing was completed and much work had to be rerun.

While it is not unforgivable for an operator to mount the wrong input tape it is unforgivable for the program to accept it. Serious errors should not be overridden by operator action. Many computer installations demand strict control of console override buttons. Daily audit of console printout might have discovered this error. Balancing the daily reports would have indicated the error immediately.

There is usually no control over console printouts, which is a serious error since these printouts supply a log of errors, inputs, and console modifications. Console printouts should also be reviewed by a knowledgeable person for errors. Knowledge by the operator that the console printout is audited will prevent some errors or frauds.

Console printouts can be prenumbered to insure all the printout is obtained. Since most computer installations do not use numbered forms, the operator normally just throws the printed messages away when they might indicate a major goof-up or fraud. Some installations have gone so far as to install another console printout device in a locked cabinet to insure control over the console printout. This is a very safe but expensive means of control. A less expensive solution is to record all console input/output messages on a disk file and dump them once a day. Of course, if no knowledgeable audit is done, this is all a waste of time—except for the fact it does provide a deterrent for fraud.

Also, if all the control totals such as record counts, tape counts, and process time are not checked, they are also a waste of time. Recently a bank customer brought in several hundred identical delinquency notices, which he had received in the mail the previous day. The customer thought it was a trick to embarrass him into paying his overdue bill. The manager apologized and convinced him all the delinquent notices were simply a program error.

In this case the extra notices were caused by a program change where the last notice on file was repeatedly printed until the end of the file was reached.

This error might have been caught since the programmer had provided for a type-out of the total number of notices produced by the main run, and in the subsequent print program he provided a count of the notices actually printed, for comparison purposes. Apparently this comparison was made for a time while the programs were new, but dropped after a few weeks.

In order to insure that these bookkeeping totals are actually checked out, it is normally necessary to formalize the actual balancing instead of just relying on eye checks. Accounting books for a separate clerical staff (not the computer center) should be set up. In these books will be recorded record counts, transaction counts, crossfoot totals, reel numbers, etc. If these books are properly set up, all the counts can be balanced easily.

The processing of input errors offers a good chance for operator error. Rather than have the computer stop (too expensive), errors should be punched out, sent back to the control section, and recycled by the control department. Operators cannot be expected to handle many input errors correctly and efficiently so it is best not to ask them.

Tight controls of input errors can also offer other dividends. A good control system will provide a built-in method of error analysis, including information on the type, quantity, value, and age of errors, so that the sources can be determined and corrective action taken.

In a case where large volumes of data are processed there is the possibility that a significant number of mistakes (even though the percentage is small) will at least attempt to enter the files. Large files can justify a master file of detected errors. These error files can be analyzed for quantity, type, seriousness, source, and magnitude. Information from this file will provide management with computerized analysis of error trends and allow quick corrective action.

OPERATOR ERROR CHECKLIST

1. Are operators well trained and closely supervised?
2. Are the programs used to check for as many operator errors as possible?
3. Can operators easily override error routines? If so, this is dangerous.
4. Do programs provide bookkeeping totals that could indicate errors, such as record counts, reel counts, etc.?

5. Is computer console output saved and periodically checked?
6. Are all input errors resubmitted by a control section?

References

Allen, Brandt. "Danger Ahead! Safeguard Your Computer," HARVARD BUSINESS REVIEW, November-December, 1968.

Carmichael, Dr. D. R. "Fraud in EDP Systems," THE INTERNAL AUDITOR, May-June, 1969.

Wasserman, Joseph J. "Plugging the Leaks in Computer Security," HARVARD BUSINESS REVIEW, September-October, 1969.

Whelan, Thomas. "Software Security," talk given before the American Management Association Conference on Security and Catastrophe Prevention Management of the Computer Complex, November, 1969.

OPERATOR
FRAUD

Basically, there are two types of operator fraud: data manipulation and program modification. Data manipulation means that the operator changes input data (usually data processing cards) before the program is run. Prevention of this has been discussed in the chapter of EDP fraud so I need only repeat here that this type of fraud can be at least discouraged by establishing a separate control section. If the computer center does its own balancing of reports, one can assume only that management is unconcerned with the possibility of computer-related fraud.

TYPES OF OPERATOR FRAUD

There are many areas in which a computer operator could benefit from computer-related fraud. If disbursement checks are prepared by the computer, or if checks with machine-sensible coding are input to the computer, the operator would have sufficient motivation and access to cash. No unusual actions would be necessary for the computer operator. The computer operator's access to these valuable assets in this situation would be an integral part of normal routine.

66

Access to many types of records is all that is necessary for manipulation frauds. These include the modifying of credit records, personnel records, or school records. In these cases it is desired that the record itself is to be changed. Credit ratings can be improved, school grades can be modified, or unpleasant personnel records can be destroyed. This type of manipulation fraud is seldom discovered.

One rather amusing case happened in a large company that was trying to decrease its phone bill. Each month a secretary would get on the phone and trace out all the long distance phone numbers. Once the names were acquired header cards were punched and the new unaccounted for phone numbers were supposed to be watched to see if they created large phone tolls the following month. The only trouble was that the phone list was run through the computer each month. One of the operators would go through the new header cards each month and throw away all the phone numbers that he was responsible for. That way there would be no continual pattern of phone charges to his particular number. Instead the operator's phone calls would appear new each month and would not be checked. The operator never was caught. A count on the phone number header cards would have uncovered this scheme.

A better understood but not necessarily more frequently used type of manipulation fraud is the increasing or decreasing of accounts that are valuable to the defrauder or his accomplices. This can be done by program modification or input manipulation. Since these accounts are usually in the accounts receivable or accounts payable category, a fraudulent increase in accounts payable (or similar account) would cause a payment to the defrauder in the normal routine. All that is necessary in this type of fraud is a transfer of value. It is not necessary to have access to valuable assets themselves. Payment would be handled normally along with legitimate payments.

In the March 31, 1971, issue of COMPUTERWORLD, it was reported that a U.S. attorney suspected that someone inside the Penn Central computer center modified input data to cover up the stealing of 217 missing boxcars. Computer data had been modified to record that the boxcars were scrapped or wrecked. These boxcars were discovered in the yards of the La Salle and Bureau County Railroad, a line located some 100 miles West of Chicago with a total of 15 miles of track. This is a good example of how the modification of computer records can cover up a theft.

Another case of operator fraud occurred at the Chicago office of ENCYCLOPEDIA BRITANNICA (EB) in 1970. According to a suit filed in Cook County Circuit Court, three operators sold copies of the company's confidential list of customers' names and addresses. The operators used EB equipment to copy reels of tapes containing two million names and addresses. The names were then sold to a mailing house. EB estimated the actual loss in excess of $3 million.

Accounts receivable are another especially tempting target in these days of easy credit. And if done with an accomplice it is difficult to uncover and trace. Examples are:

1. *Charge accounts.* Stores readily give charge accounts to their employees. An operator could use his own account but most fraudulent charge accounts would use an accomplice or pseudonym.
2. *Banks.* Both savings or checking accounts files would be readily available to a computer operator. Several bank frauds have been linked to the computer center.
3. *Brokerage accounts.* A brokerage firm employee often has a trading account with his employer. Some of the most spectacular computer-related crimes uncovered have involved brokerage firms.
4. *Accounts with third parties employing accomplices.* An account with a legitimate supplier or customer could be used for fraudulent purposes if such a business employed an accomplice of an employee-defrauder in a strategic position.

All companies usually have at least one of the above accounts which thus leaves them open to some type of manipulation fraud.

The above illegal manipulations could have been committed by program modification. Completely preventing this type of fraud is quite difficult, but there are several simple measures which can lessen the chances of illegal program modification. The primary method of prevention is not to allow source program listings or source programs in the computer center for production jobs. All production jobs should be run by using object decks; that is, binary decks or compiled programs cataloged on a storage device. Any programmer can verify the fact that it is quite difficult to modify an object deck without a source listing. Source program decks should be used only when the program is being tested.

Programs can be written so they have keys; that is, a correct password is necessary before the program will operate correctly. It is a good idea to have some control over the password in order to prevent the situation where only the operator knows the password. What if the operator quits or gets sick? Program keys will not stop the operator from misusing a program, but will stop most others.

Computer programs (both object and source decks), run instruction books, and input/output media should all be under the control of a computer center librarian. When production jobs are to be run the librarian can check out all necessary material. If the job is to be run at night when no librarian is on duty, the job can be laid out before the librarian goes home. By keeping all the programs and data under the control of the librarian much illegal manipulation can be stopped. Programs and data are not around for anyone to modify them at his leisure. Only programmers should have access to source programs and only the operation staff should have access to data. Both have to have a reason for using them. The situation where programs and data are readily available to anyone opens a much wider possibility of fraud.

Computer library procedures need strong backing by management if they are to succeed. Often a good strong library control situation is established, but the first time a production job is not run because something was not laid out for a production run, the whole system collapses. Supervisors, operators, and clerks are given keys to the library and people take things without supervision. Sometimes the library just deteriorates into a storage room with the door propped open or the key hanging on the wall. An occasional failure of the operation of the library should not be justification to discontinue the library. Library control of programs and input/output media is one of the most important measures to discourage fraud and other types of loss.

Modification of a program can be either modification of the program deck or modification through the use of the computer console. This would probably be the nature of a temporary program change. Modification of a program through use of the computer console requires detailed knowledge of programming and the computer program. Elimination of the source program listings in the computer room will discourage console modification. The second step is control of console printouts. Normally a console log would provide a record of all irregular stops and program changes, but the operator would simply throw away the offending console printout to destroy any evidence. Storing all console communications on a disk file and maintaining periodic audits will discourage this type of program change. Audit of the console printout also gives management an idea of what troubles the operators are having.

If source decks aren't available to the computer operator, most program deck modifications will not take place. This also means that source program listings should not be available. There is really no way to stop someone from modifying a binary program deck, but few people are able to without the aid of a source program listing.

Some companies attempt to avoid this type of situation by discouraging the computer operators from knowing programming. This type of action will create personnel problems since operators usually hope to become programmers. Also, company discouragement is usually not very successful.

One successful operator fraud took place in a bank where operators were discouraged from learning programming. This particular operator was self-educated. By studying the program-run book, he gained enough knowledge of the savings-account interest program in order to manipulate the file. The control system did not permit opportunities for the operator to modify the program for calculating and posting interest income to savings accounts, so the operator purchased time of a computer service bureau and modified the bank interest program there.

Then the operator proceeded to reprocess the savings-account tape and transfer interest funds to an account under his control. Next, the operator took the tape back to the computer room in the bank. During the running of the banking accounts he just switched tapes—his modified one for the correct one. This was a particularly well-designed and executed fraud. But library control of the computer tapes and program source listings and rotating duties of the operators would have made it quite a bit more difficult.

1. Is the control section for balancing reports separate from the computer center?

2. Are source programs and listings inaccessible to computer operators?
3. Are programs inaccessible when not needed?
4. Are files inaccessible when not needed?
5. Are critical programs provided with a password so they will run only with the correct password?
6. Are files stored in the library and checked out only when needed for scheduled runs?
7. Is the computer center library properly controlled?
8. Are console printouts kept and audited?
9. Are rotating duties used to prevent one operator from dominating a particular file?
10. Can operators rerun programs without authorization?
11. Are there always at least two people in the machine room?
12. Are input errors sent back to the control section for resubmitting, instead of allowing operators to correct errors?
13. Are critical forms such as checks kept locked up?

Allen, Brandt. "Danger Ahead! Safeguard Your Computer," HARVARD BUSINESS REVIEW, November-December, 1968.
Carmichael, Dr. D. R. "Fraud in EDP Systems," THE INTERNAL AUDITOR, May-June, 1969.
Wasserman, Joseph J. "Plugging the Leaks in Computer Security," HARVARD BUSINESS REVIEW, September-October, 1969.
Whelan, Thomas. "Software Security," talk given before the American Management Association Conference on Security and Catastrophe Prevention Management of the Computer Complex, November, 1969.

PROGRAMMER FRAUD

Anyone authorized to instigate program changes is suspect when it comes to programming fraud—this includes programmers, system analysts, or management. The "integrity" of programs is usually the concern of management and the internal auditor. What the management and the internal auditor must do to protect programs from unauthorized changes is to establish a sound and orderly manner for changing and implementing programs. Prevention of programming fraud necessitates the following controls: library control of programs and documentation; authorization of all program changes; and separation of duties.

LIBRARY CONTROL OF PROGRAMS

Library control of programs is an attempt to have the library keeping all input/output media as well as all operational programs and documentation. Operational programs (in the form of binary decks) are checked out when the production job is to be run. After the job is completed programs, tapes, and reports are returned to the library.

The library is also responsible for source program decks and these are also checked out from the librarian. But only the programming staff can check out source programs and programmers can check out production programs only by submitting a prenumbered change notice.

Because of the importance of program maintenance, formal program change procedures are desirable. The prenumbered program change notices contain brief descriptions of the program change and carry the signature of the program or system manager. When the changed program is checked out and certified it is submitted to the librarian. Then, a new object deck is created and the old object deck and source deck is sent to storage. Copies of the change are sent to the internal auditor if necessary.

Meanwhile, the librarian has complete records of who is making program changes and, in case of questionable action, could compare old and new object decks to ascertain what changes were made.

Controlling program changes through the library presents several formidable forms of protection:

1. Program changes are recorded and restricted to programmers. Since only object decks are available to operating staff for production jobs, program modification by the operators will be eliminated.
2. Strict control of programs prevents others (control clerks, supervisors) from surreptitiously modifying programs. Library control of programs should stop even programmers from having access to very many programs. There is at least one case where a programmer stole several hundred programs and tried to sell them.
3. Records are kept by the librarian of what program version was used for a particular production run. Thus you do not have the situation where a programmer changes a program five minutes before a scheduled run and then does not know a month later what form the program was in when a mistake in output is discovered.
4. Library control will eliminate lost programs.
5. The librarian who has all programs can be responsible for making sure copies of all programs are kept elsewhere in case of a major disaster such as flood or fire.
6. If the computer is set up so programs are cataloged on a

storage device, added protection is available. Operators should be instructed to delete and load programs only on requests from the librarian.

AUTHORIZATION OF PROGRAM CHANGES

Documentation and authorization of all program changes are an important step in control of program integrity. Formal rather than casual procedures are desired. The three phases in the process of changing a program are:

1. Request and approval.
2. Implementation and testing.
3. Feedback and confirmation.

The accounting manager and the internal auditor should insist that all changes in production programs be requested and approved in writing. This removes any possibility for later misunderstanding about who authorized a program change. A printed request form should be available for this purpose. Information necessary should include effective date (calendar date, accounting period, etc.), description of the change, and the effect on input and output files.

Other departments, including the data processing manager, should be notified of each proposed change. Otherwise, unforseen aspects could affect other users of the operating staff.

New documentation and testing are necessary for all program changes. Change sheets can be added to the program documentation. This program documentation would not be the same program documentation that the operations staff uses.

Once the testing and checkout by all concerned departments is completed, a correct source deck can be submitted to the librarian. Then a new compiled program can be added to the operations programs at the desired date.

The above program controls will not prevent all fraudulent program changes, but they will discourage most program frauds. By specifying who can make a program change, the possibility of fraud is lessened. Also, establishing each time the reason program changes are made tends to discourage most frauds.

Due to the complexity of computer programs, fraudulent routines could be concealed within a program indefinitely. Either the programmer could insert them or someone else with enough authority, such as a systems supervisor, could request the change. Control of program changes by people authorized to make program changes is a particularly difficult problem.

Separation of duties means that programmers do not operate the computer and operators do not program. The operating staff is also not permitted access to program listings. It is generally agreed that when programmers are allowed to operate the computer the chances for fraud increase.

SEPARATION OF DUTIES

    Many computer installations have adopted the "closed shop"; that is, only operations staff is allowed in the computer room. The operations staff and auditors usually prefer this setup. Some leeway is occasionally necessary when programmers need special testing or on high priority jobs. But it is important that the exception does not become the rule.

Programming fraud has become a much more serious problem since authorization and approval for routine tasks became incorporated in the computer system. These include programming shrinkage allowances, breakage allowances, writing off delinquent accounts, authorizing returns and allowances, approving invoices, preparing checks, reordering stock, and granting credit. All these decisions can be programmed and many are already in existence in various systems. Putting authorization and approval of these decisions in the computer program means putting the decision within the control of the personnel who control the programs.

CONCLUSION

1. Is there a formal policy for program changes?
2. Are programs and documentation controlled by a librarian?
3. Is the auditor informed of all program changes that involve him?
4. Is programmer access into the machine room tightly controlled?
5. Are programmers forbidden to operate the computer?
6. Are operators also used for programming? If so, this is undesirable.

PROGRAMMING FRAUD CHECKLIST

7. Has the manager of programming developed a plan to protect the integrity of programs?

References

Allen, Brandt. "Danger Ahead! Safeguard Your Computer." HARVARD BUSINESS REVIEW, November-December, 1968.

Carmichael, Dr. D. R. "Fraud in EDP Systems," THE INTERNAL AUDITOR, May-June, 1969.

Whelan, Thomas. "Software Security," talk given before the American Management Association Conference on Security and Catastrophe Prevention Management of the Computer Complex, November, 1969.

SOFTWARE PROTECTION

When the library controls the programs, software thefts can be prevented by limiting the number of people who can check out source decks. Since only programmers can get their hands on source programs, control clerks, supervisors, and computer operators cannot steal or sell programs. Programmers must have a reason for checking out programs in most computer libraries and they normally will have access only to those programs they are working on so there is some restriction on the number of programs even a programmer can steal.

However, not all software is given restricted distribution; many programs are given away or traded, and there are program-sharing organizations where software is freely interchanged. Sometimes the programs are interchanged because the giver hopes to get something in return—but often it is interchanged solely because of pride of authorship. It appears doubtful at the present time whether this give-away will continue after the unbundling of computer services. The computer industry has, after all, benefited from this free interchange of ideas and programs in the past.

Readers should be cautioned that the opinions given here   **77** should not be relied upon as legal advice. If they wish legal advice, they should seek it from their own attorneys.

Since there are obvious physical similarities between writing a literary work and writing a program, it is not surprising that a similar protection of programs, as is available with copyrights and patents, was obtained. If a man writes an original sonnet or invents a better wheel, there are legal procedures available to secure to himself the benefits of his originality or inventiveness, and it has seemed that similar protection should be available to those who have written computer programs.

The developer of programs is interested in the protection of the program developer's proprietary interests in the software against unauthorized use. The protection available is of two main types. The first is included with the law of intellectual property. primarily expressed by statute in patent, copyright, and trademark laws. The second type of protection has been developed by common law, including the law of trade secrets, unfair competition, and the law of contracts.

COPYRIGHT PROTECTION

In 1964, in response to an application by John F. Banzhaf III, the U.S. Copyright Office held that computer programs are copyrightable. Since then over a hundred program copyrights have been registered, and no serious objection has been offered to their copyrightability.

The first efforts to secure legal protection for programs took the direction of applying for a copyright much like published manuscripts. The copyright law gives the author or other copyright owner exclusive control for 28 years of the right to reproduce the form of expression. Under proper circumstances, a copyright can be renewed for an additional 28 years, bringing the life of the copyright to 56 years.

In order to obtain a copyright the program must claim to be "an original writing of an author, with some degree of originality." The program must be capable of being read by human beings. This does not exclude a program being written in code. Numerous products (mathematical tables, graphs, codes) that are just as difficult to read and understand as a program have been copyrighted as books. Also many works such as directories, catalogs, and games—which probably require less intellectual effort to produce than computer programs—have also been copyrighted.

In order to maintain a copyright, several rules must be followed. All published copies must bear the copyright notice, which is simply the word copyright, or the symbol for copyright © followed by the name of the owner, followed by the year in which it was first published. Publication without copyright notice irrevocably precludes copyright. Publication is the act, literally, of making the program publicly available to others by sale, or lease, or gift.

It is good practice to include the copyright automatically in all programs to avoid accidental publication without notice, since any publication without copyright will make it impossible to copyright later. After publishing, a formal copyright request can be made if so desired. The registration fee is $6. If not, nothing is lost. The copyright should be incorporated into the identification of all programs. In addition it should show in all object program decks or tapes. The goal is that the copyright notice should appear in all versions of the program.

Copyright protection is very limited because independent creation is not precluded; only copying a substantial amount is prohibited. Rewriting the program from memory or writing the program by analyzing the computer output is not prohibited. Some protection is available under the doctrine of fair use. In case of program infringement damages are difficult to prove, just as they are with literary works. Nevertheless, copyright offers a wide measure of protection and is available quickly and cheaply for almost all programs.

Even if copyright may not give as much protection as desired for programs, the proprietary software owner should consider the usefulness of copyright for written documentation such as programming or operations manuals. Copyright of these items, coupled with the user's contractual commitments not to disclose the program, can provide some protection to the software proprietor.

The Copyright Office has a small circular entitled "General Information on Copyright" which provides most of the information needed to follow general copyrighting procedures. There is also a circular 61 on copyrighting computer programs shown in

Figure 10-1. Both of these free circulars can be obtained by writing Copyright Office, Library of Congress, Washington, D.C. 20540.

PATENT PROTECTION

Before 1968, the Patent Office took the approach that programs were not patentable because they are not methods or apparatus, but rather mathematical processes or formulae. But in April, 1968, a patent was issued to Martin A. Goetz, vice-president of Applied Data Research in Princeton, N.J. The patent appeared to cover a computer program, but when Edwin L. Reynolds, the first assistant commissioner of the Patent Office, was asked about the Goetz patent, he stated that the Patent Office didn't think a program was patentable.

In November, 1968, the court of customs and patents appeals handed down the Prater and Wei decision which allowed the claim of applicant with a program to a patent. This was the first clearly defined patent for a program. Since then others have tried to obtain patents with varying degrees of success.

It is not yet clear exactly what programs can be patented. But it is generally agreed that most business programs are probably not patentable. When the court handed down its decision it stated that a computer process performing only what amounted to a mental step would not be patentable. It provided the Prater and Wei decision on the grounds that the program possessed a high degree of novelty and inventiveness.

In combination with a computer, the program performed a sequence or combination of steps without human intervention, and was directed to an industrial technology which is a useful art within the intention of the constitution.

A patent is more difficult to obtain, but is the best protection for a program. While a copyright prohibits wholesale copying, a patent prohibits the making, using, selling, or independent creation of even similar products. The last clause is why many are against programs being patentable—with some justification.

Patents allow the owner exclusive control of his product for 17 years. When obtaining a copyright, any legal question is usually settled afterwards. But when applying for a patent the Patent Office examines the records to see whether the applicant meets the criteria of not already invented and not obvious. If these two

COPYRIGHT OFFICE

THE LIBRARY OF CONGRESS

WASHINGTON, D.C. 20540

COMPUTER PROGRAMS

What Is a Computer Program?

In general, a computer program is either a set of operating instructions for a computer or a compilation of reference information to be drawn upon by the computer in solving problems. In most cases the preparation of computer programs involves substantial elements of gathering, choosing, rejecting, editing, and arranging material. Some programs also embody verbal material which is written by the programmer and can be considered literary expression.

Are Computer Programs Registrable for Copyright?

The registrability of computer programs involves two basic questions: (1) Is a program the "writing of an author" and thus copyrightable, and (2) Can a reproduction of the program in a form actually used to operate or be "read" by a machine be considered an acceptable "copy" for copyright registration?

Both of these are doubtful questions. However, in accordance with its policy of resolving doubtful issues in favor of registration wherever possible, the Copyright Office will consider registration for a computer program if certain requirements have been met.

Registration Requirements for Computer Programs

Registration for a computer program will be considered if:

- The elements of assembling, selecting, arranging, editing, and literary expression that went into the compilation of the program are sufficient to constitute original authorship.

- The program has been published with the required copyright notice; that is, "copies" (i.e., reproductions of the program in a form perceptible or capable of being made perceptible to the human eye) bearing the notice have been distributed or made available to the public.

- The copies deposited for registration consist of or include reproductions in a language intelligible to human beings. If the first publication was in a form (such as machine-readable tape) that cannot be perceived visually or read by humans, a visually perceptible reproduction or description (such as a print-out of the entire program) must be deposited with two complete copies of the program as first published.

- An application for registration is submitted on Form A. Detailed instructions for registration are given on the application form.

- The applicant also submits a brief explanation of the way in which the program was first made available to the public, and the form in which the copies were published. This explanation is not essential in every case, but it will generally facilitate examination of the claim.

conditions are satisfied, a patent is issued. Patents can be denied or revoked if they constitute a monopoly.

The principal legal issue involved in the question of the patentability of programs is similar to a legal distinction that Norman Wiener pointed out. If an inventor develops a new electronic circuit, he can readily obtain a patent. But if the mathematician develops a series of equations whereby a whole class of circuits (including the previously patented one) can be designed, the mathematician will receive no patent. But if the mathematician is clever, he can do some dealing with the inventor and obtain his patent.

This seeming incongruity is because mathematical equations as such do not fall within any of the statutory classes of patentable subject matter (a process or an apparatus).

Those who fail to appreciate the distinctions drawn by lawyers overlook the many fine lines of distinctions that exist elsewhere. Specifications for a machine part, distinctions that the botanist makes between species or plants, or the differences between a correct or incorrect computer algorithm are some examples of similar fine distinctions.

TRADEMARKS

An often overlooked method of protecting proprietary software is the use of the trademark protection. According to an article in DATAMATION (October 1968), Calvin Mooers registered for trademark protection an acronym TRAC for a family of programming languages. Calvin Mooers states:

> In connection with TRAC, I have taken specific protective action by (1) delegating to my organization, Rockford Research, the authority for the development and publication of authentic standards and specifications for TRAC languages; and (2) adopting TRAC as the trademark and service mark which publicly and authentically identify the languages, the standards, and any computer services offered in connection with these standard languages, whether offered by me or by licensees. These actions preclude others from publicly identifying deviant language dialects or services by the trademark TRAC, or by any misleading combined forms such

as 'Improved TRAC' or 'NU-TRAC.' I believe this approach directly serves the public interest by providing users with explicit standardization and compatibility, together with a means of accurate identification of the computer service facilities offered to them"

Other programs have obtained trademark protection too.

Trademarks have the advantage of being fairly easy to obtain and are not very expensive. But they also have the disadvantage of being difficult to defend. Trademarks, where applicable, do establish some legal rights of ownership and are thus a larger deterrent to misuse than no protection at all. Information on trademarks is obtainable from U.S. Patent Office, Washington, D.C. 20231.

Software can be protected under the laws applying to trade secrets. The program must be kept secret, must be competitively useful to the owner, and must be a process not generally known. In an excellent article in the HARVARD BUSINESS REVIEW (March-April, 1969) Milton Wessel gave the following definition for a trade secret: "A trade secret is any confidential formula, pattern, device or compilation of information which is used in one's business and which gives the owner an opportunity to obtain advantage over competitors who do not have it." He goes on to give six tests to insure the validity of the trade secret:

TRADE SECRET PROTECTION

1. Is the program really secret? It must be clearly established by the holder of the program that attempts were made to keep the program secret.
2. Is the program really valuable? The best tangible evidence of value is a log showing proof of continual use of the program.
3. Was the program developed and owned by the company? Records must be provided to show that the company developed the program. If the program was developed by an individual rather than a team, it must be proven that the development is not the work of a single employee using simply the ordinary tools and skills of his trade, and therefore, not a company-owned trade secret.
4. Was it difficult to develop the program? A log should provide detail on the expense and time necessary for developing the program.

5. Has the program been copied? In order to prove damages it must be shown that a substantial part of the program has been copied.
6. Is it fair to protect the program? A company cannot stop a former employee from exercising his skills to support himself. In addition a claim for program protection cannot be so broad and all-pervasive that it, in effect, gives a monopoly over a large area of potential competitive activity.

If the program meets these six conditions, the owner may bring legal action against anyone who uses improper means to obtain copies of the program. But anyone can develop the program themselves, and if they obtain knowledge through any legal method there is no preventing their use of it. That is, the program must be kept secret. Any publishing or selling of the program can void any right to a trade secret.

Since the law varies from state to state, legal advice will be necessary in guarding any trade secret. In most states good protection can be obtained for trade secrets if the owner is content and able to keep the program "in the house" and use necessary care to keep it secret. The trade secret protection is of no use in a system of wide-scale distribution such as by a computer manufacturer or software house. Unauthorized use of someone's trade secret subjects the user to a law suit for damages. In some states it can also be a criminal act.

Massachusetts enacted a statute in March, 1968, that defines a trade secret to mean "anything tangible which constitutes, represents, evidences or records a secret scientific, technical, merchandising, production, or management information, design, process, procedure, formula, invention or improvement." Under this statute anyone who steals or gets such a trade secret by false pretenses or copies with intent to convert to his own use, and whoever buys or sells such a trade secret, commits larceny and, if convicted, may be sentenced to five years in jail. In addition he may be liable for double damages resulting from his act to the offended person or corporation.

The owner of a trade secret does not really have a property right over the secret. Instead, all he has is the right to prevent others from taking the trade secret by improper or unfair means;

that is, if a competitor can inspect a publicly available printed output of a computer report and ascertain how the program works, he has a perfect right to write his own program to duplicate the results. But he is not entitled to get this information by improperly obtaining a computer printout of the report or program.

Another type of software protection available is the relationship between the employer and employee. Quite often today in any research-oriented industry a written agreement is given the employee to sign. Although many of the restrictions in some agreements are probably not enforceable, such an agreement does give the employer some protection and indicates to the employee what is expected of him. The practice of springing a restrictive agreement on the employee after employment is not fair. Rather, the potential employee should be made aware before accepting a position that he will be requested to sign a restrictive agreement.

EMPLOYEE-EMPLOYER AGREEMENTS

Agreements may include the following: (1) An agreement to disclose all intellectual accomplishments of interest to the company, whether made on company time or the employee's time, if the accomplishment is capable of being used by the company. (2) An agreement to execute such assignments and other papers as the company may request to give it appropriate rights in such discovery.

Furthermore, the employer will probably require the employee to keep all company confidential information secret forever. The employee should also agree that when he leaves he will not take any company property with him, without written permission of the employer.

In addition, in the programming field, an agreement that the programmer will provide some advice after he leaves for a fee on programming projects he worked on is useful to the employer. Considering how difficult it is to modify someone else's program, this agreement may be quite helpful.

There are many interesting legal cases involving relationsships between employer and employee. The courts will not always enforce restrictive agreements to the length desired by the employer. For instance, as already stated, the employer cannot do anything that will deprive an ex-employee of his right of livelihood. In addition, control over the knowledge a person can take in his head is quite limited. If a former employee takes a program with him, it is illegal; but if the ex-employee writes the program from memory, no recourse is usually available to the previous employer.

CONCLUSION

The largest software loss is due to the loss of programmers and their skills to competitors. Efforts to eliminate this loss will probably pay the highest dividends.

SOFTWARE PROTECTION CHECKLIST

1. Are programs and documentation stored in a library so they are inaccessible to those who do not have a reason to need them?
2. Do you have any programs that should be copyrighted?
3. Do you have any programs that would justify patent protection?
4. Has trademark protection been considered?
5. Are trade secret precautions enforced on important programs?
6. Are employees requested to sign a restrictive agreement?

References

Banzhof, John F. "When Your Computer Needs a Lawyer," COMMUNICATIONS OF THE ACM, August, 1968.

Bigelow, Robert B. "Legal Aspects of Proprietary Software," DATAMATION, October, 1968.

Duggan, Michael A. "Software Protection," DATAMATION, June, 1969.

Freed, Roy N. MATERIALS AND CASES ON COMPUTERS AND LAW, Boston University Bookstore, 1969.

"General Information Concerning Patents," U.S. Department of Commerce, August, 1969.

"General Information on Copyrights," U.S. Copyright Office, October, 1969.

Holmes, F. W. "Software Security," American Management Briefing Session, #6373-60.

Jacobs, Morton C. "Patent Protection of Computer Programs," COMMUNICATIONS OF THE ACM, October, 1964.

"THE LAW ON SOFTWARE, 1968 Proceedings," Computers-In-Law Institute, National Law Center, George Washington University.

Lawlor, Reed C. "Copyright Aspects of Computer Usage," COMMUNICATIONS OF THE ACM, October, 1964.

"Proprietary Programs Progress: 10 copyrights, One Jail Sentence," DATAMATION, October, 1965, 11.

"SOFTWARE PROTECTION, by Trade Secret, Contract, Patent: Law, Practice and Forms," Patent Resources Group, 2011 Eye Street N.W. Washington, D.C. 20006, 1969.

Wessel, Milton R. "Legal Protection of Computer Programs," HARVARD BUSINESS REVIEW, March-April, 1965.

Whelan, Thomas. "Software Protection," American Management Association on Security and Catastrophe Prevention Management of the Computer Complex. November, 1969.

FIRE

PROTECTION

Possibly because fire is often an after effect of other types of disasters such as earthquake, riot, or tornado, fire is the most commonly feared disaster for a computer center. Actually fire is less of a danger today than in the precomputer or early EDP days simply because there is less to burn today. Tons of paper records have been disposed of and put on difficult to burn magnetic tapes. In addition, magnetic tapes allow businesses to copy large files in minutes and cheaply store them off premises later.

Even in case of fire, magnetic tapes can sometimes be saved. During a fire, magnetic tape behaves similarly to a tightly rolled paper; that is, it resists burning because of lack of oxygen. Polyester-backed tape will not self-ignite until temperatures of 1,000°F are reached, but temperatures as low as 250°F will cause distortion. A larger danger is steam generated during a fire since even with temperatures higher than 250°F information can sometimes be saved. But steam can cause the tape layers to stick together, thus removing any chance of saving the stored information. Likewise, disk files do not always lose information if the heat does not get too high.

Rather than belabor how much information can be saved after a fire it is more optimistic to discuss prevention of computer center fires. The first precaution is the most obvious and is generally performed free by your fire department. Ask your fire department to come and inspect your computer room and storage rooms for fire hazards. Experienced eyes can point out individual hazards and conditions that no magazine article or book could possibly find.

FIRE INSPECTION

Another source of fire prevention inspections is businesses that sell fire alarms, extinguishers, and fireproof building materials. These companies are usually very happy to send a salesman out to look over your computer room and point out fire hazards as well as their own fire-preventive products.

LOCATION

There are several obvious things a manager can do before the computer center is established and without the aid of a fire inspector. One of the first precautions is that the computer center should be in a separate building and constructed of noncombustible materials. If more than one computer is used, separate rooms are desirable to limit any disaster to just one site. If the building is detached from other buildings, there is no need to worry about a fire in different parts of the building causing damage in the computer center.

New structures built to house essential electronic equipment should be of fire-resistive or noncombustible construction. All structural members of noncombustible construction, including walls, columns, piers, beams, girders, trusses, floors, and roofs, should be of materials which are inherently noncombustible such as steel, iron, aluminum, brick, concrete, glass, ceramic tile, slag, asbestos, plaster, etc., as opposed to materials which are inherently combustible but have been treated to give them fire-retardant qualities. Materials used for interior finishes, insulation, vapor barriers, or acoustical treatments should meet the criteria of noncombustibility.

Recently, a computer center that had taken all normal fire precautions was completely destroyed because a fire started on the first floor and the computer, which was located on the second floor, fell through the floor that was weakened by fire. This illustrates the need for careful consideration of the location of the computer center. Locating the computer center in a large building where the adjacent rooms have a high fire hazard is only asking for trouble. One company, for example, recently located their computer center at the end of a large airplane runway which seems to be an open invitation for disaster. Undoubtedly the computer center should be away from natural disaster areas such as near airport runways or rivers.

If the computer center itself cannot be located in a separate building (and it usually can't) then at least it should be separated from the rest of the premises by fire-resistant or noncombustible walls and floors. In an office building two hours' fire resistance is recommended for the walls, ceiling, and floor housing the computer center. If the computer center is located in a factory or warehouse building, four hours' fire resistance is recommended. If it is not possible to have fire-resistive or noncombustible floors and walls, special emphasis must be paid to providing an automatic sprinkler system.

Also all openings into the computer center must be fire-resistant; that is, doors must be fire-resistant and other openings, such as ducts carrying cables and pipes, should be fire stopped at the perimeter of the computer center.

FIRE ALARMS   Automatic fire alarms offer the best protection against fire because the fire is detected even if the premises are empty. Many computer installations are open 24 hours a day, seven days a week, which adds protection against fire or other types of disaster. Smoke detectors are one of the best fire alarm devices. These should be put in all rooms and in closed partitions such as raised floors and air ducts. Ideally, alarms can be connected to the local fire department, in addition to guard services. All fire alarms should give an audible alarm indicating a fire and if the computer center is not always occupied the alarm should be transmitted to a constantly supervised location.

Automatic fire detection equipment capable of detecting fire in the incipient stage is desirable. The Federal Fire Council recommends the product-of-combustion (ionization) type. Due consideration must be given to air currents and patterns within the space, under floor areas, false ceiling spaces, cable ways and tunnels, and return air ducts connected directly to equipment. A specific performance objective for the fire detection equipment is desirable, such as detection of a certain size and type of fire within a fixed period of time. Care must be taken so the performance objective does not cause false alarms. Detection equipment should be arranged to shut down all power and air conditioning to the involved equipment, except where air handling equipment is specifically designed for smoke removal.

Careful consideration should be given to fire-fighting equipment and automatic extinguishers. Water is not always the best thing to use with electrical equipment. Usually water is just a last resort; that is, when the fire is out of control. Carbon dioxide and BCF (bromochlorodifluoromethane) are two agents that can be used for fires in computer centers. Both are available for automatic systems and portable extinguishers. One British article, however, warns that carbon dioxide has the disadvantage of being toxic. Thus, the use of carbon dioxide is questionable since an accidental discharge or a real fire may trigger the automatic system. This has happened and people have been killed by its use. ("Fire Protection Systems," W. A. Jackson).

Fire-Fighting Equipment

Automatic sprinkler equipment provides the first line of defense against a serious fire. Each automatic sprinkler system should be provided with both local and automatically transmitted water flow alarms. The sprinkler system should preferably be valved independently from other sprinkler systems. The purpose of sprinkler protection is to limit and control major fire incidents and prevent total destruction of the electronic system. Sprinkler protection does not provide the first line of defense, but is included to prevent an incident which may progress beyond control or from developing into a major disaster involving total destruction of all equipment in the area.

To minimize water damage to the electronic computer equipment located in sprinkler protected areas, it is important that power be off prior to the application of water on the fire. In facilities which are under the supervision of an operator or other person familiar with the equipment (during all periods that equipment is energized), the normal delay between the initial outbreak of a fire and the operation of a sprinkler system will provide adequate time for operators to shut down the power by using the emergency shutdown switches. In other instances where a fire may operate sprinkler heads before discovery by personnel, a method of automatic detection should be provided to automatically de-energize the electronic equipment as quickly as possible.

While water may be a last resort method around electrical equipment it is still used with conventional fires. The possibility of the use of water hoses should not be overlooked, but if they are installed near the computer center there should be instructions on their use. A frantic employee spraying water all over to put out a small fire could cause more damage than the original fire.

If water is used in another part of a building or on an upper floor to put out a fire, it can cause extensive damage in a computer center. For this reason walls and floors should be waterproof as well as fire-resistant. The floor above the computer center should be made watertight and doors should be likewise protected. Raised floors which are common in computer centers offer some protection against water damage. An additional precaution is that structural floors underlying the raised floors of computer rooms should have positive drainage. This will allow for quick drainage of water that could accumulate from either an accidental or fire-triggered sprinkling system. Proper drainage helps prevent flooding from natural causes or something like a burst water main. If the electronic equipment or storage facilities are located in a basement, special consideration must be given to protecting the equipment from water that would tend to run to the lowest portion of the building as a result of fire-fighting efforts elsewhere, or from floods.

In any case a complete waterproof membrane should be provided where there is a large quantity of water or a high potential of water spill or flow other than that which might result from fire-fighting operations on a floor above an electronic equipment area. Where any serious potential of water spillage exists on the floor within the electronic equipment area, the necessary curbs, sills, and floor drains should be provided.

Fire Extinguishers

The best fire extinguisher is of no avail unless employees know how to use and locate it. All employees should at least read the label on the extinguisher and it is advisable that they try to operate it once. Carbon dioxide fire extinguishers should be prominently located so that no electrically powered machine or other electrical equipment is more than fifty feet travel distance from a carbon dioxide fire extinguisher of at least 15-pound capacity. Water-type extinguishers should be available for the many types of combustible items around a computer center.

Emergency master switches are of no avail if no one knows where they are or if they cannot be reached in case of a fire. A prominently labelled master control switch should be located at each principal entrance to the computer area immediately within the entrance. These switches should disconnect power to all electronic equipment.

Schools have fire drills but businesses very seldom have any. It would be interesting to determine how valuable a fire drill is in an emergency. An interesting test is to ask a couple of the employees where a fire extinguisher is or where the master power switch is. The normal response is that they have seen one but can't remember where it is.

General fire prevention measures should not be overlooked. The banning of smoking in the computer center not only lessens the possibility of fire but helps to keep the computer equipment cleaner.

GENERAL PRECAUTIONS

Most computer centers are kept clean. This is desirable in order to avoid clutter that could cause a fire. Metal trash containers are preferable and they should be emptied regularly. Electrical equipment and wiring should be adequately maintained and inspected.

Only small supervisory office areas and similar light hazard occupancies directly related to the electronic equipment operations should be located within the computer area. All furnishings such as desks and office equipment should be made of metal. Supplies of paper or other combustible material should be strictly limited to that needed for efficient operation. Special attention must be paid to maintenance areas and only maintenance areas which are impractical to remove from the computer area should be in the vicinity.

There should be a special storage room for tapes, disks, and card files. These items should not be left out in the computer room. The storage room should be a separate room. The storage of office supplies, forms, stationary, and other combustible material in the

STORAGE PROTECTION

computer area or the computer storage area should be discouraged.

Magnetic tapes and disks should be stored in a noncombustible area. No combustible materials should be stored in the vicinity. For maximum protection, tapes and disks can be stored in a fireproof vault that is also capable of maintaining a desirable internal temperature and relative humidity for a reasonable length of time. Metal shelves should be used to hold the tapes. Fireproof cabinets are available for card files.

The majority of plastic tapes are kept on reels constructed of readily combustible polystyrene or other plastic material. Tape reels are usually inserted in individual cases also made of readily combustible polystyrene, although some reels are stored by means of a combustible plastic or polystyrene wrap-around band covering the slot in the reel. All these tape containers present a serious fire development potential, particularly when large quantities of tape are stored. In fact, these containers are usually a higher fire hazard than traditional paper records. The potential fire hazard of these containers is usually overlooked.

CONCLUSION

Fire damage is like looking at an iceberg. The part you see, hundreds of thousands of dollars worth of wrecked equipment, is bad enough. But the hardware loss is usually only part of the loss. The loss of programs, information files, and documentation may easily exceed the value of the lost hardware. Inadequate fire prevention may also cause bodily injury. Much additional detail information on fire prevention is available in the pamphlet, "Fire Protection for Essential Electronic Equipment," which is distributed by the Federal Fire Council.

FIRE PROTECTION CHECKLIST

1. Is the computer center located in safe surroundings? If not, are enough additional physical protection measures provided?
2. Are building materials noncombustible?
3. Is the ventilation system safe?
4. Are there fire detectors and automatic fire extinguishers under the raised floor?
5. Are emergency master switches near an exit?

6. Is the computer center protected against both water and fire damage from another part of the building?
7. Is there a fire protection plan with a responsible executive in charge?
8. Are copies of computer files, software, system software, documentation, and hardware configuration stored off the premises?
9. Are automatic fire detection devices installed?
10. Have automatic fire extinguishers been installed?
11. Are portable fire extinguishers available for small fires?
12. Are employees trained in using fire-fighting equipment, shutting down equipment, reporting a fire and evacuating personnel?
13. Are clean housekeeping and good maintenance practices enforced?
14. Are combustibles such as forms kept to a minimum in the computer area?
15. Is the computer center, as well as fire equipment, checked periodically by a fire expert?
16. Is the local fire department familiar with the layout of the computer installations?

References

Baker, H. R., P. B. Leach, and C. R. Singleterry. SURFACE CHEMICAL METHODS OF DISPLACING WATER AND/OR OILS AND SALVAGING FLOODED EQUIPMENT: Part Two, "Field Experience in Recovering Equipment Damaged by Fire Aboard USS Constellation and Equipment Subjected to Salt-Spray Acceptance Test," NRL Report 5680; Surface Chemistry Branch Chemistry Division, September 19, 1961, U.S. Naval Research Laboratory Washington, D.C.

—— R. N. Bolster, and P. B. Leach. SURFACE CHEMICAL METHODS of DISPLACING WATER and/or OILS and SALVAGING FLOODED EQUIPMENT: Part Six, "Field Experience in Removing Seawater Salt Residues from Aircraft Cockpits and Avionics Equipment. NRL Report 6809; Surface Chemistry Branch Chemistry Division, December 12, 1968. Naval Research Laboratory Washington, D.C.

"ELECTRONIC COMPUTER SYSTEMS 1964," NFPA No. 75, National Fire Protection Association, 60 Batterymarch Street, Boston, Mass. 02110.

"Fire Defenses for Computer Rooms," OCCUPATIONAL HAZARDS, December, 1968.

"FIRE PROTECTION FOR ESSENTIAL ELECTRONIC EQUIPMENT," Federal Fire Council, Washington, D.C. 20405, July, 1969.

Jackson, W. A. "Fire Protection Systems," DATA PROCESSING. March-April, 1969.

Koefod, Curtis F. "The Handling and Storage of Computer Tape," DATA PROCESSING, MAGAZINE. July, 1969.

"PROTECTION OF RECORDS 1970," NFPA NO. 232, National Fire Protection Association, 60 Batterymarch Street, Boston, Mass. 02110.

"RECOMMENDED GOOD PRACTICE FOR THE PROTECTION OF ELECTRONIC DATA PROCESSING AND INDUSTRIAL AUTOMATION'" Factory Insurance Association, 85 Woodland Street, Hartford, Conn. 06102.

DISASTER AND CATASTROPHE PREVENTION *

Every computer system is vulnerable to disaster, accident, and sabotage as well as plain mismanagement. As a result, security measures such as entry controls, fire alarms, and off-site storage sites should be considered. Considering the large investment business and universities usually put into their computer center some catastrophe security measures are usually a must. If your computer center is such that your company could continue to function for days or weeks after a sudden disaster to the computer complex while trying to recover from a disaster, it is probable that much of the computer center is not needed. In a more typical situation, when the computer center goes down all company work is affected and in some situations all work stops.

Disasters, fire, flood, riot, bombing, environmental problems, hardware and software failures, and sabotage can and do happen. Yet very often management ignores this possibility, and the security and protection that was given journals and ledgers in

---

*Reprinted with permission of DATAMATION ®, copyright, Technical Publishing Co., Barrington, Ill. 60010, 1971.

precomputer days is not given computer files. If management considers disaster protection for the computer center and decides that the possibility is not serious enough to warrant taking precautions, this may be a sound management decision. However, if management looks ahead and decides to implement such a security system, it may mean the difference between the life and death of the computer complex. The important thing is that management should face the problem and decide what, if anything, should be done.

MAJOR DISASTERS

There have been several major disasters in computer centers in recent years. One of the most spectacular took place on July 3, 1959, in the Pentagon computer center. Most people would expect this to be one of the safest and best protected computer sites, but at that time it obviously was not.

At 10 a.m. there was a need for some tapes from the vault. This was the first trip to the tape vault for the day. When the clerk opened the vault door, flames shot out.

An electrician had left a 300-watt bulb burning on a supposedly fireproof ceiling. The fire had smoldered all night and the minute the vault door was opened oxygen hit the smoldering particles and in seconds a sheet of flame and smoke blocked all visibility in the room. People tried to shut off the power switch, but could not find it in its remote location in the rear of the computer room. Before the fire was over 19 firemen had to be treated for smoke inhalation and the entire computer area was destroyed. All tapes were lost but programs were saved because they were stored in fireproof cabinets.

After the fire, it was discovered that the supposedly fireproof ceiling was only fire resistant. Several other things were also wrong. The master switch was located where it was difficult to reach instead of being near an outside door. It was almost impossible for firemen to get near the fire because of the way the center was designed. During the fire, no one could get to the switch to shut off the power. Consequently, the firemen were pouring water on electrical gear which was still running.

Now all this has changed. Since that day all military computer center managers are supposed to establish accessible routes and exits. Master power switches capable of turning off all power are to be strategically located near an outside door. All rooms are installed with smoke detectors as well as fire alarms that are hooked directly to the base fire station. Rooms, including floors, are installed with fireproof material. Good housekeeping of trash and maintenance work is required. Fire prevention inspections are encouraged by the fire department.

The long-run effect of catastrophe prevention on an entire computer center should be obvious from this example. It is only one good reason why somewhere in the corporate management there should be an explicit response to potential disaster. Fire is not the only type of potential disaster. Here are other types of disasters for management to consider.

A different type of disaster took place when Dow Chemical's computer center at Midland, Michigan, was invaded by war protestors on November 8, 1969. No employees were in the center at the time. A thousand tapes were damaged and cards and manuals were thrown around. Damage was said to be about $100,000.

A similar, albeit more spectacular and widely publicized case took place at Montreal, Canada, at Sir George Williams University. On January 29, 1969, students set fire to the computer center, causing $2 million damage to computer equipment. An IBM 1620 and a CDC 3300 were destroyed. In addition all magnetic tapes, programs, and cards were thrown out ninth floor windows and destroyed. In this case, besides the equipment which can be easily although expensively replaced, the administrative and research files and programs were also destroyed.

College is not the only place susceptible to attack by dissatisfied people. During a bitter strike in New York, management was able to keep their computerized business running. The management people could keep the computer fed as long as they didn't have to make any modifications of existing programs or files. In order to make the strike more effective strikers gained access to the computer center and destroyed a large number of master tapes, thus effectively stopping the computerized part of the business and making the demands more significant.

Dissatisfied employees sometimes believe the risk of punishment is more than offset by the urgency of bringing to the employer's attention their own plight. In precomputer days there were several cases of plug boards being destroyed or stolen. In a similar case an EDP employee used magnets to destroy every file possible. Extensive damage was done in a very short time and his revenge was almost more than he had even hoped. In fact, for a while the auditors were not sure whether the company could reconstruct enough information to stay in business. In a case such as this, the consequences of inadequate security may be fatal to the company.

The important thing to notice in these incidents is that dissatisfied people are learning what to destroy. Not very long ago in Los Angeles someone took a couple of shots at a computer. This was a naive approach, for if the culprit had aimed his shots at the tape storage room he would have done considerably more damage. All it takes is one elementary course on computers in order to learn what to damage.

Companies with large computer files are particularly vulnerable. The manager of a major airline in the United States recently assessed the value of their current seat reservation system. When asked what would happen if a dissatisfied employee fouled up the computer system for at least a day, his pessimistic but realistic response was: "First, it is entirely possible for many members of our computing staff as well as software or hardware problems to do this to our reservation system. And it could cost us as high as a million dollars a day of revenue during the down period." Other cases where loss of on-line files could cause serious repercussions are inventory files and bank files.

In one unusual case a computer center disaster which would have wiped out many an installation is being used as an advertising bonanza. On November 13, 1969, the president of an exterminating firm landed his out-of-gas light plane on the roof of the Applied Data Research, Inc., in Princeton, New Jersey. The plane caught fire, but some 100 ADR personnel and the pilot escaped without serious injury. The upper two stories of the three-story building burned, destroying the card files and some tapes, while the first floor, housing most of the tapes plus the 360/50 and PDP-10 computer, was flooded by water from firemen's hoses.

Among the software packages ADR sells are Autoflow and Librarian. The latter package allows users to store all programs on tapes. Because ADR had these back-up reels, they lost no programs. Autoflow permitted flowcharts of the rescued programs to be regenerated immediately and ADR was back in business within a week. Here is a company whose major assets were computer software and its loss would have been disasterous. Good thing they use their own products!

Proper site security can do much to reduce the risk of disaster. **SITE SECURITY** The main element is the location of each building. Is the building away from flood areas, earthquake faults, airplane runways, etc.? The next step to consider is what sort of natural disaster is most common in your area. Each part of the world has some type of natural phenomenon. In the United States the west coast has earthquakes, the southeast has hurricanes, and the midwest has tornadoes. The type of local natural phenomenon should be considered in locating the computer center. For example, a computer center should be in an earthquake resistant building in earthquake country, or not near plate-glass windows in tornado country.

The building should be evaluated for possible water damage. Is there a large water pipe concealed in the ceiling of the computer center? If the pipe should burst, water would flood the computer center.

The ideal setting for a computer center is an upper floor interior location. This way the computer center is not susceptible to fire bombing or wind-broken windows. The structure should be fire resistant as much as possible.

The building must be air conditioned and humidity tightly controlled. The air conditioning unit must be protected from sabotage since most computer systems cannot function without their air conditioning.

Catastrophe normally connotes an impression of finality or total **LEVELS OF** disaster. Instead, management should consider a catastrophe as **INTERRUPTIONS** any event that significantly disrupts the normal order of the system. As this definition implies, there are hierarchies or levels of catastrophes. A catastrophe may run the gamut from a temporary shutdown of the system caused by a power failure, software problem, equipment malfunction, or a self-inflicted wound by an improperly trained or misoriented employee, to the more critical conditions brought on by flood, riot, fire, earthquake, tornado, or the complete loss of electric power for a prolonged period, as was experienced within New York City in early 1965.

Since the level of catastrophe can range from the trivial to total, it is best to develop levels of responses. Where there is no contingency plan, there is a tendency to treat all processing interruptions the same—usually with panic.

LEVELS OF RESPONSE

The response to an interruption in processing will normally depend on its duration. Generally there are three approaches to a processing interruption. If the interruption is too brief to have any significant effect on operations, nothing is done. The second type of interruption is of longer duration and management usually reschedules work so that critical applications are given priority when operations resume. Either extra operating hours or off-premise computer time is scheduled to allow delayed work to be processed. The third type of interruption falls in the total disaster area—flood, fire, vandalism, etc. In this case operations are shifted as soon as possible to a back-up computer site so that essential computer functions can still operate.

CONTINGENCY PLANS

It is not always clear what level of response should be taken. Power failure, software trouble, or hardware problems can range from the trivial to the serious and still not be obvious at the inception. Emergencies are more likely to appear on weekends or night shifts than the short day shifts.

To avoid waiting too long for a "trivial" software bug or hardware problem to be fixed, the contingency plan should indicate what immediate actions have to be taken, including who to notify and how to get corrective action started. Such a strategy might include an immediate call to the data processing manager, a call to the computer engineer, and notification of the back-up site that back-up time may be needed.

Establishment of wait periods will avoid the situation of the computer going down Friday night and staying down all weekend and no one knowing about it until Monday morning. The idea of the wait period is that after a certain length of time (say, 4 hours), no matter what the reason, certain responses are necessary. The allowable wait period will depend on the amount of down time which can be accepted without the need for action. In a heavily used center a short down-time period is serious while a computer center that normally runs only 12 to 16 hours a day will not be seriously affected by an 8-hour loss.

On-line systems can usually tolerate little down time. A back-up system must be available at all times. Usually this is too expensive for most users. But installation with one system for on-line processing and another for batch processing can switch the batch processor on-line if necessary for back-up.

Time-sharing companies are an obvious place where interruptions can be quite expensive, since no revenue is coming in while the computer is down and long periods of down time will lose customers. The dollar cost of a one-day delay in clearing transit checks can be calculated fairly accurately by a bank. If a wholesaler is unable to process incoming orders promptly, customer dissatisfaction will cause loss of business. Because of the rather large loss possible under these circumstances, it is best for such installations to appoint one person responsible for the computer center processing, should an emergency arise.

DISASTER MONITOR

A disaster and emergency monitor would have full responsibility for developing emergency guidelines. These duties usually fall on the shoulders of the data processing manager. He should be responsible for deciding when an emergency situation exists. His responsibilities should also include location of a back-up site, scheduling necessary personnel, off-site file maintenance, and software availability.

Off-Site Files

The day-to-day maintenance of off-site files can be left to the computer librarian. But the decision of which files and how often to store files off-site must be made by those responsible for the files. Because the actual user should share in the decision and cost of maintaining back-up files at another storage site, it is not fair to make the disaster monitor carry the whole responsibility.

Today it is actually easier and cheaper to maintain a duplicate file at another site than in the days before computers, or in the EDP card days. Today all types of computer files, including source programs, can be copied in minutes on magnetic tape and cheaply stored. These back-up tapes should be occasionally checked. This will insure that the correct tapes are being stored. Also care must be taken so tapes are not stored near magnetic fields (motors, power cables). Otherwise, when you actually need the tapes for data recovery you may find that the information has been destroyed.

There have been reports that tapes grow errors if stored for long periods of time. This is probably not very serious. Occasional testing of stored reels will indicate how serious a problem this is. Several special types of magnetic tapes are sold which are supposed to resist these kinds of errors.

An Internal Revenue Service office at Nashville, Tennessee, learned that one cannot always forget about back-up tapes once they are created. Their computer center is within about 200 yards of a radar installation. According to an article in the December 30, 1970, issue of *Computerworld,* magnetic tapes containing thousands of tax records were erased by airport radar. Other reports have indicated that radar can cause errors to computers which are running if proper grounding to shielding is not used.

Some installations rely on on-premise libraries to protect computer files, but this overlooks at least two catastrophe possibilities: (1) total disaster, and (2) that it is not at all uncommon for the source program and documentation to be on some programmer's desk.

No matter how good your off-site storage procedures are, some loss will occur such as the current day's processing. But care must be taken to include as much current information as possible in back-up files.

Basic file security includes never releasing a current file for processing until it can be reconstructed should it be damaged. This usually means son, father, and grandfather files. Periodically (weekly or monthy), a reserve copy should be stored off-premise. Old copies of the file should not be released from the off-premise storage site until the new copy is safely stored. Access to these off-premise files should be severly restricted. The surest approach is to allow no one access to both on-premise and off-premise files. This way no single disgruntled employee could destroy all files.

One unhappy employee in California simply took off all the external tape labels. This caused an immense amount of confusion.

If files are stored in some fail-proof safe, that may help but it will do no good if supporting documentation is not provided so someone can use the files. The programs and files that are important enough to store in an off-site location are important enough to store with the supporting documentation. As software and file contents change, so must the supporting documentation. Periodic microfilming and storage of the film in a safe deposit box at least 3 miles away is a good solution to this problem.

Documentation Back-up

No computer installation is immune from electrical power failure. The power failure can be for minutes or several hours. The necessity of power back-up will depend on how essential it is that computer operations are never interrupted and the risks the center can take. Emergency power will be needed for both the computer and the air conditioning. Emergency power equipment is similar to insurance and should be weighed by businesses strictly in dollar-and-cents costs and risks involved.

Power Back-up

Because of precise power requirements some computer centers have installed on-site electric utilities. This also eliminates the need for special equipment to protect against power fluctuations. The Internal Revenue Service computer center in Brookhaven, New York, has their own on-site electric utility.

It is generally possible to provide for some system back-up in case of disaster to the computer system in the normal maintenance contract with equipment vendors. Since it is much easier to negotiate before signing the contract than afterwards, this factor should always be considered before signing a hardware contract.

Equipment Back-up

On-call maintenance support will generally satisfy the requirements of most batch-type systems. Large-scale, real-time, and time-sharing installations will require around-the-clock on-site engineering support. In addition, redundancy of system will be usually necessary.

If the installation is depending on off-site back-up, it is not very wise to make preliminary agreements and then forget about them. Instead, a periodic check should be made to see if the agreement still holds. One manager who had made arrangements for back-up with another installation was surprised when he found that the installation he was depending on had changed hardware three months earlier without notifying him. Another manager discovered that the computer center which previously had guaranteed him 8 hours a day if necessary, had increased their work load so much that no time was available.

In another case where a utility company was depending on using a neighboring company's IBM 1401, they had overlooked the fact that the other company did not have the "multiply-divide" function and all the company's programs used the multiply-divide function. Obvious things to check for when considering back-up hardware include machine type/model, core size, tape density and tracks, type of disk facilities, and special modifications.

It is doubtful that any back-up computer could handle the full load of most installations since normally the back-up computer has a work load of its own. Instead, limited essential processing is the most that is hoped for.

A factor usually overlooked is that after a computer center disaster additional processing time will be necessary. Debugging and testing time will be needed to make sure the programs run correctly on the new system. Files must be reconstructed, programs must be restored, salvage operations completed, libraries duplicated, and a million other housekeeping chores completed before normal processing can start again.

In addition, the functional problems of personnel supervision, communications, work flow, security, orderly transfer of machine operators, shift breaks, transportation, and changed environmental and different shift conditions will all substantially reduce normal efficiency.

Software Back-up

Software catastrophe is the most common headache for management. When having software problems, it is difficult to determine the exact cause of disruption. Software errors often look like hardware errors at first glance. Since the greater majority of these errors are usually software, the necessity of thorough testing cannot be overemphasized.

Software error can cause an installation to have to turn to outside computer help in a hurry. In business applications, output for one file is often input for the next job. Thus troubles can multiply rapidly.

Along with maintaining operational software (programs) at a back-up site there is also the job of supplying the software for the system. If the hardware of the back-up site is compatible to present software, there is no reason why a copy of the system software cannot be sent to the off-site storage location in case of total disaster. After each software revision a new back-up copy will be necessary.

Successful operation at an alternate computer site is possible only if arrangements have been made in advance. If management feels that a back-up site is necessary, then an attempted run at the back-up site should be tried.

Testing Back-up Sites

Not only must the hardware be compatible but so must the software. Whether your software or the back-up site's software is used, problems can develop. The back-up site's software may be incompatible. On the other hand, if company-owned software is used, both computers must have identical memory size and peripherals and logical addresses must be the same. If your company has two computer sites, this problem can be overcome by company control of software and hardware. Some state installations (California State Colleges, California Water Resources) have acquired identical computers and maintained identical software to guarantee compatibility of both software and hardware.

If a computer center is not fortunate enough to have such tight control over the back-up site, the only conclusive proof of compatibility of software and hardware is to successfuly run production programs. This will also give an opportunity to test out the back-up maintenance of files, operator instructions, program documentation, and programs. Only back-up site programs and files stored at the off-site location should be available for a trial run. If you can't run by using just the programs stored off-site, you would not be able to run after a disaster either. A test run also will point out problems of alternate input media, handling source documents at the alternate facility, available working space, and storage space.

Management must keep up-to-date knowledge of the availability of back-up sites, firm reciprocal agreements, interchange rehearsals, and thorough preparations for emergency processing. If two computer sites are depending on each other for back-up sites, then both have an incentive to keep each other informed of hardware and software changes. Also there is a possibility of a reciprocal trial run. One-way agreements do not offer these advantages.

The possiblity of temporary manual processing should not be overlooked. If it is impossible to resume computer processing for a week, it normally would be better to revert to manual processing than no processing at all and possibly closing down the business.

Even if a periodic test cannot be made of the off-site computer preparation, there should be an occassional audit of duplication and storage of off-site files. Checks should be made to see that original procedures are still being followed, new files are added, and obsolete files are returned to the center.

Personnel Back-up

Improperly trained or motivated people can be the cause of a disaster in a computer center. Prevention of this situation is part of the over-all security program. During an emergency situation, overtime hours will usually be needed. In addition, critical people may be unavailable. Both these situations should be considered in advance. Any conditional approval of overtime should be established. There should be some freedom in using people in positions that they do not normally work. The use of rotating duties for personnel will help provide trained people during critical periods.

DISASTER RECOVERY

In order to recover from a disaster it is essential that accurate records of the type of equipment and software used, and particularly any modifications or changes made after installation, should be kept in a location separate from the computer equipment, to aid the manufacturer in prompt replacement of any destroyed equipment.

In the event of fire or water damage, prompt salvage operations can aid greatly in rapid restoration of operations and limitation of damage. Immediate action is one of the main keys to a successful salvage operation. And preplanning is usually the key to immediate action. Because of the importance of preplanned salvage operations, all the possibilities should be formalized in written emergency operation plans.

There have been several large examples of disasters involving computer centers. The most widely reported one was the bombing of the University of Wisconsin Army Mathematics Research Center in 1970. Several computers were damaged, but more damage took place from the hurricane Celia when it sped through Corpus Christi at speeds of 162 mph earlier in 1970.

Two facts become evident from these two examples. Protection against a well-planned bombing or 162-mph hurricanes is almost impossible. But damage can be lessened by simple precautionary measures and site location.

Users without back-up files were ruined after the large disaster. Site location was important. Computers surrounded by glass showcases were ruined by the hurricane. After the hurricane, users who had auxiliary power sources were the first to start running again. Other users who had back-up sources in other cities were able to start work sooner than those who had to wait for machine replacement or repair.

The greater the preparation, the less the risk. Such a small thing as keeping off-premise back-up files can mean the difference between a total disaster and just a major set-back. Each computer installation must decide the necessary precautions needed as well as their resulting expenses and the chances they wish to take.

CONCLUSION

1. Do you have a contingency plan to implement in case of disaster? Does the plan respond differently to each level of interruption of service?
2. Who is responsible for restarting production, should disaster occur?
3. Does everyone have specific duties assigned to him if a disaster should strike?
4. Are son, father, and grandfather files always kept?
5. Have you decided which files and programs are critical to your operation?
6. Are these critical files, programs, and documentation stored off-premise?
7. Is a back-up system available? Can your programs actually run on this system?
8. Is there a back-up of the system software?
9. Are accurate records kept of current hardware specifica-

DISASTER CHECKLIST

tions in case replacement is necessary? Are these records off-site?

10. Where would you find additional personnel to help you during an emergency situation?
11. Are fluctuations in power supply serious enough to warrant power back-up?
12. If the computer center is on the ground floor, are windows protected by diamond steel mesh to prevent fire bombings?
13. How safe is the general location of the computer center? Is the air conditioning likewise protected?

References

Allen, Brandt. "Danger Ahead! Safeguard Your Computer," HARVARD BUSINESS REVIEW, November-December, 1968.

Anderson, B. G. "The Systems Executive's Responsibility in Guarding the Data Resource," American Management Association Conference on Security and Catastrophe Prevention Management of the Computer Complex, November, 1969.

Brock, Eugene H. "Maximizing Computer Systems Reliability at the Manned Spacecraft Center," American Management Association Conference on Security and Catastrophe Prevention Management of the Computer Complex, November, 1969.

Compton, Laurence B., Lt. Col., USAF. "The Air Forces' Internal Control Program for Personnel and Physical Facilities," American Management Association Conference on Security and Catastrophe Prevention Management of the Computer Complex, November, 1969.

"Computer Security," INDUSTRIAL SECURITY. December, 1969.

Grant, D. B. S. "Will Students Wreck your Computer Center?" DATA PROCESSING MAGAZINE, May, 1969.

Hines, Harold, H., and Haig G. Neville. Letter Re: "Danger Ahead! Safeguard Your Computer." HARVARD BUSINESS REVIEW, May-June, 1969.

Jacobson, Robert V. "Planning for Back-up Facilities," American Management Association Conference on Security and Catastrophe Prevention Management of the Computer Complex, November, 1969.

Jacobson, Robert V. "Providing Security Protection of Computer Files," American Management Association Conference on Security and Catastrophe Prevention Management of the Computer Complex, November, 1969.

"Light Plane Lights ADR's Fire," DATAMATION, January, 1970, page 174.

Scoma, Jr., Louis. "Catastrophe Prevention in the Computer Complex. Environmental Factors: How Vulnerable Are You?" American Management Association Conference on Security and Catastrophe Prevention in the Computer Complex, November, 1969.

Supp, Robert J. "Catastrophe Prevention Management of the Computer Complex," American Management Briefing Session #6373-60, April 13-15, 1970.

Wasserman, Joseph J. "Plugging the Leaks in Computer Security," HARVARD BUSINESS REVIEW, September-October, 1969.

——. "Protecting your Computer's Security," DATA SYSTEMS NEWS, February, 1970.

INSURANCE

If a company's total assets are computer hardware and software, then it is obvious that they should be insured. But if the computer center is just a small part of the business, then the computer center is usually not completely insured. Data processing insurance can insure against environmental disaster, mechanical failure, operator error, theft, fraud, or sabotage. Your policy can provide 100 percent coverage, specific equipment coverage, or deductible coverage. It is not safe to depend on conventional business insurance to cover data processing insurance needs. For example, while conventional insurance may pay the cost of replacing a damaged reel of magnetic tape, it usually will not pay for reconstructing the information on the tape. The price of the tape is small in comparison to the value of the information stored on the tape.

It is also a mistake to overlook data processing insurance because the computer is rented. Rented computers are normally insured by the owner, that is, the computer company or leasing company. If you lease equipment, the lessor may have complete insurance on his equipment. But some lessors carry protection

INSURANCE INVENTORY FOR DATA PROCESSING EQUIPMENT						
Equipment	Number of Units	Total Value	Lessor's Coverage	Coverage Needed	Premium Rate	Policy Due Date
ADDING MACHINE AIRCONDITIONING AUDIO RESPONSE UNIT						
BINDING EQUIPMENT BURSTER						
CALCULATOR CARD DUPLICATOR CARTS CARTRIDGES CHAIRS COMPUTER						
DATA COLLECTION SYSTEM DATA CONVERTER DATA TERMINAL DECOLLATOR DESK DESK CALCULATOR DISK FILE DISK PACK						
EMBOSSER						
FILING SYSTEMS						
INPUT SUPPLIES INTERCOM SYSTEM INTERPRETER						
KEYPUNCH KEYVERIFIER						
LIBRARY EQUIPMENT						
MAILING EQUIPMENT MAINTENANCE PARTS MEMORY UNITS						
OPTICAL SCANNER						
PRINTER						
REPRODUCER						
SAFE SCRATCH TAPES SOFTWARE SORTER SPLICER						
TABLE TAPE DRIVES TAPE DUPLICATOR TAPE PUNCH TAPE READER TESTING DEVICES TYPEWRITER						
UNWIRED PANELS						
WIRED PANELS						
TOTAL						

Use this checklist to help you determine the data processing protection you need and what it will cost.

(Reprinted from the May, 1966, issue of MODERN OFFICE PROCEDURES; copyrighted 1966 by Industrial Publishing Company, Division Pittway Corporation.)

only for common perils such as fire or windstorm. Other equipment companies insure only specified percentages of the value of the equipment. The lessee is usually liable for the uninsured risk. Check your leasing contracts! Most data processing installations own part of the peripheral equipment. In addition, insurance for the media is often overlooked.

Another area of concern is the value of software. Software and its supporting documentation is quite expensive and often near the value of the hardware. Insurance is an individual judgment. One can go bankrupt buying insurance and go bankrupt because you didn't buy it. But insurance is a form of protection for the computer center which should be considered.

Data processing insurance offered by the St. Paul Insurance Companies provides six separate categories of coverage: equipment, media, extra expense, valuable papers and records, accounts receivable, and business interruption. This insurance is available with deductibles ranging from $500 to $100,000. Similar data processing insurance is available from Chubb & Son, Inc., of New York. Appendix 3 contains a sample data processing insurance policy.

EQUIPMENT INSURANCE

Equipment insurance can insure all or part of owned, leased, or rented equipment. The insurance can be designed to cover actual cash value or replacement cost. Equipment insurance can also include the air conditioning system. Equipment insurance can cover "difference in conditions" if equipment is leased. One should be careful not to overlook insurance for bursters, decollators, filing equipment, maintenance and testing equipment, or owned input/output devices. Insurance for the air conditioning system should also not be overlooked.

Insurance can be purchased for all hazards or specific hazards such as fire, water, building collapse, smoke, or explosion. Insurance never covers war hazards or intentional destruction. Insurance seldom covers earthquake damage. The lessee often is responsible for any damage not covered by the lessor's insurance. As already stated, some leasing companies carry insurance only for common perils such as fire or water damage.

The premiums will depend on insurance company, on the amount of coverage needed, and the perils of the equipment. The checklist can be used to determine the protection and resulting cost.

Media insurance is the most complex type of data processing insurance. It includes insuring physical loss or damage to all forms of media and can include magnetic tapes, perforated paper tapes, punch cards, disks, drums, and other forms of communication related to the data processing unit. The general distinction is between source documents and media that can be used as input to the processing system. Source documents are not insured under this type of insurance, but input is insured. Either all the media or any part can be insured.

MEDIA INSURANCE

Media insurance normally covers losses due to fire, water, smoke, or other selected hazards. Intentional destruction or war damage are excluded. In addition, insurance will not cover accidental loss due to machine, programming, or operator error or loss resulting from misplaced files.

The most difficult part is determining a proper value for media. Not only is it difficult to place a cost on media, but after a total computer center disaster it would be much more expensive to replace the media because of destroyed data. There are two methods of selecting media insurance. The insurer can establish a fixed value on each item—for example, so much per reel of tape or so much per punch card. The other method is to use actual reproduction cost. Reproduction cost is what it would cost to replace the media after a loss. This cost is figured not only on the basis of what it cost originally to produce records, but the additional expense that must be incurred as a result of a loss.

Extra-expense insurance is designed to cover the extra expense necessary to continue to conduct, as nearly as practicable, the normal operation of business immediately following damage to or destruction of the data processing center. The cost includes expense of using other facilities or other necessary emergency expense.

EXTRA-EXPENSE INSURANCE

Extra expenses are those that are above the normal operating costs. These expenses would normally include additional temporary employees such as delivery personnel, clerks, keypunchers, machine operators, and guards. In addition, overtime pay and travel expenses would probably be necessary. Rental of temporary quarters, machines, filing equipment, and transportation equipment can be included.

Extra expenses must be predicted prior to the loss in order to insure that enough coverage is available. The most obvious way to get some idea of the extra cost is to price the renting of computer services similar to present services. Don't forget courier services, travel expenses, and other expenses necessary to maintain computer services in an off-site location. Once temporary location costs are estimated, they can be compared to actual expenses to determine extra expense needs.

Valuable Papers and Accounts Receivable

The valuable papers insurance is designed to cover source documents plus other valuable papers. Source document insurance is not covered under media insurance. Accounts-receivable insurance covers loss of sums due the insured from customers when the insured is unable to collect payments because of loss or damage to records of accounts receivable.

Business-Interruption Insurance

Business-interruption insurance covers monetary loss resulting from total or partial suspension of operations due to damage to the data processing center. Loss of profits can be quite severe due to temporary shutdown of the data processing center. Since computer centers have wide impact on their companies, it is not unreasonable to expect a company to have to shut down until the computer center is functioning again. Warehousing operations, banking, or ticket reservation systems are examples of where heavy damage can be caused by prolonged interruption of the computer center.

Customers cannot wait until the computer system is replaced, but must normally place orders elsewhere. Business-interruption insurance can pay the company for lost income. You must decide what type of interruptions you are going to insure against (fire, flood, or explosion) and length of the suspension period to insure against.

Service bureaus can obtain insurance to cover their data processing center like any other center. But insurance is also available for service bureaus to protect them from losses due to errors in processing or malfunction in machine operation. It is designed to protect against lawsuits based on erroneous data processing results for customers. This type of insurance can be quite expensive, but there has been a trend toward lawsuits resulting from damages caused by incorrect data processing. This type of insurance is covered in more detail in the chapter on service bureaus.

Insurance is no substitute for good computer security. Insurance is another business expense and with a good computer security program an insurance policy with a large deductible, and thus lower rate, would be feasible. In addition, good computer management and security will result in lower premiums. No insurance covers loss of business momentum. Such damage can be done to customer relations that the competitive position may never be regained.

On the following pages a sample of values of a data processing center and insurance costs developed by Gordon M. Paine, Assistant Secretary of St. Paul Insurance Companies, is given. Premiums are provided only to complete the example and vary with each installation and insurance carrier. The rate depends on the insurance requested, the location of the data processing center, room construction, and the protection from exposure provided.

1. Have you checked your conventional insurance to see how much of your computer operation is covered?   **INSURANCE CHECKLIST**

2. Are you responsible for part of the insurance on your rented equipment?

3. Is your equipment insured for the following: fire, water, building collapse, smoke, explosion, earthquake?

4. Are the input/output media covered by insurance?

5. Do you have extra-expense insurance?

6. Are your valuable papers covered by insurance?

7. Does your insurance cover loss of profit due to business interruption?

8. Can your present insurance be modified to cover your data processing risks? If so, which is cheaper, modifying your present policy or buying a new data processing policy?

9. Have your insurance needs been checked by an insurance expert?

10. Could you reduce your insurance premiums by better computer security measures?

EXAMPLE OF VALUES AND COSTS

Hypothetical Insured—ABC Insurance Company
Has owned and leased equipment.
Rents time to others.
Operates on maximum four-week cycle.
Duplicates and updates programs continously and keeps duplicates elsewhere.
Keeps back-ups of master and transaction tapes elsewhere.

OWNED EQUIPMENT

1401 System, incl. 3 tape drives	$ 275,000
7080 System, incl. 11 tape drives	2,650,000
360/50 System main frame and console	792,000
Scanner typewriter	10,300
Tabulator	9,700
Raw Tapes	150,000
TOTAL	$3,887,000

This is the amount to insure.

LEASED EQUIPMENT

H 1250 System	$ 625,000
360/50 Peripheral Equipment	568,500
Scanner Page Reader	180,000
30 Card Punch	75,000
17 Verifiers	48,800
2 Sorters	16,700
2 Card Proving Machines	80,000
1 Interpreter	10,000
TOTAL	$1,604,000

MEDIA VALUES

Program Tapes
Duplicated, kept in separate building.
Updated as changes occur.

No. of tapes	12
Machine time to duplicate	1 hour
Machine rental per hour	$30.00
No. of operators	1
Average OT hourly rate	$5.25
Cost to Replace	$35.25

Master and Transaction Tapes
Personnel Costs:

Keypunch—77 operators and supervisory personnel Monthly salaries 35,000 x 1 1/2 (for overtime)	$52,000
EAM operators—7 Monthly salaries 3,000 x 1 1/2 (for overtime)	4,500
EDPM—19 operators regular - 4 operators additional Monthly salaries regular 10,000 x 1 1/2 (for overtime)	15,000
Monthly salaries additional 2,000 x 1 1/2 (for overtime)	3,000
TOTAL Data Processing Operations Personnel Exp.	$74,500

Equipment Costs:

1401 System	$ 7,300
7080 System	56,600
360/50 System	29,000
1250 System	13,300
Scanner	3,800
EAM Equipment	4,000
TOTAL	$114,000

Other Costs:
    Hotels, meals, etc., 10 men @ $30
      per day for 30 days $ 9,000
    Travel expense, 10 men @ $300   3,000
    Postage, telephone, telegraph   500
    Relocating source material, 20 girls
      $7,000 x 1 1/2   10,500
    TOTAL $23,000

MEDIA SUMMARY

Program Tapes $ 35

Master and transaction tapes
    (A) DPO personnel $ 74,500
    (B) Equipment rental   114,000
    (C) Other costs   23,000
TOTAL Media Value $211,535
    Insure for $225,000.

EXTRA EXPENSE

Extra Personnel 2,000 x 6   12,000
Equipment Rental 84,000 x 6   504,000
Other Expense 12,500 x 6   75,000
                    $591,000

Less: Servicing Contracts 4,000 x 6 = 24,000
    Power   300 x 6 = 1,800
    Light, heat, security 100 x 6 = 600
                   $26,400

    Deduct proportion applicable
      to BI   2,025
                   24,375
                       $ 24,375
Net Extra Expense $566,625
    Insure for $575,000.

BUSINESS INTERRUPTION

40 x 200 x 6 = $ 48,000
Less: Servicing Contract 40/500 x 4,000 x 6 = 1,920
    Power   40/500 x 190 x 6 = 90
    Light, heat, etc.   40/500 x 30 x 6 = 15
                   $2,025
                     $ 2,025
Net Business Interruption $45,975
    Insure for $50,000.

SUMMARY OF VALUES AND PREMIUMS

	Amount	Premium
Equipment owned	$3,887,000	$10,495
Equipment rented	1,604,000	875
Media	225,000	563
Extra Expense	575,000	1,438
Business Interruption	50,000	190
TOTALS	$6,341,000	$13,661

References   Allen, Brandt. "Letter to the Editor," HARVARD BUSINESS REVIEW, May-June 1969.

Carr, Peter F. "Datafile Reconstruction Insurance Left to Unaware," COM-PUTERWORLD, August 19, 1970.

Hines, Jr., Harold H. "Letter to the Editor," HARVARD BUSINESS REVIEW, May-June 1969.

"Protect Your Business Secrets," MODERN OFFICE PROCEDURES, May 1966.

"The St. Paul Data Processing Policy," St. Paul Insurance Companies, 385 Washington St., St. Paul, Minn. 55102.

CRYPTOGRAPHIC
TECHNIQUES*

The use of systems of secret communication can provide an economical method to increase the security of confidential computerized files. During Congressman Gallagher's congressional hearings on privacy, it was repeatedly suggested that cryptographic-type protection should be used for data communication lines and storage of confidential information in order to make eavesdropping an extremely difficult task. An often overlooked fact is that not only can time-sharing files be protected by cryptography, but many sensitive in-house files can also be economically protected in this manner.

Today one finds the very nature of computerized information systems actually facilitates its unlawful reproduction and transmission to anyone with the tools and know-how. Unlike information which is stored with scrambling techniques, information stored in clear form requires no sophisticated technology, nor complex deciphering systems for either decoding or dissemination. More importantly, there is good reason to assume that organized

*Part of this section is from the author's paper in PROCEEDINGS SPRING JOINT COMPUTER CONFERENCE, 1969.

crime and industrial spies have, or will have, the knowledge and financial resources necessary to acquire and misuse the information in most systems now being considered, including the tapping of communication lines. Finally, once a piece of information is lost, its original confidentiality can never be regained. Since information which has previously been scattered among several rather protected and widespread sources is being collected into one place, wholesale theft of information is very likely to become a continuing fact of life for the American public.

A high degree of secrecy at minimum cost can be achieved through the use of cryptographic techniques for the protection of confidential information. The general principle behind the use of cryptographic techniques to protect confidential information is that if unauthorized use is inexpedient and costly, the price of such use is raised to such an extent that it is generally uneconomical to attempt it.

Traditional cryptographic techniques were designed long before computers were thought of, so many of these techniques are not particularly well suited to computers. But a short discussion of the traditional techniques will show some of their possibilities and weaknesses, and at the same time indicate methods of realizing low-level security. The reason traditional cryptographic methods do not suit computers is that computer files have a great deal of repetition. Record formats are usually similar and all this would give an enemy a handle for breaking a cryptographic method. Low-level techniques will offer some protection against the casual snooper.

In order to explain the use of cryptographic techniques for computers it is necessary to preface the discussion with a brief definition of terms. A PLAINTEXT message is the input message. A CIPHER or CRYPTOGRAM is the output message; that is, the message after it has been changed to hide its meaning. CRYPTANALYSIS is the act of resolving cryptograms into their intelligible texts without having possession of the system or key employed. Throughout this chapter the word ENEMY will be used to designate any persons not authorized access to the messages.

There are two principal classes of traditional cryptography, transposition and substitution. A TRANSPOSITION cipher is one in which the letters of the plaintext are unchanged, but the order is rearranged so that the cipher message apparently conceals the clear message. The agreed upon manner of writing the clear message into the agreed upon pattern is called the INSCRIPTION of the message. The method of taking off the letters from the cipher sequence is called the TRANSCRIPTION.

In a SUBSTITUTION cipher the elements of the plaintext keep their relative position, but they are replaced in the cipher text by other letters of symbols. Most cipher systems consist of two parts: a general method which is fixed, and a key-variable which changes at the will of the correspondents and which controls the operation of the basic method. Keys are either literal, consisting of words, phrases, or sentences; or numerical, composed of figures. Examples of keys will be provided with each method.

Just as locks and bank-vault combinations are occasionally changed to void the use of any past information or keys, the same principle should be used with cryptographic keys. The cryptographic key should be changed as often as is practical. This not only eliminates the use of any past information, but also discourages anyone from taking the time to figure out the key. It is rather discouraging to spend two weeks figuring out a cryptographic key that is changed each week.

Transposition techniques consist of changing the natural order of a record so that the original meaning is hidden. A common game with children is to write a message backwards. The message JACK LONDON would be enciphered as NODNOL KCAJ. This is a simple example of a transposition cipher. Another type of transposition which is not very complicated is called a RAIL FENCE transposition. This method is commonly used by military in the field for sending short messages because of its ease of memory and enciphering. In this system the message "LONDON, JACK071816WRITER1876" would be inscribed by first writing it along a "rail fence" route as follows:

TRANSPOSITION METHODS

```
L N O , A K 7 8 6 R T R 8 6
O D N J C 0 1 1 W I E 1 7
```

Then the first row in groups of five would be transcribed and followed by the second row as follows:

```
LNO,A K786R TR86O DNJC0 11WIE 17
```

There are many more geometric patterns that can be used to change the order of records. These records are explained in the book by Gaines and in my 1969 Spring Joint Computer Conference paper. Both are listed in the references. These methods offer very little security and will not be further discussed.

SUBSTITUTION METHODS*

One of the simplest substitution systems is called the Caesar System, supposedly because Julius Caesar used it. Caesar replaced each plaintext letter by the one three letters further on in the alphabet. The correspondence of each plaintext letter with its cipher letter may be represented as in the following table:

Plain: A B C D E F G H I J K L M N O P Q R S T U V W X Y Z
Cipher: D E F G H I J K L M N O P Q R S T U V W X Y Z A B C

The record COBOL is enciphered as FRERO. In enciphering a record by a Caesar substitution, the mathematical interpretation of the operation is similar to module-26 arithmetic. A value K is chosen and is kept as a constant for the full message. In the above alphabet the K is 3 and this is called the key. The key can be changed as often as desired.

There are several variations of the Caesar substitution. One is the Reversed Normal Cipher Alphabet. This consists just of reversing the sequence of the cipher alphabet as in the following table:

Plain: A B C D E F G H I J K L M N O P Q R S T U V W X Y Z
Cipher: N M L K J I H G F E D C B A Z Y X W V U T S R Q P O

The record COBOL is enciphered as LZMZC. Both of these methods give very little security since anyone who knows a little about cryptanalysis would be able to decipher the record.

One additional variation of the Caesar substitution should be examined since it is very simple to use and offers a bit more security. This type of system is called a key-word method. The key-word is written first and followed by other letters of the alphabet not in the key-word. Any letter which is repeated in the

---

*Reprinted from an article by the author in INFORMATION STORAGE AND RETRIEVAL, June, 1970.

key-word is dropped. If the key-word is STENOGRAPHIC, the key-word would be as follows:

Plain: A B C D E F G H I J K L M N O P Q R S T U V W X Y Z
Cipher: S T E N O G R A P H I C B D F J K L M Q U V W X Y Z

This is a key-word Caesar alphabet. The plaintext record COBOL would be enciphered as EFTFC.

In the first example, the key was just the number which indicated how much the alphabet is rotated. The last method has a higher degree of security and avails itself to be used as a program subroutine because the keys are words, and if the words are well chosen, the protection is the individuality of each word. But unless the key is changed quite often (every record), little security will be gained.

When a key-word alphabet sequence is used to produce a mixed alphabet those letters that occur later alphabetically than the "latest" letter of the key-word will remain unchanged. If the key-word is BEAD, the encipherment would be worthless. For every plaintext letter from F on would be "enciphered" as itself, as may be seen from the following table:

Plain: A B C D E F G H I J K L M N O P Q R S T U V W X Y Z
Cipher: B E A D C F G H I J K L M N O P Q R S T U V W X Y Z

Moreover, many key-words whose letters are closely grouped alphabetically do not scramble the normal alphabet sequence very well, as can be seen from the two long unbroken sequences in the following illustration of the key-word STORM;

Cipher: S T O R M A B C D E F G H I J K L N P Q U V W X Y Z

On the other hand, words like BANKRUPTCY and LOGA-RITHMS avoid both of these problems and the word UNCOPY-RIGHTABLE is nearly perfect.

If the cipher alphabet is a normal one, whether direct or reversed, it is possible for the enemy to find the solution by a simple hit and miss method, or with the help of the expected frequencies of the letters.

There are many varieties of substitution methods. They were all invented long before the computer and most are not well suited to computers. These methods are amply explained in Gaines's book and my papers.

ADVANCED CRYPTOGRAPHIC TECHNIQUES FOR COMPUTERS*

If scrambling techniques are to be successfully used for computers, it is necessary to understand some of the unique characteristics of computer files for cryptographic computerized usage. Computer files would offer an enemy cryptanalyst a large amount of data to work on. Supposedly the enemy would know what type of information is in the stolen file (programs, address file, scientific information); otherwise he would not steal it. In computer files all records are usually similar. That is, an address file will be all addresses, probably in zip code sequence. Programs have a high rate of repeated characteristics (COBOL, FORTRAN). Also, quite often, the structure of computer files can be guessed at. For example, an address file usually would start each record with name, proceed through the address, and end with the zip code. All this helps an enemy cryptanalyst to decode even when fairly sophisticated cryptographic techniques are used.

Now that some of the unique characteristics of computer files have been demonstrated it can be determined what precautions are necessary to maintain cryptographic security of computer files.

1. Repetition of the cryptographic keys must be avoided. Some repetition is all right as long as the location of the repetition is not obvious. If the whole file uses the same key, security is extremely low.
2. The system (such as Vigenere Substitution) is often of only secondary importance to the method of using it.
3. Use of transposition, substitution, and nulls will help solve the problem of repeated structure characteristics.
4. The best system will use a unique key for each record. In sequential files the key can be calculated on the basis of the number of the record. On nonsequential files a key number will have to be inserted into the record.

---

*Copyright © 1969, Association for Computing Machinery, Inc. Reprinted from Communications of the ACM, Vol. 12, No. 12, 1969 with permission of Association for Computing Machinery.

5. Large groups of nulls will tend to discourage analysis by statistical methods. But, of course, if too large a number of nulls is used, core and time will be wasted. Nulls can be placed within each record or complete null records can be placed in the file.

6. Cryptographic techniques are of no value if other basic protection is ignored. If security is lax the enemy will simply steal the key.

There are several cryptographic methods besides the traditional transposition and substitution methods. In a very good paper, E. V. Krishnamurthy (*International Journal of Control*, November, 1970) surveys the general cryptographic techniques available. He distinguishes between old-style cryptography where small amounts of data were communicated and presently where computers will compute large amounts of data. Therefore, Krishnamurthy suggests that precomputer cryptography be called communication cryptography and computer cryptographic be called computational cryptography. I will use his terminology.

In looking for a new method for computational cryptography it is necessary to make sure that there always is a good set of rules so a unique inverse can always be found for any method. In addition, hopefully methods would be developed that are easy to use on computers.

Arithmetic Operations

The four arithmetic operations of addition, subtraction, multiplication, and division can be used in computational cryptography. Since information is stored in binary form, all one must do is generate a pseudo-random binary string and use this for subtraction or addition to the computer record. One must make sure the record with all 0's or all 1's does not cause trouble, but this is not difficult.

Krishnamurthy points out that multiplication or division also can be used, but if multiplication is used the size of the record expands, and this is undesirable. If division is used care must be taken to use perfect division, and this is a disadvantage.

Base-Conversions

Converting numbers from one number base to another is a possible cryptographic tool. This operation is unique and done quite efficiently on computers. Krishnamurthy points out that statistical parameters involved in a language—such as frequency of single letters, diagrams, trigrams, vowel percentages are nearly destroyed by this technique. But it seems that a new set of frequencies is created. Base-conversions are simple to use and would give some low-level security at minimal cost.

Matrix Operations

Matrix operations offer some interesting possibilities for computational cryptography.

Multiplication of matrices has been investigated by Hill (1929) and Krishnamurthy (1970). These techniques are usually called algebraic cryptography which refers to any method of secret communication that utilizes an algebraic system such as a group, ring, or field to encipher or decipher a message.

The general idea in using matrices is to use n × n matrices to multiply the information to be enciphered. This method removes all the frequencies of the original matrix. By changing the matrix, security would probably be quite good.

Logic Operations

The use of logic operations and pseudo-random numbers presently seems to offer the greatest possibility for computational cryptography. These methods have been explored by both Skatrud and Krishnamurthy.

Of the possible binary operations only negation, equivalence, and exclusive-or possess inverse operations. The use of exclusive-or seems to have the best characteristics for computers. Information is usually stored in binary form. Then if pseudo-random binary strings are generated, the use application of the exclusive-or will completely change the stored records.

The general process is illustrated in the following example:

		Rules
Data	10011001110	
Key	11010101101	$0+0=0$
Cipher	01001100011	
		$0+1=1$
		$1+0=1$
		$1+1=0$

Cipher	01001100011
Key	11010101101
Data	10011001110

If the key is very long, preferably as long as the file, security is very good. This type of operation is simple and fast to do on a computer. One cannot discover the data by analysis, but must steal the key.

Even the high repetition that is present in computer files will not help enemy decipherment. Skatrud goes into some detail, using this type of method in his paper.

CONCLUSION

Much work remains to be done in this area but it is probable that computational cryptography will have some use in protecting information in stored memory or information that is sent over telephone lines.

There are several different criteria that should be considered when designing a computational cryptographic method. They are:

1. It should not be necessary to keep the method secret, only the keys.
2. The amount of secrecy obtained should be directly related to the amount of computing time necessary to use the system.
3. The method should destroy the statistical parameters or natural structure of the language.
4. An error should not destroy successive information.

Cryptographic techniques are not a panacea for file security. Other normal security measures must be used in the protection of confidential files since if other types of security are lax the enemy will simply steal the cryptographic key.

References

Baran, Paul. "MEMORANDUM ON DISTRIBUTED COMMUNICATIONS: SECURITY, SECRECY, AND TAMPER-FREE CONSIDERATIONS, The RAND Corporation, Santa Monica, Calif., August, 1964, RM-3765-PR.

Carroll, J. M., and P. M. McLelland. "Fast 'Infinite-Key' Privacy Transformation for Resource-sharing Systems," PROCEEDINGS FJCC, 1970.

"THE COMPUTER AND INVASION OF PRIVACY," hearings before a subcommittee on Governmental Operations, House of Representatives, July 26-28, 1966, U.S. Governmental Printing Office, Washington, D.C. 1966.

Gaines, H. F. CRYPTANALYSIS. Dover, New York, 1956.

Goode, George E. "Data Encryption: Fundamentals for Communications and Computer File Security." Available from Datotek Inc., Dallas, Texas.

Kahn, David. THE CODE BREAKERS, Macmillan Company, 1967.

Krishnamurthy, E. V. "Computer Cryptographic Techniques for Processing and Storage of Confidential Information," INTERNATIONAL JOURNAL OF CONTROL, November, 1970.

Shannon, C. E. "Communication Theory of System Systems," BELL SYSTEMS TECHNICAL JOURNAL, October, 1949.

Skatrud, Ralph O. "A Consideration of the Application of Cryptographic Techniques to Data Processing," PROCEEDINGS OF FJCC, 1969.

Turn, Rein, and Harold E. Petersen. "Security of Computerized Information Systems," PROCEEDINGS OF CARNAHAN CONFERENCE ON ELECTRONIC CRIME COUNTERMEASURES, PB 190 589. Available from U.S. Clearinghouse.

Van Tassel, D. "Advanced Cryptographic Techniques for Computers," COMMUNICATIONS OF THE ACM, December, 1969.

Van Tassel, D. "Cryptographic Techniques for Computers," PROCEEDINGS SJCC, 1969.

———. "Keeping Confidential Information Confidential," JOURNAL OF SYSTEMS MANAGEMENT, February, 1969.

SERVICE BUREAUS

Security for a service bureau involves two points of view: the service bureau and the customer. These two viewpoints will be covered separately.

The central fact about security in a service bureau is that all normal computer security measures must be taken. This would involve the following which already have been discussed: site security, library control of files and programs, back-up facilities, and auditibility. It is assumed that the service bureau takes normal business precautions reported in this book to protect customers' information. In addition, there are a few new problems to consider.

Service bureaus must be careful that they don't inadvertently give away confidential information to competitors. This is especially true when handling accounts for competing companies. A system analyst or salesman could inadvertently give away confidential information while telling a customer that they should process their files in a new way "since ABCD company does it that way."

SERVICE BUREAU VIEWPOINT

Some service bureaus offer "package processing" for one type of business. Because all input and files and reports are similar, great care must be taken not to mix up information and give output to incorrect customers.

Independent Certification

If security is a major concern to some of a service bureau's customers, an outside computer security agency can be called in to certify the security in the service bureau. There are several reputable computer security firms in the business and some are listed in Appendix 1.

Service bureaus are not immune from computer-related crime. In 1970 two employees of Trenton Data Centre in Helsingborg, Sweden, copied tapes and sold them at reduced prices to the service bureau's customers. These tapes contained specialized population data. The theft was discovered when some tapes were found missing prior to a special run. The two employees were tried and found guilty, and sentenced to six months' imprisonment.

SERVICE BUREAU INSURANCE

Insurance is available which is specially designed for service bureaus to cover errors and omissions. This insurance is sold by Chubb & Son, Inc. of New York as part of their data processing insurance. It does not cover punitive damages and it does impose a deductible ($10,000 per claim is the most economical in rate). St. Paul Insurance Company also has this type of policy.

The Data Processing Errors and Omissions insurance covers claims against the insured arising out of negligent act, error, or omission of the service data processing. It covers actual costs of reprocessing, the actual income lost by others, and the additional expenses incurred by others due to the negligent act, error, or omission. In addition, consequential damage for which the service bureau is held liable in a court of law is covered.

CUSTOMER VIEWPOINT

The major difficulty in developing a security program for the customer will be the customer himself; that is, the customer must be able to indicate how much security is necessary with his data and he must be willing to pay the additional cost.

First, some general notes about the business of a service bureau. Service bureaus, like any other type of business, are set up to handle their business in the most efficient manner. Thus, if a customer wants all his data reports, programs, and files handled separately, he must be willing to pay the additional cost. Service bureaus would normally store several customers' data on the same disk. This might be objected to by some customers from a security angle.

The next systematic step is to establish what special precautions are necessary. The key here is that these precautions should all be established before a contract is signed. Any protection wanted after the original contract is signed will be expensive and more difficult to agree to later.

SPECIAL PRECAUTIONS

    Unneeded precautions are time consuming and expensive. Thus realistic appraisals of security needs are needed. If no precautions are provided for data and reports at the customer location, the requesting of special handling procedures at the service bureau is of questionable value. At the same time, if data are of little value to anyone else, additional precautions are expensive and wasteful. People only steal what is of value.

An area of concern that is unique to the service bureau and its customers is the failure to deliver service that was promised. There have been at least three major companies held liable for failure to deliver promised service. A Minneapolis decision, which was appealed, resulted in a half-million dollar liability on the service bureau, despite contractual disclaimers and no proven intent to misrepresent. Thus, the user should be sure that the contract spells out the service bureau commitment and its liability for failure to perform as agreed.

Failure to Deliver Service

A similar concern involves the responsibility for errors in data processing service. There have been several lawsuits over mistakes in data processing service. It is not inconceivable that future lawsuits could involve service bureaus. Because victims of data processing mistakes have collected damages, the question of who is responsible for the mistakes in case of lawsuits when using a service bureau should be considered. There also seems to be a legal trend of making businesses responsible for computer-generated

Responsibility for Errors

errors which will complicate the service bureau and customer relationship. Thus, it is evident that users and service bureau should agree on the liability for misinformation or mistakes. Insurance is available to cover damages done to customers of service bureaus.

The Association of Data Processing Service Organizations (ADAPSO) suggests that the following disclaimer be added to its reports: "The foregoing presentation has been processed electronically by computer from data furnished to us, has not been analyzed by professional (accountants) (engineers) (architects) (doctors) (lawyers) or other persons purporting to have expert knowledge of (accounting) (engineering) (architecture) (medicine) (law) and is furnished without (accounting) (engineering) (architectural) (medical) (legal) opinion of any kind." This disclaimer tends to tell the customer that he must check his own reports for errors. The customer is better equipped to discover errors in computer output since he should know what is reasonable. Companies having their own computer center cannot guarantee against all mistakes, so it is not reasonable to expect service bureaus to either. Most lawsuits by wronged customers have materialized only after repeated attempts to get obvious errors corrected have failed. Processing of data without computers is not error-free but it was often easier to get errors corrected.

Contracts

Contracts between the user and service bureau should clearly establish the responsibility for service and errors. Other questions that should be agreed on before using a service bureau are: How will pickups and deliveries of data and reports be handled? Who is authorized to pick up reports? Without these precautions, an industrial spy could easily call in to ask when the accounting reports will be ready and simply walk in and pick them up.

Another question is: Who is eligible to request changes in data or program? Conflicting changes by different or unauthorized personnel could drastically change output reports.

Critical Files

Specifying which files and programs are critical is often overlooked. It may be obvious that a certain file or program is critical to the customer, but it wouldn't be obvious to the service bureau. Which files, programs, and documentation require back-up? How long must these files be maintained? Customers can request that back-up files, programs, and documentation be stored on their premises. This not only takes care of off-site storage of files, but provides the customer with physical possession of his own files, programs, and documentation.

The question of who own the files, programs, and documentation when the service bureau contract is terminated is often not clear. Information is normally stored on media (such as tapes or disks) owned by the service bureau. In addition, information stored this way has a rather tenative physical existence. While it may be obvious that the user owns the input information, it is not always obvious that he also owns the computer developed information.

Ownership of Files and Programs

Ownership of the programs is another critical question. Who owns the programs? Usually the party who pays to develop them. But if the user pays a fee for development, ownership may not be clearly defined. A rather bitter termination of a contract with a Los Angeles service bureau resulted in a one-million dollar lawsuit involving ownership of files and programs. Both sides not only claimed ownership of files and programs, but disagreed on who was to take the blame for unreliable and late reports.

Even if the customer does own the files, programs, and documentation, other problems must be investigated. Is documentation inadequate to allow the user use of the information? Furthermore, will the programs and files run on someone else's computer? Are similar computers available? The service bureau computer may be so unusual or modified that similar, additional, or back-up service is not available elsewhere.

The user would normally want some guarantee that back-up service is available in case the service bureau has its present site damaged or if equipment becomes inoperative for lengthy periods; otherwise, the customer may just have to wait until the service bureau center is repaired or until replacement equipment can be obtained. Users using time-sharing services will quite often be concerned over loss of service.

Back-up Service

Reasonable measures must be taken by the service bureau to protect the confidentiality of the users' information. The service bureau can be helped by having the user point out information that should be kept confidential. The service bureau can help maintain privacy by locking up files and programs and destroying old reports so browsers can't use them.

SERVICE BUREAU CHECKLIST

1. Does the service bureau satisfy basic rules for protecting the confidentiality of information?
2. Is the service bureau site protected from sudden disasters such as fire, flood, tornadoes, or riot?
3. Is there back-up equipment available for service bureau use?
4. Are files and programs protected with back-up files where needed?
5. Who owns the files, programs, and documentation in case service is discontinued?
6. Are files auditible? Do they satisfy federal and state laws such as tax record regulations?
7. Is the type and amount of service clearly understood by both parties?
8. Who is responsible for errors and what are the limits of responsibility?
9. Who is authorized to pick up reports or request changes?
10. Which files are critical from a privacy or company point of view?
11. Has your lawyer checked over the service bureau contract?

References

Bigelow, Robert P. "Some Legal Aspects of Commercial Remote Access Computer Services," DATAMATION, August, 1969.

Davis, Morton. "Service Bureaus Need to Improve Data Security," COMPUTERWORLD, August 26, 1970.

Delair, W. E. "Security Responsibilities of a Time-Sharing Service Company," October 25, 1969. Available from TRANSDATA Corporation.

"Electronic Data Processing Errors and Omissions," insurance policy provided by Chubb & Son, Inc., 90 John St., New York, N.Y. 10038.

Scaletta, Jr., Phillip J. "Legal Ramifications of the Computer," DATA MANAGEMENT, November 1970.

"Scandinavia's First Data Theft Occurs at Service Bureau," COMPUTERWORLD, November 18, 1970.

Wessel, Milton R. "Problems of Liability for the EDP Service Industry," COMPUTERS AND AUTOMATION, September, 1970.

TIME-SHARING

Large quantities of private information are presently being accumulated in computer files. Concurrent with this accumulation is the steady growth in the use of remote terminal devices and time-sharing systems to make this information available to a wide variety of users for widely diverse applications. In 1970 there were about 70,000 terminals connected to computers, and the number is growing rapidly. There is a natural momentum towards the pooling of resources since it is normally cheaper to use somebody else's data file than create your own.

As these systems grow and their data increase the incentive to penetrate the safeguards will likewise grow. Unless security measures keep up with the value of the information there will soon exist a situation where the temptation to breach the security of a large time-sharing center will be greater than the deterrent provided. Figure 16-1 illustrates a typical resource sharing system.

Existing laws have proven inadequate to protect non-computerized information, so it is unlikely they will be of much help with time-sharing information. Therefore, any privacy of information will have to be designated by the holder of the information.

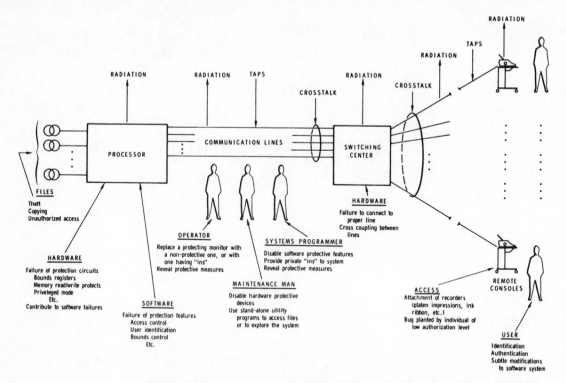

Figure 16-1 *Typical configuration of resource-sharing computer system*

From "Security and Privacy in Computer Systems" by Dr. Willis H. Ware. Used with permission of the RAND Corporation, Santa Monica, Calif. Reprinted from the Proceedings of the Spring Joint Computer Conference, 1967. AFIPS Press, Montvale, New Jersey.

Not only is there concern with security of data in these systems, but also with the integrity of the data. That is, is the information correct or, through accidental or intentional but unauthorized modification, have the data been changed? In addition, are authorized people the only ones receiving the data? Are users being charged correctly for use?

Time-sharing systems require as much security protection as any other important computer file. There are many examples of individual misuse of time-sharing systems, and large-scale fraud using a time-sharing system is far from being a remote possibility. More than likely, it just hasn't been uncovered.

Several rather minor crimes have been discovered with time-sharing. In the July 29, 1970, issue of *Computerworld* there is an article on the arrest of a man for illegally copying data files from a time-sharing system. The government, at the time of arrest, claimed that the man extracted information from Metridata Computing, Inc., of Louisville, Kentucky.

The FBI arrested the man in Cincinnati, Ohio, which was the location the man used for his interstate thefts. He signed onto the system by using several customers' account numbers and pass-words, and knew the unlisted telephone number for the time-sharing service. It is not clear how he obtained this information. According to the FBI, he was building a program that would have bypassed the security system for all of his future accesses.

In March, 1971, another story appeared in many newspapers with the title "Computer Raped Over the Phone." In this case an employee of the Palo Alto, California, office of University Com-puting Co., Dallas, was charged with grand theft in Oakland, California, for allegedly stealing a graphics program by telephone from Information Systems Design Inc., of Oakland. This EDP service company stated that someone with the correct account and identification had accessed the computer by phone to get a copy of this $25,000 program. The company filed a $6 million damage suit over loss of the program. Figure 16-2 lists some countermea-sures that can be taken to increase and improve information privacy.

Time sharing is the ability of many users to be served by a single computer simultaneously. Their programs, their systems, and their data are residing in the computer, some parts in memory or storage simultaneously. Generally, the users are geographically spread around, although not necessarily, and are usually using terminals. In addition to terminal usage, multiple card readers or line printers can be hooked up and often jobs are being processed at the main computer center at the same time.

Because of the vast difference between electronic and human speeds, each terminal user usually feels he is obtaining almost instantaneous response. All the resources of the computer are being shared and each user's problem is broken up into many small bits and each user is given a few milliseconds of time. No user is allowed to take too much time if other users are waiting. If jobs

WHAT IS TIME SHARING

SUMMARY OF COUNTERMEASURES

Countermeasure / Threat	Access Control (passwords, authentication, authorization)	Processing Restrictions (storage, protect, privileged operations)	Privacy Transformations	Threat Monitoring (audits, logs)	Integrity Management (hardware, software, personnel)
Accidental: User error	Good protection, unless the error produces correct password	Reduce susceptibility	No protection if depend on password; otherwise, good protection	Identifies the "accident prone"; provides post facto knowledge of possible loss	Not applicable
System error	Good protection, unless bypassed due to error	Reduce susceptibility	Good protection in case of communication system switching errors	May help in diagnosis or provide post facto knowledge	Minimizes possibilities for accidents
Deliberate, passive: Electromagnetic pick-up	No protection	No protection	Reduces susceptibility; work factor determines the amount of protection	No protection	Reduces susceptibility
Wiretapping	No protection	No protection	Reduces susceptibility; work factor determines the amount of protection	No protection	If applied to communication circuits may reduce susceptibility
Waste Basket	Not applicable	Not applicable	Not applicable	Not applicable	Proper disposal procedures
Deliberate, active: "Browsing"	Good protection (may make masquerading necessary)	Reduces ease to obtain desired information	Good protection	Identifies unsuccessful attempts; may provide post facto knowledge or operate real-time alarms	Aides other countermeasures
"Masquerading"	Must know authenticating passwords (work factor to obtain these)	Reduces ease to obtain desired information	No protection if depends on password; otherwise, sufficient	Identifies unsuccessful attempts; may provide post facto knowledge or operate real-time alarms	Makes harder to obtain information for masquerading; since masquerading is deception, may inhibit browsers
"Between lines" entry	No protection unless used for every message	Limits the infiltrator to the same potential as the user whose line he shares	Good protection if privacy transformation changed in less time than required by work factor	Post facto analysis of activity may provide knowledge of possible loss	Communication network integrity helps
"Piggy-back" entry	No protection but reverse (processor-to-user) authentication may help	Limits the infiltrator to the same potential as the user whose line he shares	Good protection if privacy transformation changed in less time than required by work factor	Post facto analysis of activity may provide knowledge of possible loss	Communication network integrity helps
Entry by system personnel	May have to masquerade	Reduces ease of obtaining desired information	Work factor, unless depend on password and masquerading is successful	Post facto analysis of activity may provide knowledge of possible loss	Key to the entire privacy protection system
Entry via "trap doors"	No protection	Probably no protection	Work factor, unless access to keys	Possible alarms, post facto analysis	Protection through initial verification and subsequent maintenance of hardware and software integrity
Core dumping to get residual information	No protection	Erase private core areas at swapping time	No protection unless encoded processing feasible	Possible alarms, post facto analysis	Not applicable
Physical acquisition of removable files	Not applicable	Not applicable	Work factor, unless access to keys obtained	Post facto knowledge form audits of personnel movements	Physical preventative measures and devices

Figure 16-2 *Summary of countermeasures to threat to information privacy*

are also being fed in at the computer center, then they usually get low priority which means whenever there is spare time the computer center jobs are processed. These are commonly called background jobs while the terminal jobs are called foreground jobs. Time-sharing systems allow for the highest possible efficiency of the computer and thus its popularity.

Time-shared on-line systems usually have most of the following: a central processing facility of one or more processors, associated memory hierarchy, information files (disk, drum, or tape), either public or private query terminals at remote locations, and a communications network (common carrier, leased or private lines). In this chapter this type of time-shared on-line system will be referred to as the "system."

Time-sharing systems offer one large security advantage. In normal computer operations, programs are designed and reports are run at the computer center and then sent over to the requesting department. In this situation the computer operator, or anyone else around the computer, can (and usually does) look at reports and can also copy data and programs. By using terminals the programs can be designed at the terminal, data read in at the terminal, and the final processing printed at the terminal. All this can be done by the user. Even if only part of the work is done at the department's terminal, such as input or output, security should be better if there are normal security measures in the time-sharing center. Thus a secure time-sharing system offers the possibility of computerizing information that before was too sensitive.

Threats to "in-company" time-sharing systems are similar to threats that can develop with outside services or a computer utility. In the latter case, the user actually entrusts his data base to a third party. It is then the responsibility of the third party to explain and assure the user that sufficient protection is available. In order for the user to evaluate the provided protection, he must

**THREATS TO
INFORMATION
SECURITY**

Figure 16-2 on the facing page is taken from "System Implication of Information Privacy" by H. E. Petersen and R. Turn. Used with permission of the RAND Corporation, Santa Monica, Calif. Reprinted from the Proceedings of the Spring Joint Computer Conference, 1967. AFIPS Press, Montvale, New Jersey.

have some knowledge of computer systems, types of security threats, and possible safeguards.

Both accidental and deliberate attempts can result in computer information being divulged to unauthorized people. Accidental destruction of data through human or machine error can be just as damaging as intentional destruction, and accidental disclosures can be as embarrassing as intentional ones. Many of the protecting features developed for hardware and software were originally developed to prevent accidental misuse of data by un-debugged programs. Write bounds were developed so a program could not branch out of its core area and write in someone else's data or program. New protection has been added such as read bounds since, from a security point of view, reading someone's data is as serious as destroying someone's data. Most of the features developed to prevent accidental misuse will also prevent deliberate misuse, and vice versa.

A great deal has been done to protect military computer files and we are occasionally given a brief glimpse of some of the possibilities developed here (Bernard Peters, "Security Considerations in a Multi-programmed Computer System"). But most of this information is kept secret so nonmilitary computer users are forced to "re-invent the wheel," or in this case develop their own security measures. The sad fact is that most of the computer security problems have been solved at taxpayer expense, but the results are kept secret by the governmental agencies.

Business espionage is a well-developed and profitable field, so it is not unlikely that industrial spying will soon attack the time-sharing computer system. The possible payoff for a well-organized computer raid is immense because there is so much information available.

In addition, legal restrictions are rather vague and untested, thus offering another inducement to attack the computer. Some people feel that since an all-out effort to intrude on a time-sharing system would involve a great deal of organization, money, and expertly trained people, it will not happen. The military, of course, disagrees. This assumption does overlook a similar situation and that is the drug market, which involves a great deal of organization, finances, and well-trained chemists, and all these have been readily available. A general rule in regard to crime or industrial espionage is that when the possible payoff exceeds the deterrent, then the crime will probably be committed, and the same general rule will apply to time-sharing situations. As computer networks continue to grow and go international, foreign governments and industry might find it quite profitable to tap this source of information.

Much business information is company-confidential because it relates to proprietary processes or technology, payroll, customer credit, marketing, or to the success, failure, or state-of-health of the company. Since technological skills necessary to interpret computerized data are widespread, time-sharing systems themselves can be expected to offer no more protection than telephone conversations or Morse code.

There are several types of threats to any system which should be considered. A nonuser, for example, can try to use the system without authorization. By watching others use the terminal, he could learn how to use the system. His purpose could be to use the system without paying for it, or to use the system to obtain information not readily available elsewhere. Once in the system, he would be able to modify as much information as the legitimate user could.

TYPES OF VIOLATIONS

A speaker at an industrial security conference ("Computer Security," INDUSTRIAL SECURITY, December, 1969) recently bragged that he could dial up the legislative system in Florida and determine what bills are currently in what committees. He is also able to dial up the Missouri passenger automotive registration system and find out the kind of car Harry Truman currently owns. There are many other systems which one can get into simply by having the telephone number. And once into the system, instructions are given on how to use it.

Another type of security problem is the copying of files. If complete files were copied and given to unauthorized persons, serious damage could result. Possession of such files as marketing, research files, or customer name and address files might do a lot of damage.

In any situation where personnel confidential information is available there is the problem of people browsing through files. Computer systems will have the same temptation as noncomputerized files. This includes looking up a neighbor's bank account, an office rival's pay scale, or even personnel records.

A legitimate user could use the system to obtain unauthorized facts. This could be as simple as requesting available information for personal use or copying files for later sale. By phrasing questions in the proper manner, he could find out more information than allowed; for example, by asking for the largest salary in his department he could discover his department head's salary. Lance Hoffman and W. F. Miller ("Getting a Personal Dossier from a Statistical Data Bank," DATAMATION, May, 1970) have lucidly explained these techniques. Phil Hirsch ("The World's Biggest Data Bank," DATAMATION, May, 1970) also demonstrates how information as seemly innocent as U.S. Census information can be used to manipulate people.

Certain people will have access to the system by virtue of their position. These include the computer operator, system programmer, maintenance engineer, and certain management personnel. Normally these people will be able to read, modify, or copy files and programs.

Wire tapping would normally give the passwords and terminal identification away and in most cases allow the setting of an infiltrator's terminal. A similar approach is called "piggy back" in which the entry into the system is by selective interception of communications between a user and the processor. Messages can be modified or substituted while returning an "error" message. Between line entry involves using the system when an authorized user is inactive but still connected to the system.

In addition, it is possible to cancel the user's sign-off signal and thus continue operation. In all these cases only the legitimate users files will be available, but this is probably sufficient for obtaining the information desired.

PERSONNEL Intimately involved with the system are three types of personnel: operators, programmers, and maintenance engineers. In contrast to the potential outside intruder, these three people are much more capable of executing undiscovered intrusion simply because they are in a position of trust. And it is always trustworthy people who commit large embezzlements since only trustworthy people have access to assets.

Presently all systems require an operator who can override

many system security measures as part of his normal duties. Care must be taken so there is some record of operator-originated overrides. Operators should not be able to ignore log and audit procedures.

In addition, the operator could replace the correct monitor with a rigged monitor of his own which has special "ins" for unauthorized parties. He could also reveal to unauthorized parties some of the protective measures which are designed into his particular system.

An operator can copy files or modify files, but in order to make any use of these files he would need documentation on the files. Descriptive documentation, source listing, and other supporting documentation should not be available to the operator. Limiting computer printout is one option that can prevent misuse by the operator. Inquiries can be limited to terminal users.

The system programmers have great freedom to make changes in the system that override software security and allow browsing or the modifying or copying of files. System changes should be strictly controlled and written authorization should be necessary for all system changes.

A maintenance engineer could alter hardware so unauthorized entries can be made in files, or he could snoop in files while doing maintenance work. While attempting to diagnose a system failure, an engineer could easily locate enough information to reveal how the software protections are coded. Then the machine could be rewired so that protection features appear normal, but, in fact, can be bypassed.

While all these are deliberate acts it is also quite possible that an operator error, program change, or engineering change could weaken some of the security measures. This type of error could go unnoticed for quite a long time if testing procedures do not uncover it.

An integral part of any personnel security plan is that personnel must be aware and be able to respond to security measures. The operating doctrine should be written and be clear enough so it can be easily followed.

Maintenance of security demands competence, loyalty, and integrity from all personnel connected with the system. In addition, it requires continuing training for them, both in operating procedures and security measures. The purpose of this training is to insure that each individual recognizes his vital role in installation security and does not, through familiarity, become careless.

The selection of these people is an especially sensitive issue. In fact, trustworthy people in the computer center are the key to any secure situation—without them all security efforts will fail. Since these people could have access to customer or sensitive files, careful screening and bonding are recommended where necessary.

System integrity should depend on as few people as possible and, where necessary, overlapping of duties and dual authorization should be considered. Sensitive systems should require two people checking out software modifications. No one, regardless of position or level of competence, should be able to circumvent the security procedures, logs, and audit trails.

A realistic evaluation must be made of the information available. Too much security is oppressing and expensive. The lower the value of the information, the less security needed. If the information is of high value, the possibility exists of someone being bribed or planted in the center. Because of the high turnover of help in the computer field, it is not inconceivable for an intruder to hire away a crucial person and then send someone eminently qualified to take his place.

Some system of control of outsiders would seem desirable. As computing systems and peripheral devices become increasingly more complex, the nature and variety of those who traditionally participate becomes wider. During times of crisis (power failures, hardware problems) there is a steady pressure to bypass security measures to get things going again. A reasonable judgment must be made so security is not overly compromised is the name of expediency. A leak in many security situations is the computer maintenance personnel. Most security-conscious installations should exercise some control over who the maintenance people are. Often this is left to the manufacturer.

USER SECURITY   The user is responsible for his share of the security problem whether he is using an in-house computer or a time-sharing service bureau. He will want to restrict his terminals to authorized personnel only. This can be accomplished by company policy, restrictive location of the terminals, or personnel identification for terminal entry.

Terminals should be placed so they are not readily available to unauthorized users. If care is not taken when locating terminals, an operator can leave the terminal for a couple of minutes and access would be available by any passerby.

If sensitive information is available through a terminal, some method should be available to physically shut down the terminal. That is, if the terminal is used only during day hours, then a key lock could turn off the terminal so that it could not be used during off-hours.

There has been some talk of using voiceprints, fingerprints, or retina images but these devices are not yet available and, if available, would be quite expensive. Problems may develop in their adaptation; otherwise, someone could come to work with a sore throat or bloodshot eyes and not be able to use the terminal. Voice recordings or eye snapshots might be able to circumvent this type of identification device anyway.

Both keys and ID cards have been used successfully to access terminals. Banks regularly use keys and airline systems have used ID badges. Since a user must have his key or badge to use the system, he is bound to recognize and report a loss if it occurs. Keys and badges have the advantage that they make the sign-on procedure easier, but have the disadvantage that they can be lost or duplicated.

Standardized identification cards with magnetic stripes are available and seem to presently offer the most advantages. These cards can be designed to have no human readable information except an address to send it to if found. Then if one is found, no one will know who it belongs to. If it is stolen or lost, the owner will usually know it and can report its disappearance so it can't be used.

A user would have to insert his card to use the terminal and if the card is used incorrectly, it can be held by the device until a security officer gets there to release it. In order to avoid the situation where someone leaves the card in the terminal, military users have surrounded the terminal by a small booth. Then the card must be used to enter and leave the booth.

TERMINAL IDENTIFICATION

In order to establish billing and locate the level of privacy of the terminal it is necessary to identify the terminal. Petersen and

Turn, in an excellent paper, suggest that this could involve transmission of an internally (to the terminal) generated or user-entered code word consisting, for example, of two parts: one containing a description or name of the terminal; the other, a password which authenticates that the particular terminal is indeed the one claimed in the first part of the code.

The terminal device can have interlocks so that only certain types of files and/or information are allowed to be put out on this particular terminal. This is similar to software locks where only individuals providing passwords are allowed certain files.

Verification of terminal can be accomplished by using the computer to hang up and call back before starting processing. This will verify the processor is talking with the correct terminal. Then computerized tables can establish the privacy level and processing restrictions of that particular terminal.

Some terminals have special features providing the ability to respond to computer-generated queries with a unique tamperproof identification code. The only problem created is that when the terminal stops working and the user wishes to switch to another terminal, the necessary changes in authorization must be accomplished first. This sometimes can be time consuming and this is one reason user identification is often preferred over terminal identification.

In nonsensitive situations it is not unusual that the only identification necessary is the terminal identification. A terminal in an accounting office may be considered secure and everyone in the office has authority to request information. No user identification is necessary. Additional verification or security is usually a waste of money. Proper physical placing of the terminal will provide enough protection.

But if more than one user shares the same terminal and different privacy levels are imposed on the individual users of the same terminal, then it is necessary not only to identify the terminal but also the user. This can be done by user name and passwords.

ACCESS MANAGEMENT

Normally there are some restrictions on who can use the system. The user must identify himself and prove authorization by providing a password. He may also have to show an account number. Permanently assigned passwords used for user identification are not uncommon. While passwords do provide some protection, it is simple to see that the same password does not provide a great deal of protection simply because there is an inverse relationship between the length of time it is used and the degree of security it maintains. Nevertheless, passwords do serve their purpose in a relatively low-security situation.

There are several things which can be done to improve password protection. Passwords should be changed aperiodically, so an unauthorized user will not know how long he can use a password. Passwords should not be printed or should be over-printed when accepted. But with overprinting the password is normally available from the ribbon.

Lists of one-time passwords have been suggested and these would obviously provide more protection if people do not forget their list. Lists of one-time passwords are used in the following manner. A list is generated with one copy being stored in the computer and one copy going to the user. Each time the system is activated the user uses the first password that hasn't been used and the user and system cross that password off the list. Attempts at using old passwords or passwords out of order should cause an immediate cutoff of the terminal.

Use of once-only passwords will not stop piggy-back infiltrators, especially if the password is used only at initial sign-in time. But lists of one-time passwords can be automatically generated and included when each message is generated. These passwords can be stored in the terminal on punched paper tape and generated internally by special circuits. Still another suggestion includes keeping passwords in special secure housing with only a single password visible. A special key would be used to advance the list. Finally, Paul Baran has suggested the use of random numbers.

Among the variations of the random number techniques is one where the computer supplies a pseudorandom number to the user. The user then performs some simple mental transformation on the number and provides the result of transformation to the computer. Then the computer does the same transformation and checks the answer. In this way very little information is provided a wire-tapper and the security is almost as good as the one-time password lists without the cumbersome vulnerability of an actual list.

Some installations have tried using personal information about the user to maintain security. The user is asked his birthdate, mother's maiden name, or some such similar question. This system does not provide much more security than passwords because if each user is asked the same questions, it is not difficult to find this kind of personal data on users.

The more questions that are asked, the more boring and time consuming the sign-on procedure becomes. All this becomes quite tedious to the terminal user with steady repetition. In addition, storage and programming requirements may make lengthy verifications impractical in systems with many or frequently changing systems. This may be why keys or badges are gaining favor for verification.

The second failure to provide the correct password should cause the system to completely abort the user's line; that is, completely disconnect the telephone line. The user would then have to call back and start all over again. And the computer operator could be warned to watch the terminal. Failure to provide the password could also be used to send a signal to the terminal area and warn the user area that something strange may be going on. Disconnecting the terminal prevents multiple tries at determining the password.

Passwords have several drawbacks, the major one being that people don't protect their passwords. They write the password on the wall so they won't lose it, or loan their password to a friend. The second drawback is that people forget their passwords. In some systems as high as 30 percent of the users forget the password. And the more often you change the password, the higher is the possibility of forgetting. Now, if a customer is buying computer time and can't use his own data because he forgot the password, he is not going to be very happy. He expects the center to do something about it. This usually results in the center operator keeping a list of the passwords and giving them out on request. Thus the operator has a list of passwords, too. Not only is there sometimes trouble over forgetting passwords, but if different levels of security are used for different users, the codes must be remembered, too.

Level of Authorization

After determining authorization to use the system, the next step is to establish level of authorization. This is necessary only if the system contains files with different levels of security or users with individual files.

If each user has his own files, then the authorization function becomes the relatively simple one of restricting each user to his own files. If, however, users share files and have different degrees of authorization, the job of protecting files becomes much more complicated.

A file may be read only with no modifications allowed. Or the researcher may be allowed to take only summary totals. Another situation would be where the person would be allowed to read information from some fields, but be prohibited from using others. A statistician may be allowed to tabulate salary ranges, but not allowed to correlate the names with the salary.

Just as files must be protected, so must some programs; that is, some programs will be available for use but the user cannot alter the program. Alteration of the program could lead to obtaining unauthorized information. Similarly, if programs can be altered, shared programs could be in a constant state of flux which would result in inconsistent results.

Others may be allowed to examine old records and modify, but not set up, new records. An example would be when a bank teller was allowed to examine an account to see if a balance is sufficient to cash the check. Or a store would want to check a credit card to make sure it is still valid and not stolen before allowing a large purchase. In this case read-only would be allowed.

Read-only restrictions are the most common in time-sharing systems. Tables, credit information, or statistical data are examples of where users are allowed to read-only. Write-only restrictions are less common but exist when an operator is allowed to make additions (a personnel file or outstanding traffic ticket file), but not allowed to read current entries.

The originator of the file is in the best position to know how sensitive information is. It is, therefore, up to him to decide the level of security necessary. In addition, liberty must be given to change authorization by the originator of the files. Then the owner of the file can change authorization by changing security codes or lockwords as they are occassionally called.

As creator and owner of the file this person can give out the proper lockword for each user. One lockword would allow read-only. By adding a suffix, users could be allowed to write or update the file or be allowed to read restricted data.

This user-originated and controlled lockword technique is

currently used on many systems. It will successfully protect files from most casual intruders. However, since any authorized user of the file will know part of the lockword, it is necessary to prevent experimentation to gain access to unauthorized files.

Incorrect lockwords should cause complete cancellation of the job and disconnecting of the telephone line. Otherwise, users can use multiple tries to obtain a higher security than authorized. It is very important that no one be able to write a program to test out the different possible combinations. One way to prevent this is to abort the user on incorrect tries.

The extent and complexity of the protection will be determined by the center. At the time the system is built it is very difficult to forsee all possible restrictions necessary. The situation becomes more complex in a large dynamic system where new files and records are frequently added and modified.

In an excellent paper, Lance Hoffman ("Computers and Privacy: A Survey" COMPUTING SURVEYS, January, 1969) discusses some of the problems connected with designing secure file-handling systems. It is worth reading because these security methods can be quite time consuming and each user has to pay for the security in loss of efficiency and higher user costs.

Security considerations are discussed in some detail by Clark Weissman ("Security Controls in the ADEPT-50 Time Sharing System," Proceedings, Fall Joint Computer Conference, 1969). Weissman offers a method of automatic file classification based on the cumulative security history of referenced files.

Besides establishing security of files by originators, the originator should also be able to shut the file down when it is not in use. If the file user uses the file only during day shift, he should have the option of preventing misuse after-hours by imposters. Also, if the file owner is going on vacation for two weeks, he should be able to close the file and keep it closed while on vacation. Demountable files should be demounted when not in use, such as weekends.

PROCESSING RESTRICTIONS   Read-only memory protection has already been discussed here, but there are other types of processing restrictions which also deserve mention. Users should not be able to modify anything connected with the monitor, memory bounds, or input/output commands. Each computer will need privileged instructions; that is, instructions that can be executed only by privileged programs such as the operating system.

Restrictions might be added to the copying of files or deletion of files. Or maybe an upper bound could be set on how many records could be modified during a period. Files can be put on removable devices so authorization is necessary before access is allowed.

Sophisticated users could follow in after a high-security job and pick up as much information as possible from core and work areas such as disk files, magnetic tapes, or drums. If core images of programs can be obtained, decompilers can be used to translate binary programs into higher-level languages. This information would make the work of any enemy much easier. For these reasons core should be "cleansed" where necessary. New information should be written over the old information such as all zeros.

INFORMATION DESTRUCTION

Another problem is the destroying of old information on storage media. Most people think that if you write over information on a tape you destroy the old information. This is not actually true. What you really do is fix the old information so the computer can't read it. The computer is designed to read only the most recently written information. But any removable storage device such as tapes or disks could be subject to laboratory processing where old information can be still read.

For that reason a few additional safeguards used with removable storage media should be discussed. The Air Force specifies that streams of random digits written over classified information at least three times is sufficient to declassify. The reason for multiple writing is simply to make certain that all the classified areas have been covered. There are certain kinds of software failures and certain kinds of hardware failures in a computer which could negate the intent of this overwriting of nonsense information.

This procedure will certainly work for magnetic drums and core storage. The tape and disk problems are more complicated because tapes or disks can be removed. A reel of magnetic tape can be taken from the machine and subjected to electronic or magnetic tampering. Experiments have been performed to demonstrate that it is possible to recover information which has been overwritten by other information. Presumably the same conditions apply to magnetic disks. For these reasons magnetic tapes and disks once used in a classified mode are physically destroyed when no longer of use. There are large economic reasons (the saving of the tape or disk) to be able to insure that no old information can be read after certain types of "cleansing," but so far none have been accepted by the military.

This problem does not come up with magnetic core. Streams of nonsense information should destroy any classified information. Also magnetic core is not usually removed and thus is not subject to laboratory techniques.

MONITOR PROTECTION   Bernard Peters describes a number of protection features available through use of a monitor. In a later paper Clark Weissman describes some of these same features that were implemented on an IBM system 360/50. These papers are listed in the references.

The monitor acts as the overall guard to the system. An appropriate monitor must have a set of rules by which it judges all requested actions. After checking its rules it obeys only those requests for action which conform to the security principles necessary for the particular operation.

Bernard Peters' paper and various other sources agree that the monitor must perform all input/output (I/O). User programs cannot be allowed to control any I/O device, except by call to the monitor. The monitor must control systems clocks and the main console. Ideally the monitor would also control the maintenance panel, but if not, the panel must otherwise be secured.

Monitors must take into consideration un-debugged programs, interrupts, or system failures. During these situations sections of core could be unprotected. Adequate memory protect and privileged instruction set contain all input/output commands, but also every command that could change a memory bound or protection barrier.

Bernard Peters describes what makes up an appropriate monitor for security. Peters estimates that a properly designed monitor is probably not more than 10 percent greater than that of a monitor which is minimally acceptable for multiprogramming.

Information can be divulged by wiretapping or by electronic-magnetic pickup of traffic at any point in the system. One normally assumes that communications lines are secure, but in fact they are no more secure than telephone conversations.

Techniques for unauthorized use of communications lines are well developed. For this reason, digital transmission of information should not be considered any more secure than Morse code messages since there are sufficient people and equipment to violate the communications lines. Maybe a basic test should be the risk involved by sending the information over a regular telephone conversation line; similar precautions should be taken to protect computer messages.

Petersen and Turn suggested that a one-hundred-dollar tape recorder and code conversion table is sufficient to tap digital transmission of information.

The central computer can be used to encode information prior to transmission, but this means that the terminal will also need special coordinated equipment to encode and decode the messages. Hardware and software are now available to encode data.

This type of protection will help eliminate wire tapping, electronic-magnetic pickups, infiltrator terminals, piggy-back entries, and similar threats. Physically protected cables are possible for in-house communications, but not if a common carrier is used to send messages to widely scattered geographic locations.

There are a number of privacy transformations available from traditional cryptographic methods, mathematical methods, and newer computational cryptography. Privacy transformations offer several advantages. For one, if someone is able to enter a file surreptitiously but does not have the key necessary for decoding, he gains nothing. Basically, privacy transformation raises the price of infiltration at a very reasonable cost. The CPU-I/O balance is not usually adversely affected by adding privacy transformations.

In addition the copying of files offers much less of a temptation if files are not readily decoded. Coded files discourage snooping, too. Privacy transformations offer some protection against intrusion by virtue of position, such as the system manager, operator, or maintenance engineers.

**PRIVACY
TRANSFORMATION**

**TESTING
THE SYSTEM**

Deliberate and periodic security violations should be a part of any system. Programs can be designed to violate memory bounds protection to verify that the bounds protection checker is working. The security system should be tested and audited not only at regular intervals but at random intervals.

Initially there should be complete checking of the system to verify that the programs and hardware work as they are supposed to. Usually it is possible to save these tests to use as periodic tests. Careful control over hardware and software must be established; otherwise, accidental or deliberate changes may weaken controls.

Several people have suggested that one or two persons be given the job of trying to break the security of the system. If one person can divert the security precautions, it is not too much to expect others to do the same thing. It would seem best to have someone who was not responsible for designing security try to break it. This way he would have no incentive to cover up past errors. Proper motivation, such as a bonus or free vacation, might be a good incentive for trying to find a way into the system.

Besides, this is probably one of the best ways to check out the system. The "authorized" infiltrator should be forced to work under the same conditions as a real infiltrator, except that he would not be punished if caught; but likewise if it becomes obvious to the operator that an infiltrator is trying to "bug" the system, then he has not succeeded.

Very often the same people who design the system test out the system. While it is expected that the designer test out his own system, it seems preferable that others also test it out. Special training and experience can be used to establish a group of system testers. These people would probably come from the most experienced and talented of the system group.

**THREAT
MONITORING**

A log of all significant events should be maintained both by the computer and the operating personnel. The computer log can be stored on a disk or tape and then printed out once a day. Care must be taken so the operator is not able to throw away any offensive computer console printout. Locked consoles and consecutively numbered console forms are one alternative, but storage of messages on disks with special later printouts seems more desirable.

Since the log is the ultimate defense against penetration, care must be taken to protect the log and assure that sufficient, but not unnecessary, information is included. Some systems may want to record all inquiries while others may need to record only file use. The log must be able to answer the question of whether or not some data has gone astray. In fact, the log will normally be the chief source that reveals some information has been lost.

The log should be used to record all illegal attempts to use the system. In addition, the log should record the utilization of files. Logs normally identify each user and terminal. And in some high-security cases each attempt to access restricted data will be recorded.

The recording of all attempted illegal activity will indicate trouble spots. Users can then be provided with periodic reports of file use and denied requests. These reports may indicate misuse or attempted misuse which may warrant closer scrutiny or increase security.

If security restrictions are unnecessarily hampering use of the system, then the log should help indicate this. But the log will also provide factual information for increasing security if previous security has proven ineffective.

Logs provide a deterrent since people hesitate to do something illegal that will undoubtably be discovered. Logs can provide records of unusually high levels of activity in particular files or unusual high usage of particular terminals. Logs should also be some help in protecting abuses of statistical banks to disclose personal dossiers.

If the area of concern can be predetermined, the system can actually do the checking, but the log normally will have to be audited by some knowledgeable person to discover new abuses.

A review of all the various audit logs will help management consider relaxing security or strengthening it as the need may be. Here are some of the questions to check: Are security measures still effective, or do security breaks regularly occur? Are all new changes to the system properly authorized and tested out? How often is a security test run on the system? Was one run after the last system change? Have techniques been developed to bypass security by users? Are original procedures for passwords, identifi-

ANALYZING THE AUDIT TRAIL

cation cards, access restrictions, and keys still being followed? Are they sufficient or necessary? Have special programs been developed to provide demonstrations or to speed up processing during emergencies or high-priority work schedules? Are stand alone utility programs used and able to bypass system security?

Security should also be checked to see if it is cumbersome. Are the security measures measurably slowing processing or discouraging authorized use? If so are they really necessary? Finally, is previous security still necessary or sufficient?

Certain files may be found to have very high use. If so, it may be possible to redesign the files so the high-security parts can be separated out and the nonsecurity parts of the file may still be of use or be able to be used at a lower level of security. Low use of a file may indicate it does not belong on the system, or that security procedures are so complex that people have avoided using the file or found ways to get around security measures.

Actual lists of users can indicate that some people never use a file and thus should never have been authorized to use it in the first place. On the other hand, if everyone is authorized, security may well be a waste of time.

A complete log would list all inquiries each user makes each day. The information can include time of inquiry, type of inquiry, and total time used. If the inquiry was unsuccessful, the type of error can be listed. When this information is obtained it can be sorted into user sequence, dates, and times. By sending the user a copy, the user can uncover misuse of his files.

Listings of unsuccessful inquiries should also make it easy to spot attempts at misuse and show how successful they are. Experimentation with authorization codes becomes apparent. This will serve as a major deterrent to potential violators since they will know that even if they are successful, they will probably be discovered. Some trial and error is almost always necessary when experimenting.

CONCLUSIONS

Most of the techniques necessary for protecting a time-sharing system are either already available or probably could be developed very soon. Economic considerations along with the need for protection will probably control their adoption. While few business systems would consider adopting all the security measures mentioned in this chapter, their possible use should be at least considered and evaluated, and rejected if found unnecessary. Unfortunately, security measures are often accepted only after some instance points out their need.

TIME-SHARING CHECKLIST

1. Is the terminal in a protected location so unauthorized people cannot get to it?
2. Are terminals locked so they cannot be used during off-hours?
3. What policy is used when users forget their passwords or lockwords?
4. Are execute-only programs available?
5. Are read-only, write-only protections available?
6. Is it possible to have different levels of security in the same file?
7. Are files demounted during periods of non-use?
8. Are terminals identified at sign-in time?
9. Do users have to identify themselves before using a terminal?
10. Must the user authenticate himself by use of password before using a terminal?
11. Are users prevented from experimenting on passwords or lockwords by disconnecting their telephone line when incorrect ones are tried?
12. Is the system reliable enough so that excess down time does not prohibit use or cause loss of data?
13. Are operators closely supervised?
14. Are operators and programmers prohibited from browsing through files?
15. Are terminal users prohibited from modifying the monitor or anything that might change their security level?
16. Is privacy transformation necessary to protect data being transmitted over telephone lines?
17. Has the system been verified as being secure?
18. Is a log kept of all significant events such as identification of users, file use, and attempts at unauthorized use?

References

Babcock, J. D. "A Brief Description of Privacy Measures in the RUSH Time-Sharing System," PROCEEDINGS SPRING JOINT COMPUTER CONFERENCE, 1967.

Bingham, H. W. "Security Techniques for EDP of Multi-Level Classified Information," ROME AIR DEVELOPMENT CENTER, December, 1965, RADC-TR-65-415.

"Considerations of Data Security in a Computer Environment," IBM 520-2169-0.

"Computer Security," INDUSTRIAL SECURITY, December, 1969.

Courtney, Robert H. "Data Security and Privacy," PROCEEDINGS, 6th Annual Natl. Colloq. on Information Retrieval.

DeLair, W. E. "Security Responsibilities of a Time-Sharing Service Company," TRANSDATA Corporation. October 25, 1969.

Dennis, Robert L. "Security in the Computer Environment," System Development Corporation, SP 2440/000/02, August 18, 1966.

Ellis, Terrance C. "Time-Sharing Security," speech at the American Management Association Catastrophe Prevention Seminar, April 15, 1970.

Fanwick, Charles. "Maintaining Privacy of Computerized Data," System Development Corporation, SP-2647, December 1, 1966.

Glaser, Edward L. "A Brief Description of Privacy Measures in the Multics Operating System," SPRING JOINT COMPUTER CONFERENCE, 1967.

Hirsch, Phil. "The World's Biggest Data Bank," DATAMATION, May, 1970.

Hoffman, Lance J. "Computers and Privacy: A Survey," COMPUTING SURVEYS, June, 1969.

——. "The Formulary Model for Access Control and Privacy in Computer Systems," SLAC Report No. 117, May 1970. Stanford Linear Accelerator Center, Stanford University, Stanford, Calif.

—— and W. F. Miller. "Getting a Personal Dossier from a Statistical Data Bank," DATAMATION, May, 1970.

Peters, Bernard. "Security Considerations in a Multi-Programmed Computer System," PROCEEDINGS SPRING JOINT COMPUTER CONFERENCE, 1967.

Petersen, H. E., and R. Turn. "System Implications of Information Privacy," PROCEEDINGS SPRING JOINT COMPUTER CONFERENCE, 1967.

RYE, CAPRI, COINS, OCTOPUS, SADIE Systems. Network of Computers Workshop, National Security Agency, October, 1968.

"Safeguarding Time-Sharing Privacy—An All-out War on Data Snooping," ELECTRONICS, April 17, 1967.

Van Tassel, D. "Information Security in a Computer Environment," COMPUTERS AND AUTOMATION, July, 1969.

Ware, Willis H. "Security and Privacy in Computer Systems," PROCEEDINGS SPRING JOINT COMPUTER CONFERENCE, 1967.

——. "Security and Privacy: Similarities and Differences," PROCEEDINGS SPRING JOINT COMPUTER CONFERENCE, 1967.

Weissman, Clark. "Security Controls in the ADEPT-50 Time-Sharing System," PROCEEDINGS FALL JOINT COMPUTER CONFERENCE, 1969.

COMPUTER
PRIVACY

Computer privacy can be guaranteed only if computer security is complete. Without computer security any promises of computer privacy will be easily violated. But good computer security is no justification for computer misuse. Rather, computer security should be thought of as guaranteeing that original security is kept. Daily in the mass media there are anticomputer stories, cartoons, and jokes. Many are based on good reasons. Loss of job, loss of privacy, loss of prestige, or loss of personal relations are just some of the fears common to many in and out of the computer profession.

The clerk who loses his job or the executive who loses some of his prestige or control does not accept the fact that computers seldom put people out of work. Similarly, people who are turned down for loans for credit or a new job, and when asking why are told that a computer did the evaluation but they are not allowed to see what facts and what criteria were used, are normally not very happy.

Everyone has tried to communicate with a large bureaucracy where all replies come back on printed forms with boxes checked **161** that seem to have nothing to do with the original question. Now on top of this we have added the computer, thus supplying an obvious scapegoat—the computer.

Very often management too readily uses the computer as the scapegoat. Some bills have instructions written on them to blame the computer if mistakes occur, just as if no humans were involved. Many people have learned that if the computer is unreliable so is the rest of the company, and it is best to take your business elsewhere.

Very little hostility is generated toward the computer that does a matrix manipulation or calculates gamma rays. What people normally fear is unseen control and with some reason. Any system that can accurately keep track of a Venus rocket can as easily keep track of individuals.

This fear is as well understood and felt among computer professionals as the public at large. The surprising thing is that so little has been done about it. The magazine COMPUTERS AND AUTOMATION and the newsweekly COMPUTER WORLD have been the most vocal in their covering of the privacy problem.

Since the computer industry has failed to come to grips with the privacy situation, the methods of control will be decided in the political arena. The computer industry and computer professional groups have not yet accepted privacy guidelines, even though a great deal of talk and discussion has been devoted to the subject. During this same period the industry has adopted standard computer languages (COBOL and FORTRAN) and an American National Standard for identifying persons in large data files (THE OFFICE, June 1970). It is interesting that the standard identification code was adopted before any privacy standards were adopted.

The computer industry badly needs some face lifting and good public relations. I did not say whitewashing. A great deal of hostility is building up against computers which many politicians will be very eager to take advantage of and ride the wave of votes to follow. I think some people will be surprised at the restrictiveness of the type of laws governing computer data banks. The credit reporting agencies have already got an idea of what is about to happen. Credit bureaus are now supporting laws they fought against tooth and nail a few years ago, in order to ward off even more restrictive laws. Given the wide diversity of accepted habits and beliefs, the last quarter of this century may produce a privacy movement. Then new laws will certainly result.

It is well worth the trouble of introducing some of the more important privacy measures discussed today. A rule widely accepted is that all persons shall have a right to inspect their own dossiers. This is already partly practiced by some credit bureaus, but most other government and nongovernmental files are still immune to this very basic protection.

The next right is the right to sue for slander and force correction of misleading information. If one can lose an FHA house loan, be denied credit or a new job, this is a very necessary protection. If a person is slandered under other circumstances, he always can sue; therefore, there is no logical reason that computer-generated and processed information should be exempt from slander suits. Mistakes can and do happen in data banks and there must be a way to correct them.

Along with this is the right to face one's accusers. If one is to sue for slander he must be able to find out who provided the slanderous information and why it was not checked. This means no anonymous information can be computerized. The saying "the computer said so" would not be accepted in court. Computer printout has an aura of veracity to it. It is usually accepted as truthful even if it goes against common sense. The concept of requiring a source to stand behind any accusations has sound legal background. The last two types of protection will either be established by the courts or new laws. Presently some information collecting groups are attempting to deny any responsibility for slander. This is an unreasonable request on their part, and an effort to avoid normal responsible behavior.

A new problem is the keeping of information forever. Some government agencies even keep track of minor crimes and traffic violations almost forever. Before computers this was not usually feasible. This trend will label our society "the one-chance society." That is, if you ever make a mistake, we will never forgive you. All chance of redemption or forgiving is lost. There probably is no better way to develop habitual criminals since no recourse is left them. If a person does some criminal offense and serves his "punishment," why is he still punished after he has been released or paid his "debt to society"? Does society not want him to join again as a respectable citizen? Some rules of destroying obsolete information must be developed. Since the Federal government is the largest employer they should take the lead in reemploying released persons, just as they did in stopping discrimination in hiring for religious or ethnic reasons.

Some control must be established over the types of information kept. If we wish to avoid the misuse of certain types of information, the easiest way is not to record the information. Arrest records are still recorded when convictions don't follow—an obvious area of abuse. There is already precedent for not recording certain types of information. Black lists are usually frowned upon even though they still exist. But asking future employees or loan applicants their religious or ethnic background is normally prohibited.

An easy way to control the types of information collected is to require that a valid reason exist for the collection of each classification of information. Under this rule, any agency which wishes to collect information must prove publicly that the information is needed to conduct its business. For example, if an insurance company wishes to collect information on spending habits, they would have to first establish why this information is necessary for their business.

Another example would be an attempt by credit bureaus to collect information on drinking habits. Since credit bureaus are concerned only with people paying their bills, this information would not be necessary for operation of their business. Presently there is a great deal of "fishing" for information that is not very relevant to the agency collecting it.

Any information taken under governmental or business coercion should automatically become private information, restricted to that one agency. Presently, the California Department of Motor Vehicles requires certain information in order to get a driver's license. Then the DMV sells this information to junk mailers and it is combined with census information which is also sold to junk mailers. All this information is combined by computer in order to tailor "personal" letters according to economic class and type of car. This behavior of the California Department of Motor Vehicles is particularly offensive and should be discontinued.

Any solutions to private data banks should also apply to governmental data banks since it is government snooping that most people fear. This is ironic since most of the laws being introduced will restrict private data banks and exempt the government's.

One idea being discussed is that each individual should have ultimate control over his own personal information. Robert P. Henderson, vice-president and general manager of Honeywell's EDP Division, suggests that legislation be introduced to make personal information a property right. Each individual yearly would receive a copy of the personal data being kept on him. Henderson suggested that the protections of due process afforded property under present laws be extended to personal information, with criminal penalties for improper conduct in gathering, storing, or releasing personal information.

There is already precedent for this type of action. If a person receives undesirable mail in the United States, he can go to a post office, get a POD Form 2150 which is a "Post Office Department Notice For Prohibitory Order Against Sender Of Pandering Advertisement in the Mail." Once this form is filled out, the post office sends an order that the mailer must remove the name and address from his file and stop sending any mail to the person filing the complaint.

Another rather novel idea is information bankruptcy. That is, just as in financial bankruptcy, whenever an individual feels that his information is so stacked against him he could go to court and declare himself "informationally bankrupt." Then his data files would be erased. It would be recorded that he declared himself informationally bankrupt and a new data file would be started, but all previous information would be destroyed. If we wish to give individuals a second chance in financial or criminal matters, then individuals should also be given a second chance in information matters.

A summary of some of the privacy proposals made thus far shows:

1. There shall be no secret computer information from the individual involved. Each individual shall receive a copy of his file at least yearly on demand.
2. Personal information shall be the property of the individual involved. And he shall have the right to have incorrect information corrected or deleted.
3. Each person shall be informed of who is inspecting his file.

4. Each person should have the right to restrict entry of information that he feels intrudes on his privacy.
5. No anonymous information shall be stored on individuals.
6. Information shall be periodically deleted after a reasonable length of time.
7. Information collection agencies will have to publicly prove that each classification of information is necessary for them to conduct their business.
8. Information collected under coercion shall be classified private and restricted to the agency that collected it.
9. Individuals shall have the right to declare themselves "informationally bankrupt" and have their file erased.

If high standards are maintained in regard to the gathering of personal data and the privacy of computer data, one form of hostility to computer systems will disappear, thus making computer security easier.

References   Halsbury, Lord. "Lord Halsbury speaks on Computer Privacy," THE COMPUTER BULLETIN, February, 1970.

Hirsch, Phil. "The World's Biggest Data Bank," DATAMATION, May, 1970.

"Honeywell Executive Proposes Legislation to Make Personal Data a Property Right," COMPUTER WORLD, June 17, 1970.

"Identity Code for Individuals," THE OFFICE, June, 1970.

Lauren, Roy H. "Reliability of Data Bank Records," DATAMATION, May, 1970.

APPENDICES

APPENDIX 1

**Firms specializing
in the field of
computer security
include:**

Bradford Associates, Inc.
592A Washington Street
Wellesley, Mass. 02181
Phone: (617) 237-3890

Robert V. Jacobson
President

Bradford Associates, Inc. was formed in 1969 to provide professional consulting services in the area of computer security, accuracy, and dependability. Its security specialists use a systematic and comprehensive set of procedures: (1) to establish the specific security requirements for a computer system; (2) to evaluate its exposure to all hazards including natural disasters; fire, smoke, flooding, structural collapse, etc., human errors and human acts such as riot, vandalism, and fraud; and (3) to devise cost-effective remedial, preventive, and recovery measures to assure that security requirements are satisfied. The Bradford staff have training and experience in computer sciences, business management, accounting systems, auditing, electrical engineering, physical security, and human resource development and motivation.

Computer Audit Systems, Inc.
725 Park Avenue
E. Orange, New Jersey 07017
Phone: (201) 676-8320

Joseph J. Wasserman
President

Computer Audit Systems, Inc. specializes in the areas of computer auditing and security. C.A.S. is currently marketing a software package called Computer Audit Retrieval System, training seminars for auditors and EDP control managers, and consultation services in the areas of auditing, controls, and security.

Data Processing Security, Inc.
15 Spinning Wheel Road
Hinsdale, Illinois 60521
Phone (312) 325-2105

Louis Scoma, Jr.
President

Data Processing Security, Inc. (DPS) provides services in these areas:

CONSULTING AND RECOMMENDATIONS

Evaluate the needs for auxiliary power
Study standby air conditioning requirements
Determine the vulnerability to theft and sabotage of vital data
Vital records storage (off site)
Review the smoke and fire protection

Consider accessibility to the EDP center
Emergency evacuation plans
Emergency recovery plans
Facilities and personnel

HARDWARE

DPS provides recommendations for physical hardware along with a professional plan for implementing the security recommendations in a logical and economical manner.

Records Retention Timetable

LEGEND FOR AUTHORITY TO DISPOSE

AD—Administrative Decision
ASPR—Armed Services Procurement Regulation
CFR—Code of Federal Regulations
FLSA—Fair Labor Standards Act
ICC—Interstate Commerce Commission
INS—Insurance Company Regulation
ISM—Industrial Security Manual, Attachment to DD Form 441

*After Disposed ** Normally

LEGEND FOR RETENTION PERIOD

AC—Dispose After Completion of Job or Contract
AE—Dispose After Expiration
AF—After End of Fiscal Year
AM—After Moving
AS—After Settlement
AT—Dispose After Termination
ATR—After Trip
OBS—Dispose When Obsolete
P—Permanent
SUP—Dispose When Superseded

† Govt R&D Contracts

TYPE OF RECORD	RETENTION PERIOD YEARS	AUTHORITY
ACCOUNTING & FISCAL		
Accounts Payable Invoices	3	ASPR-STATE, FLSA
Accounts Payable Ledger	P	AD
Accounts Receivable Ledgers	5	AD
Approvals		
Authorizations for Accounting	SUP	AD
Balance Sheets	P	AD
Bank Deposits	3	AD
Bank Statements	3	AD
Bonds	P	AD
Budgets	3	AD
Capital Asset Record	3*	AD
Cash Receipt Records	7	AD
Check Register	P	AD
Checks, Dividend	6	AD
Checks, Payroll	2	FLSA, STATE
Checks, Voucher	3	FLSA, STATE
Cost Accounting Records	5	AD
Earnings Register	3	FLSA, STATE
Entertainment Gifts & Gratuities	3	AD
Estimates, Projections	7	AD
Expense Reports	3	AD
Financial Statements, Certified	P	AD
Financial Statements, Periodic	2	AD
General Ledger Records	P	CFR
Labor Cost Records	3	ASPR, CFR
Magnetic Tape and Tab Cards	1**	AD
Note Register	P	AD
Payroll Registers	3	FLSA, STATE
Petty Cash Records	3	AD
P & L Statements	P	AD
Salesman Commission Reports	3	AD
Travel Expense Reports	3	AD
Work Papers, Rough	2	AD
ADMINISTRATIVE RECORDS		
Audit Reports	10	AD
Audit Work Papers	3	AD
Classified Documents: Inventories, Reports, Receipts	10	AD
Correspondence, Executive	P	AD
Correspondence, General	5	AD
Directives from Officers	P	AD
Forms Used, File Copies	P	AD
Systems and Procedures Records	P	AD
Work Papers, Management Projects	P	AD
COMMUNICATIONS		
Bulletins Explaining Communications	P	AD
Messenger Records	1	AD
Phone Directories	SUP	AD

TYPE OF RECORD	RETENTION PERIOD YEARS	AUTHORITY
COMMUNICATIONS (CONT'D)		
Phone Installation Records	1	AD
Postage Reports, Stamp Requisitions	1 AF	AD
Postal Records, Registered Mail & Insured Mail Logs & Meter Records	1 AF	AD, CFR
Telecommunications Copies	1	AD
CONTRACT ADMINISTRATION		
Contracts, Negotiated. Bailments, Changes, Specifications, Procedures, Correspondence	P	CFR
Customer Reports	P	AD
Materials Relating to Distribution Revisions, Forms, and Format of Reports	P	AD
Work Papers	OBS	AD
CORPORATE		
Annual Reports	P	AD
Authority to Issue Securities	P	AD
Bonds, Surety	3 AE	AD
Capital Stock Ledger	P	AD
Charters, Constitutions, Bylaws	P	AD
Contracts	20 AT	AD
Corporate Election Records	P	AD
Incorporation Records	P	AD
Licenses - Federal, State, Local	AT	AD
Stock Transfer & Stockholder	P	AD
LEGAL		
Claims and Litigation Concerning Torts and Breach of Contracts	P	AD
Law Records - Federal, State, Local	SUP	AD
Patents and Related Material	P	AD
Trademark & Copyrights	P	AD
LIBRARY, COMPANY		
Accession Lists	P	AD
Copies of Requests for Materials	6 mos.	AD
Meeting Calendars	P	AD
Research Papers, Abstracts, Bibliographies	SUP, 6 mos AC	AD
MANUFACTURING		
Bills of Material	2	AD, ASPR
Drafting Records	P	AD†
Drawings	2	AD, ASPR
Inspection Records	2	AD
Lab Test Reports	P	AD
Memos, Production	AC	AD
Product, Tooling, Design, Enginneering Research, Experiment & Specs Records	20	STATUE LIMITATIONS
Production Reports	3	AD
Quality Reports	1 AC	AD
Reliability Records	P	AD
Stock Issuing Records	3 AT	AD, ASPR
Tool Control	3 AT	AD, ASPR
Work Orders	3	AD
Work Status Reports	AC	AD
OFFICE SUPPLIES & SERVICES		
Inventories	1 AF	AD
Office Equipment Records	6 AF	AD
Requests for: Services	1 AF	AD
Requisitions for Supplies	1 AF	AD
PERSONNEL		
Accident Reports, Injury Claims, Settlements	30 AS	CFR, INS, STATE
Applications, Changes & Terminations	50	AD, ASPR, CFR
Attendance Records	7	AD
Employee Activity Files	2 or SUP	AD
Employee Contracts	6 AT	AD
Fidelity Bonds	3 AT	AD
Garnishments	5 *c	AD
Health & Safety Bulletins	P	AD

Revised, reset and printed by Electric Wastebasket Corp. ©1969, based on the April 1969 issue of MODERN OFFICE PROCEDURES.

TYPE OF RECORD	RETENTION PERIOD YEARS	AUTHORITY
PERSONNEL (CONT'D)		
Injury Frequency Charts	P	CFR
Insurance Records, Employees	11 AT	INS
Job Descriptions	2 or SUP	CFR
Rating Cards	2 or SUP	CFR
Time Cards	3	AD
Training Manuals	P	AD
Union Agreements	3	WALSH-HEALEY ACT
PLANT & PROPERTY RECORDS		
Depreciation Schedules	P	AD
Inventory Records	P	AD
Maintenance & Repair, Building	10	AD
Maintenance & Repair, Machinery	5	AD
Plant Account Cards, Equipment	P	CFR, AD
Property Deeds		
Property Deeds	P	AD
Purchase or Lease Records of Plant Facility	P	AD
Space Allocation Records	1 AT	AD
PRINTING & DUPLICATING		
Copies Produced, Tech. Pubs., Charts	1 or OBS	AD
Film Reports	5	AD
Negatives	5	AD
Photographs	1	AD
Production Records	1 AC	AD
PROCUREMENT, PURCHASING		
Acknowledgements	AC	AD
Bids, Awards	3 AT	CFR
Contracts	3 AT	AD
Exception Notices (GAO)	6	AD
Price Lists	OBS	AD
Purchase Orders, Requisitions	3 AT	CFR
Quotations	1	AD
PRODUCTS, SERVICES, MARKETING		
Correspondence	3	AD
Credit Ratings & Classifications	7	AD
Development Studies	P	AD
Presentations & Proposals	P	AD
Price Lists, Catalogs	OBS	AD
Prospect Lines	OBS	AD
Register of Sales Order	NO VALUE	AD
Surveys	P	AD
Work Papers, Pertaining to Projects	NO VALUE	AD
PUBLIC RELATIONS & ADVERTISING		
Advertising Activity Reports	5	AD
Community Affairs Records	P	AD
Contracts for Advertising	3 AT	AD
Employee Activities & Presentations	P	AD
Exhibits, Releases, Handouts	2 - 4	AD
Internal Publications	P (1 copy)	AD
Layouts	1	AD
Manuscripts	1	AD
Photos	1	AD
Public Information Activity	7	AD
Research Presentations	P	AD
Tear-Sheets	2	AD
SECURITY		
Classified Material Violations	P	AD
Courier Authorizations	1 mo. ATR	AD
Employee Clearance Lists	SUP	ISM
Employee Case Files	5	ISM
Fire Prevention Program	P	AD
Protection - Guards, Badge Lists, Protective Devices	5	AD
Subcontractor Clearances	2 AT	AD
Visitor Clearance	2	ISM

TYPE OF RECORD	RETENTION PERIOD YEARS	AUTHORITY
TAXATION		
Annuity or Deferred Payment Plan	P	CFR
Depreciation Schedules	P	CFR
Dividend Register	P	CFR
Employee Withholding	4	CFR
Excise Exemption Certificates	4	CFR
Excise Reports (Manufacturing)	4	CFR
Excise Reports (Retail)	4	CFR
Inventory Reports	P	CFR
Tax Bills and Statements	P	AD
Tax Returns	P	AD
TRAFFIC & TRANSPORTATION		
Aircraft Operating & Maintenance	P	CFR
Bills of Lading, Waybills	2	ICC, FLSA
Employee Travel	1 AF	AD
Freight Bills	3	ICC
Freight Claims	2	ICC
Household Moves	3 AM	AD
Motor Operating & Maintenance	2	AD
Rates and Tariffs	SUP	AD
Receiving Documents	2 - 10	AD, CFR
Shipping & Related Documents	2 - 10	AD, CFR

APPENDIX 3

MULTIPLE PERIL POLICY

ST. PAUL FIRE AND MARINE INSURANCE COMPANY

(A Capital Stock Insurance Company, Herein Called the Company)

In consideration of the payment of premium, this Company does insure the Insured named in the Declarations subject to all of the terms and conditions of this Policy including all of the terms and conditions of the Declarations and Insuring Agreement(s) which are made a part thereof.

GENERAL POLICY CONDITIONS AND EXCLUSIONS

UNLESS PHYSICALLY DELETED BY THE COMPANY OR UNLESS SPECIFICALLY REFERRED TO IN THE INSURING AGREEMENT(S), THE FOLLOWING CLAUSES SHALL BE PARAMOUNT AND SHALL SUPERSEDE AND NULLIFY ANY CONTRARY PROVISIONS OF THE INSURING AGREEMENT(S).

1. GENERAL CONDITIONS

A. TERRITORIAL LIMITS: This Policy insures only while the property is at locations and while in transit within and between the forty-eight contiguous states of the United States of America, the District of Columbia and Canada, unless otherwise endorsed.

B. REMOVAL: Such insurance as is afforded by this Policy applies while the property insured is being removed to and while at place of safety because of imminent danger of loss, damage or expense and while being returned from such place, provided the Insured gives written notice to this Company of such removal within ten days thereafter.

C. OTHER INSURANCE: If there is available to the Insured or any other interested party any other insurance which would apply in the absence of this Policy, the insurance under this Policy shall apply only as excess insurance over such other insurance.

D. ASSIGNMENT: Assignment of interest under this Policy shall not bind the Company until its consent is endorsed hereon; if, however, the Insured shall die, or shall be adjudged bankrupt or insolvent and written notice is given to the Company within sixty days after the date of such adjudication, this Policy shall cover the Insured's legal representative as insured; provided that notice of cancelation addressed to the Insured named in this Policy and mailed to the address shown in this Policy shall be sufficient notice to effect cancelation of this Policy.

E. MISREPRESENTATION AND FRAUD: This Policy shall be void if the Insured has concealed or misrepresented any material fact or circumstance concerning this insurance or the subject thereof or in case of any fraud, attempted fraud or false swearing by the Insured touching any matter relating to this insurance or the subject thereof, whether before or after a loss.

F. NOTICE OF LOSS: The Insured shall as soon as practicable report to this Company or its agent every loss or damage which may become a claim under this Policy and shall also file with the Company or its agent within ninety (90) days from date of loss a detailed sworn proof of loss. Failure by the Insured to report the said loss or damage and to file such sworn proof of loss as hereinbefore provided shall invalidate any claim under this Policy for such loss.

174

**This Policy is not complete unless
a Declarations Page is attached.**

G. SETTLEMENT OF LOSS: All adjusted claims shall be paid or made good to the Insured within thirty days after presentation and acceptance of satisfactory proofs of interest and loss at the office of this Company. No loss shall be paid or made good if the Insured has collected the same from others.

H. SUE & LABOR: In case of loss or damage, it shall be lawful and necessary for the Insured, or his or their factors, servants and assigns, to sue, labor and travel for, in and about the defense, safeguard and recovery of the property insured hereunder, or any part thereof, without prejudice to this insurance; nor shall the acts of the Insured or this Company, in recovering, saving and preserving the property insured in case of loss or damage, be considered a waiver or an acceptance of abandonment, to the charge whereof this Company will contribute according to the rate and quantity of the sum herein insured.

I. SUIT: No suit, action or proceeding for the recovery of any claim under this Policy shall be sustainable in any court of law or equity unless the same be commenced within twelve (12) months next after discovery by the Insured of the occurrence which gives rise to the claim. Provided, however, that if by the laws of the State within which this Policy is issued such limitation is invalid, then any such claims shall be void unless such action, suit or proceeding be commenced within the shortest limit of time permitted by the laws of such State.

J. SUBROGATION: In the event of any payment under this Policy the Company shall be subrogated to all the Insured's rights of recovery therefor against any person or organization and the Insured shall execute and deliver instruments and papers and do whatever else is necessary to secure such rights. The Insured shall do nothing after loss to prejudice such rights.

K. APPRAISAL: If the Insured and the Company fail to agree as to the amount of loss, each shall, on the written demand of either, made within sixty (60) days after receipt of proof of loss by the Company, select a competent and disinterested appraiser, and the appraisal shall be made at a reasonable time and place. The appraisers shall first select a competent and disinterested umpire, and failing for fifteen days to agree upon such umpire, then, on the request of the Insured or the Company, such umpire shall be selected by a judge of a court of record in the county and state in which such appraisal is pending. The appraisers shall then appraise the loss, and failing to agree shall submit their differences to the umpire. An award in writing of any two shall determine the amount of loss. The Insured and the Company shall each pay its chosen appraiser and shall bear equally the expenses of the umpire and the other expenses of appraisal. The Company shall not be held to have waived any of its rights by any act relating to appraisal.

L. EXAMINATION UNDER OATH: The Insured shall submit, and so far as is within his or their power shall cause all other persons interested in the property and employees to submit, to examinations under oath by any persons named by the Company, relative to any and all matters in connection with a claim and subscribe the same; and shall produce for examination all books of account, bills, invoices, and other vouchers or certified copies thereof if originals be lost, at such reasonable time and place as may be designated by the Company or its representatives, and shall permit extracts and copies thereof to be made.

M. AUTOMATIC REINSTATEMENT: Any loss hereunder shall not reduce the amount of the Policy.

N. DEBRIS REMOVAL: This Policy is extended to cover expenses incurred in the removal of all debris of the damaged property insured hereunder which may be occasioned by loss caused by any of the perils insured against in this Policy. In no event shall the additional coverage granted by this paragraph increase the Limit of Liability specified in the "Declarations".

O. CANCELATION: This Policy may be canceled by the Insured by mailing to the Company written notice stating when thereafter such cancelation shall be effective. This Policy may be canceled by the Company by mailing to the Insured at the address shown in this Policy written notice stating when not less than ten (10) days thereafter such cancelation shall be effective. The mailing of notice as aforesaid shall be sufficient proof of notice and the effective date of cancelation stated in the notice shall become the end of the policy period. Delivery of such written notice either by the Insured or by the Company shall be equivalent to mailing.

If the Insured cancels, earned premiums shall be computed in accordance with the customary short rate table and procedure. If the Company cancels, earned premiums shall be computed pro rata. Premium adjustment may be made at the time cancelation is effected and, if not then made, shall be made as soon as practicable after cancelation becomes effective. The Company's check or the check of its representative mailed or delivered as aforesaid shall be a sufficient tender of any refund of premium due to the Insured.

P. CONFORMITY TO STATUTE: Terms of this Policy which are in conflict with the statutes of the State wherein this Policy is issued are hereby amended to conform to such statutes.

2. **PERILS EXCLUDED:** This Policy does not insure against loss, damage or expense caused directly or indirectly by:

A. (1) Hostile or warlike action in time of peace or war, including action in hindering, combating or defending against an actual impending or expected attack, (a) by any government or sovereign power (de jure or de facto), or by any authority maintaining or using military, naval or air forces; or (b) by military, naval or air forces; or (c) by an agent of any such government, power, authority or forces;

(2) Any weapon of war employing atomic fission or radioactive force whether in time of peace or war;

(3) Insurrection, rebellion, revolution, civil war, usurped power, or action taken by governmental authority in hindering, combating or defending against such an occurrence, seizure or destruction under quarantine or Customs regulations, confiscation by order of any government or public authority, or risks of contraband or illegal transportation or trade;

B. Nuclear reaction or nuclear radiation or radioactive contamination, all whether controlled or uncontrolled, and whether such loss be direct or indirect, proximate or remote, or be in whole or in part caused by, contributed to, or aggravated by the peril(s) insured against in this Policy; however, subject to the foregoing and all provisions of this Policy, direct loss by fire resulting from nuclear reaction or nuclear radiation or radioactive contamination is insured against by this Policy.

THIS POLICY IS MADE AND ACCEPTED SUBJECT TO THE FOREGOING STIPULATIONS AND CONDITIONS, together with such other provisions, agreements or conditions as may be endorsed hereon or added hereto; and no officer, agent or other representative of this Company shall have power to waive or be deemed to have waived any provision or condition of this Policy unless such waiver, if any, shall be written upon or attached hereto, nor shall any privilege or permission affecting the insurance under this Policy exist or be claimed by the Insured unless so written or attached.

PROVISIONS REQUIRED BY LAW TO BE STATED IN THIS POLICY:— "This Policy is issued under and in pursuance of the laws of the State of Minnesota, relating to Guaranty Surplus and Special Reserve Funds." Chapter 437, General Laws of 1909.

IN WITNESS WHEREOF, this Company has executed and attested these presents; but this Policy shall not be valid unless countersigned on the Declarations Page by a duly authorized Agent of the Company.

Secretary.　　　　　　　　　　　　　　　　　　Carl B. Drake, Jr.
　　　　　　　　　　　　　　　　　　　　　　　President.

SHORT RATE TABLE (For One Year Policies) [Days Policy In Force — Per Cent of 1 Yr. Prem.]

14000 MPP   Rev. 11-65

ST. PAUL FIRE AND MARINE INSURANCE COMPANY
DATA PROCESSING POLICY

DECLARATIONS:

Name and address of Insured

SPECIMEN

A
G
E
N
T

FORMER POLICY NO.

The insurance afforded is only with respect to such and so many of the following Insuring Agreements as are indicated by ☒. The limit of this Company's liability shall be as stated herein, subject to all the terms of this Policy having reference thereto.

In states where required, the statutory fire conditions are made a part of this Policy.

POLICY PERIOD* FROM	TO	SUM INSURED	RATE	PREMIUM
		$		$

*AT NOON STANDARD TIME AT PLACE OF ISSUANCE AS TO EACH OF SAID DATES.

☐ **1. DATA PROCESSING SYSTEM EQUIPMENT:**

LIMITS OF LIABILITY (Paragraph 3)

A. On property of the Insured in the amount of:
  (1) $_____located at_____
  (2) $_____located at_____
B. On property leased, rented or under the control of the Insured in the amount of:
  (1) $_____located at_____
  (2) $_____located at_____
C. $_____while in transit and while temporarily within other premises.

VALUATION (Paragraph 6)		COINSURANCE CLAUSE (Paragraph 7)		DEDUCTIBLE (Paragraph 8)
☐ A. ACTUAL CASH VALUE CLAUSE	☐ B. REPLACEMENT COST CLAUSE	☐ A. ____%	☐ B. 100%	$

☐ **2. DATA PROCESSING MEDIA:**

LIMITS OF LIABILITY (Paragraph 3)

A. On property of the Insured in the amount of:
  (1) $_____located at_____
  (2) $_____located at_____
B. $_____while in transit and while temporarily within other premises.

VALUATION (Paragraph 6)	VALUE OF EACH	LIMITS OF INSURANCE
(A) Specified Articles	$	$
(B) All Others		$
		DEDUCTIBLE (Paragraph 7)
		$

☐ **3. EXTRA EXPENSE:** Subject of Insurance and Perils Insured (Paragraph 1):

AMOUNT OF INSURANCE	MEASURE OF RECOVERY (Paragraph 2)	DEDUCTIBLE (Paragraph 8)
$	$	$

COUNTERSIGNATURE DATE	COUNTERSIGNED AT	AGENT

14000 CAA Rev. 9-66 Printed in U.S.A.   (OVER)

177

☐ 4. VALUABLE PAPERS AND RECORDS

PROPERTY COVERED (Paragraph 1)

A. Specified Articles

	VALUE OF EACH	LIMITS OF INSURANCE
	$	$

B. All Others

		$

LOCATION AND OCCUPANCY OF PREMISES

PART OF BUILDING INSURED OCCUPIES	LOCATION OF BUILDING	BUSINESS INSURED CONDUCTS THEREIN

PROTECTION OF VALUABLE PAPERS AND RECORDS (Paragraph 4)

KIND OF RECEPTACLE	NAME OF MAKER	"CLASS" OR "HOUR EXPOSURE" OF LABEL	NAME OF ISSUER OF LABEL

☐ 5. ACCOUNTS RECEIVABLE

LOCATION AND OCCUPANCY OF PREMISES (Paragraph 4)

PART OF BUILDING INSURED OCCUPIES	LOCATION OF BUILDING	BUSINESS INSURED CONDUCTS THEREIN

PROTECTION OF RECORDS OF ACCOUNTS RECEIVABLE (Paragraph 4)

KIND OF RECEPTACLE	NAME OF MAKER	"CLASS" OR "HOUR EXPOSURE" OF LABEL	NAME OF ISSUER OF LABEL

LIMIT OF INSURANCE (Paragraph 5)	PROVISIONAL PREMIUM (Paragraph 2 of "Special Conditions")	
$	$ INCLUDED	

☐ 6. BUSINESS INTERRUPTION: Subject of Insurance and Perils Insured (Paragraph 1)

AMOUNT OF INSURANCE	MEASURE OF RECOVERY (Paragraph 2)	DEDUCTIBLE (Paragraph 8)
$	$ PER DAY	$

GENERAL INFORMATION
DATA PROCESSING POLICY

The Data Processing Policy has been designed to meet a real need to insure Electronic Data Processing Equipment and other machines related to the data processing operation on a broad "All Risks" basis. It is also designed to provide proper insurance on the very substantial exposure of Media as well as the Extra Expense involved to return to a normal operation after a loss to machines or media and the monetary loss due to Business Interruption.

The coverage is divided into four major sections, as follows:

Insuring Agreement No. 1. **DATA PROCESSING EQUIPMENT.** This portion insures all equipment and component parts related to the processing unit. A schedule must be obtained of the units to be covered, and it is optional whether all or part is to be insured. Many firms will rent much of the equipment, and in such cases, we are prepared to cover the Difference of Conditions to pick up the responsibility of the Insured. This, basically, would be perils over and above Fire and Extended Coverage. Valuation may be actual cash value or retail replacement cost. Coinsurance of 80%, 90%, and 100% on actual cash value is optional but 100% coinsurance is mandatory on replacement cost basis.

Insuring Agreement No. 2. **DATA PROCESSING MEDIA.** This section insures physical loss or damage to all forms of media and can include magnetic tapes, perforated paper tapes, punch cards, discs, drums, and other forms of communication related to the data processing unit—in other words, this media picks up the data after it is converted from the source material into a form which is used in the processing system. For example, in the insurance business, when the information from a policy copy is put on a punch card or magnetic tape or perforated tape, it is then in converted form. The daily report or copy of the policy is not covered in this example. The Insured may elect to insure all media or any specific part. Great care must be exercised in developing a risk to determine the proper valuation to be insured on media. We give the Insured the option of valuing on two bases. If they can establish and wish to set a fixed value on each item — for example, so much per reel of tape or so much per punch card — we will accept this valuation and it becomes valued. If no specific valuation is placed, then we pay the actual reproduction cost. Reproduction cost will mean what it would cost to replace the media after a loss. This cost, therefor, must be figured not only on the basis of what it cost to originally produce those records, but the additional expense that must be incurred as a result of a loss. This additional expense can be quite substantial because it may involve working at some other location or on an overtime basis. No coinsurance applies.

Insuring Agreement No. 3. **EXTRA EXPENSE.** This coverage is designed to insure the extra expense necessary to continue to conduct, as nearly as practicable, the normal operation of business, due to damage to or destruction of the processing system including equipment and component parts and the data processing media therefor. On the surface, this would appear to overlap Agreement No. 2, because it includes media. It was written this way to take care of situations where all media may not be insured, although it should be, and also in situations when the machines are damaged but there is no damage to the media. Here again, it is essential that great care be exercised in developing the proper exposure, not only for the protection of the Insured, but for rating the risk. It will be found that this extra expense item can be very substantial. No coinsurance applies.

Insuring Agreement No. 6. **BUSINESS INTERRUPTION.** This agreement designed for use with the Data Processing Policy to cover monetary loss resulting from total or partial suspension of operations by reason of direct physical loss to data processing equipment and active data processing media. Perils are all risk using a **valued** business interruption form.

Use of this Agreement, in combination with Extra Expense Insuring Agreement No. 3, rounds out the Insured's recovery program whenever extra expense, while compensating for extra expenses incurred, falls short in replacing production earnings lost when data processing equipment and media control daily production and when a definite loss to earnings can be demonstrated.

DEDUCTIBLES will be available in most states on Insuring Agreements Nos. 1, 2, 3 and 6 from $500 to $100,000 with appropriate credits. ($5,000 to $250,000 in New York)

(over)

14172 GID   Rev. 9-66   Printed in U.S.A.

VALUABLE PAPERS AND ACCOUNTS RECEIVABLE. These two parts tie into the general requirements of a firm and can be included in the contract. The Valuable Papers policy covers the source material plus any other valuable papers. It should be considered at the same time. Accounts Receivable is important since there may be a loss of receivables due to the destruction of the records.

INSPECTION. Each risk must be considered on its individual merits and a complete inspection will be necessary for each risk.

APPLICATION. The Application is designed to not only develop information for our own use, but to lead the Insured into a realization of his exposures and assist him in developing the proper amount of insurance. The Information Sheet should be used as a preliminary check of the exposures prior to inspection to determine the desirability of the risk.

RATES. Each risk will be rated individually, but the rates generally are based on the Fire, Extended Coverage, and Vandalism rate plus a loading to take care of the additional perils, plus any possible increase in the fire exposure not previously considered.

TERM. While it is preferable to write policies for only one year because of constant changes in valuations, exposures, equipment and procedures, policies can be written for a term of three years at the term multiple.

PROSPECTS. In addition to the obvious prospects such as insurance companies of all kinds, large manufacturers, banks and finance organizations, there are no doubt many other low hazard classes of risks that have small units of data processing equipment in various forms, which qualify, who also need this type of coverage.

180

INSURING AGREEMENT No. 1

Data Processing System Equipment

1. **PROPERTY COVERED:** Data processing systems including equipment and component parts thereof owned by the Insured or leased, rented or under the control of the Insured, all as per schedule(s) on file with this Company.

2. **PROPERTY EXCLUDED:** This Insuring Agreement does not insure:
   A. Active data processing media which is hereby defined as meaning all forms of converted data and/or program and/or instruction vehicles employed in the Insured's data processing operation;
   B. Accounts, bills, evidences of debt, valuable papers, records, abstracts, deeds, manuscripts, or other documents;
   C. Property rented or leased to others while away from the premises of the Insured.

3. **LIMITS OF LIABILITY:** See "DECLARATIONS".

4. **PERILS INSURED:** This Insuring Agreement insures against all risks of direct physical loss or damage to the property covered, except as hereinafter provided.

5. **PERILS EXCLUDED:** This Insuring Agreement does not insure against loss, damage or expense caused directly or indirectly by:
   A. Damage due to mechanical failure, faulty construction, error in design unless fire or explosion ensues, and then only for loss, damage, or expense caused by such ensuing fire or explosion;
   B. Inherent vice, wear, tear, gradual deterioration or depreciation;
   C. Any dishonest, fraudulent or criminal act by any Insured, a partner therein or an officer, director or trustee thereof, whether acting alone or in collusion with others;
   D. Dryness or dampness of atmosphere, extremes of temperature, corrosion, or rust unless directly resulting from physical damage to the data processing system's air conditioning facilities caused by a peril not excluded by the provisions of this Insuring Agreement;
   E. Short circuit, blow-out, or other electrical disturbance, other than lightning, within electrical apparatus, unless fire or explosion ensues and then only for loss, damage or expense caused by such ensuing fire or explosion;
   F. Actual work upon the property covered, unless fire or explosion ensues, and then only for loss, damage, or expense caused by such ensuing fire or explosion;
   G. Delay or loss of market;
   H. War risks or nuclear risks as excluded in the Policy to which this Insuring Agreement is attached.

6. **VALUATION:**
   A. ACTUAL CASH VALUE — The following clause shall apply if indicated in the "Declarations": This Company shall not be liable beyond the actual cash value of the property at the time any loss or damage occurs and the loss or damage shall be ascertained or estimated according to such actual value with proper deduction for depreciation, however caused, and shall in no event exceed what it would then cost to repair or replace the same with material of like kind and quality.
   B. REPLACEMENT COST — The following clause shall apply if indicated in the "Declarations": This Company shall not be liable beyond the actual retail replacement cost of the property at the time any loss or damage occurs and the loss or damage shall be ascertained or estimated on the basis of the actual cash retail replacement cost of property similar in kind to that insured at the place of and immediately preceding the time of such loss or damage, but in no event to exceed the limit of liability stipulated in the "Declarations".

7. **COINSURANCE CLAUSE:**
   A. The following clause shall apply if indicated in the "Declarations": This Company shall be liable in the event of loss for no greater proportion thereof than the amount hereby insured bears to the percent indicated in the "Declarations" of the actual cash value of all property insured hereunder at the time such loss shall happen.
   B. The following clause shall apply if indicated in the "Declarations": This Company shall be liable in the event of loss for no greater proportion thereof than the amount hereby insured bears to the percent indicated in the "Declarations" of the actual cash retail replacement cost of all property insured hereunder at the time such loss shall happen.

8. **DEDUCTIBLE:** Each and every loss occurring hereunder shall be adjusted separately and from the amount of each such loss when so adjusted the amount indicated in the "Declarations" shall be deducted.

9. **DIFFERENCE IN CONDITIONS:** It is a condition of this Insurance that the Insured shall file with this Company a copy of any lease or rental agreement pertaining to the property insured hereunder insofar as concerns the lessors' liability for loss or damage to said property, and coverage afforded hereunder shall be only for the difference in conditions between those contained in said lease or rental agreement and the terms of this Insuring Agreement. The Insured agrees to give this Company thirty days notice of any alteration, cancellation or termination of the above mentioned lease or rental agreement pertaining to the lessors' liability.

All other terms and conditions of the Policy not in conflict herewith remain unchanged.

14000 CAC 3-70 5M Rev. 12-64 Printed in U. S. A.

1. **PROPERTY INSURED:** Active data processing media, being property of the Insured or property of others for which the Insured may be liable.

2. **PROPERTY EXCLUDED:** This Insuring Agreement does not insure accounts, bills, evidences of debt, valuable papers, records, abstracts, deeds, manuscripts or other documents except as they may be converted to data processing media form, and then only in that form, or any data processing media which cannot be replaced with other of like kind and quality.

3. **LIMITS OF LIABILITY:** See "DECLARATIONS".

4. **PERILS INSURED:** This Insuring Agreement insures against all risks of direct physical loss or damage to the property covered, except as hereinafter provided.

5. **PERILS EXCLUDED:** This Insuring Agreement does not insure against loss, damage, or expense resulting from or caused directly or indirectly by:

   A. Data processing media failure or breakdown or malfunction of the data processing system including equipment and component parts while said media is being run through the system, unless fire or explosion ensues and then only for the loss, damage or expense caused by such ensuing fire or explosion;

   B. Electrical or magnetic injury, disturbance or erasure of electronic recordings, except by lightning;

   C. Dryness or dampness of atmosphere, extremes of temperature, corrosion, or rust unless directly resulting from physical damage to the data processing system's air conditioning facilities caused by a peril not excluded by the provisions of this Insuring Agreement;

   D. Delay or loss of market;

   E. Inherent vice, wear, tear, gradual deterioration or depreciation;

   F. Any dishonest, fraudulent or criminal act by any Insured, a partner therein or an officer, director or trustee thereof, whether acting alone or in collusion with others;

   G. War risks or nuclear risks as excluded in the Policy to which this Insuring Agreement is attached.

6. **VALUATION:** The limit of this Company's liability for loss or damage shall not exceed:

   A. As respects property specifically described in the "Declarations", the amount per article specified therein, said amount being the agreed value thereof for the purpose of this insurance;

   B. As respects all other property, the actual reproduction cost of the property; if not replaced or reproduced, blank value of media; all subject to the applicable limit of liability stated in the "Declarations".

7. **DEDUCTIBLE:** Each and every loss occurring hereunder shall be adjusted separately and from the amount of each loss when so adjusted the amount indicated in the "Declarations" shall be deducted.

8. **DEFINITIONS:** The term "active data processing media", wherever used in this contract, shall mean all forms of converted data and/or program and/or instruction vehicles employed in the Insured's data processing operation, except all such UNUSED property, and the following

_____

(insert names of media not to be insured)

which the Insured elects not to insure hereunder.

All other terms and conditions of the Policy not in conflict herewith remain unchanged.

14000 CAD Rev. 3-63

INSURING AGREEMENT No. 3
Extra Expense

1. **SUBJECT OF INSURANCE AND PERILS INSURED:** This Insuring Agreement insures against the necessary Extra Expense, as hereinafter defined, incurred by the Insured in order to continue as nearly as practicable the normal operation of its business, immediately following damage to or destruction of the data processing system including equipment and component parts thereof and data processing media therefor, owned, leased, rented or under the control of the Insured, as a direct result of all risks of physical loss or damage, but in no event to exceed the amount indicated in the "Declarations".

This Insuring Agreement is extended to include actual loss as covered hereunder, sustained during the period of time, hereinafter defined, (1) when as a direct result of a peril insured against the premises in which the property is located is so damaged as to prevent access to such property or (2) when as a direct result of a peril insured against, the air conditioning system or electrical system necessary for the operation of the data processing equipment is so damaged as to reduce or suspend the Insured's ability to actually perform the operations normally performed by the data processing system.

2. **MEASURE OF RECOVERY:** If the above described property is destroyed or so damaged by the perils insured against occurring during the term of this Insuring Agreement so as to necessitate the incurrence of Extra Expense (as defined in this Insuring Agreement), this Company shall be liable for the Extra Expense so incurred, not exceeding the actual loss sustained, for not exceeding such length of time, hereinafter referred to as the "period of restoration", commencing with the date of damage or destruction and not limited by the date of expiration of this Insuring Agreement, as shall be required with the exercise of due diligence and dispatch to repair, rebuild, or replace such part of said property as may be destroyed or damaged.

This Company's liability, during the determined period of restoration, shall be limited to the declared amount per period of time indicated in the "Declarations" but in no event to exceed the amount of insurance provided.

3. **EXTRA EXPENSE DEFINITION:** The term "Extra Expense" wherever employed in this Insuring Agreement is defined as the excess (if any) of the total cost during the period of restoration of the operation of the business over and above the total cost of such operation that would normally have been incurred during the same period had no loss occurred; the cost in each case to include expense of using other property or facilities of other concerns or other necessary emergency expenses. In no event, however, shall this Company be liable for loss of profits or earnings resulting from diminution of business, nor for any direct or indirect property damage loss insurable under Property Damage policies, or for expenditures incurred in the purchase, construction, repair or replacement of any physical property unless incurred for the purpose of reducing any loss under this Insuring Agreement not exceeding, however, the amount in which the loss is so reduced. Any salvage value of property so acquired which may be sold or utilized by the Insured upon resumption of normal operations, shall be taken into consideration in the adjustment of any loss hereunder.

4. **EXCLUSIONS:** It is a condition of the insurance that the Company shall not be liable for Extra Expense incurred as a result of:

A. Any local or State ordinance or law regulating construction or repair of buildings;

B. The suspension, lapse or cancellation of any lease, license, contract or order;

C. Interference at premises by strikers or other persons with repairing or replacing the property damaged or destroyed or with the resumption or continuation of the Insured's occupancy;

D. Loss or destruction of accounts, bills, evidences of debt, valuable papers, records, abstracts, deeds, manuscripts or other documents except as they may be converted to data processing media form and then only in that form;

E. Loss of or damage to property rented or leased to others while away from the premises of the Insured;

F. Error in machine programming or instructions to machine;

G. Inherent vice, wear, tear, gradual deterioration or depreciation;

H. Any dishonest, fraudulent or criminal act by any Insured, a partner therein or an officer, director or trustee thereof, whether acting alone or in collusion with others;

I. Damage due to mechanical failure, faulty construction, error in design unless fire or explosion ensues, and then only for loss, damage, or expense caused by such ensuing fire or explosion;

J. Short circuit, blow-out, or other electrical disturbance, other than lightning, within electrical apparatus, unless fire or explosion ensues and then only for loss, damage or expense caused by such ensuing fire or explosion;

K. Delay or loss of market;

L. War risks or nuclear risks as excluded in the Policy to which this Insuring Agreement is attached.

(over)

14000 CAE   Rev. 3-63

183

5. **RESUMPTION OF OPERATIONS:** As soon as practicable after any loss, the Insured shall resume complete or partial business operations of the property herein described and, in so far as practicable, reduce or dispense with such additional charges and expenses as are being incurred.

6. **INTERRUPTION BY CIVIL AUTHORITY:** Liability under this Insuring Agreement is extended to include actual loss as covered hereunder, sustained during the period of time, not exceeding two weeks, when as a direct result of a peril insured against, access to the premises in which the property described is located is prohibited by order of civil authority.

7. **DEFINITIONS:** The term "Normal" wherever used in this contract shall mean: The condition that would have existed had no loss occurred.

8. **DEDUCTIBLE:** Each and every loss occurring hereunder shall be adjusted separately and from the amount of each such loss when so adjusted the amount indicated in the "Declarations" shall be deducted.

All other terms and conditions of the Policy not in conflict herewith remain unchanged.

1. **PROPERTY COVERED:** The Company agrees to pay on valuable papers and records, as stated in the "Declarations".

2. **THIS INSURING AGREEMENT INSURES AGAINST:** All risks of direct physical loss of or damage to the property covered, except as hereinafter provided, occurring during the period of this Insuring Agreement.

3. **LOCATION AND OCCUPANCY OF PREMISES:** See "DECLARATIONS".

4. **PROTECTION OF VALUABLE PAPERS AND RECORDS:** Insurance under this Insuring Agreement shall apply only while valuable papers and records are contained in the premises described in the "Declarations", it being a condition precedent to any right of recovery hereunder that such valuable papers and records shall be kept in the receptacle(s) described in the "Declarations" at all times when the premises are not open for business, except while such valuable papers and records are in actual use or as stated in paragraph 5 of this Insuring Agreement and 1B of Policy General Conditions.

5. **AUTOMATIC EXTENSION:** Such insurance as is afforded by this Insuring Agreement applies while the valuable papers and records are being conveyed outside the premises and while temporarily within other premises, except for storage, provided the Company's liability for such loss or damage shall not exceed ten percent of the combined limits of insurance stated in paragraph 1, nor Five Thousand Dollars, whichever is less.

EXCLUSIONS

THIS INSURING AGREEMENT DOES NOT APPLY:

(a) to loss due to wear and tear, gradual deterioration, vermin or inherent vice;

(b) to loss due to any fraudulent, dishonest, or criminal act by any Insured, a partner therein, or an officer, director or trustee thereof, whether acting alone or in collusion with others;

(c) to loss to property not specifically declared and described in section (a) of paragraph 1, "Property Covered", if such property cannot be replaced with other of like kind and quality;

(d) to loss to property held as samples or for sale or for delivery after sale;

(e) to loss due to electrical or magnetic injury, disturbance or erasure of electronic recordings, except by lightning;

(f) to war risks or nuclear risks as excluded in the Policy to which this Insuring Agreement is attached;

(g) to loss directly resulting from errors or omissions in processing or copying unless fire or explosion ensues and then only for direct loss caused by such ensuing fire or explosion.

SPECIAL CONDITIONS

1. **OWNERSHIP OF PROPERTY; INTERESTS COVERED:** The insured property may be owned by the Insured or held by him in any capacity; provided, the insurance applies only to the interest of the Insured in such property, including the Insured's liability to others, and does not apply to the interest of any other person or organization in any of said property unless included in the Insured's proof of loss.

2. **LIMITS OF LIABILITY; VALUATION; SETTLEMENT OPTION:** The limit of the Company's liability for loss shall not exceed the actual cash value of the property at time of loss nor what it would then cost to repair or replace the property with other of like kind and quality, nor the applicable limit of insurance stated in this Insuring Agreement; provided, as respects property specifically described in section (a) of paragraph 1, "Property Covered", the amount per article specified therein is the agreed value thereof for the purpose of this insurance. The Company may pay for the loss in money or may repair or replace the property and may settle any claim for loss of the property either with the Insured or the owner thereof. Any property so paid for or replaced shall become the property of the Company. The Insured or the Company, upon recovery of any such property, shall give notice thereof as soon as practicable to the other and the Insured shall be entitled to the property upon reimbursing the Company for the amount so paid or the cost of replacement.

   Application of the insurance to property of more than one person shall not operate to increase the applicable limit of insurance.

3. **INSURED'S DUTIES WHEN LOSS OCCURS:** Upon knowledge of loss or of an occurrence which may give rise to a claim for loss, the Insured shall give notice thereof as soon as practicable to the Company or any of its authorized agents and, if the loss is due to a violation of law, also to the police.

4. **ACTION AGAINST COMPANY:** No action shall lie against the Company unless, as a condition precedent thereto, there shall have been full compliance with all the terms of this Insuring Agreement, nor until thirty days after the required proofs of loss have been filed with the Company, nor at all unless commenced within two years after the discovery by the Insured of the occurrence which gives rise to the loss. If this limitation of time is shorter than that prescribed by any statute controlling the construction of this Insuring Agreement, the shortest permissible statutory limitation in time shall govern and shall supersede the time limitation herein stated.

5. **DEFINITIONS:**

   (a) Valuable Papers and Records — The term "valuable papers and records" means written, printed or otherwise inscribed documents and records, including books, maps, films, drawings, abstracts, deeds, mortgages and manuscripts, but does not mean money or securities, or electronic data control tapes.

   (b) Premises — The unqualified word "premises" means the interior of that portion of the building at the location designated in paragraph 3, "Location and Occupancy of Premises" and described in the "Declarations", which is occupied by the Insured for the business purposes stated therein.

6. **CHANGES:** Notice to any agent or knowledge possessed by any agent or by any other person shall not effect a waiver or a change in any part of this Insuring Agreement or estop the Company from asserting any right under the terms of this Insuring Agreement nor shall the terms of this Insuring Agreement be waived or changed, except by endorsement issued to form a part of this Insuring Agreement.

INAPPLICABLE POLICY CONDITIONS

Paragraph 1A, 1F, 1G, 1H, 1I and 1N of General Policy Conditions do not apply to this Insuring Agreement.

All other terms and conditions of the Policy not in conflict herewith remain unchanged.

14000 CAF   Rev. 6-65

1. THE COMPANY AGREES TO PAY:

A. All sums due the Insured from customers, provided the Insured is unable to effect collection thereof as the direct result of loss of or damage to records of accounts receivable;

B. Interest charges on any loan to offset impaired collections pending repayment of such sums made uncollectible by such loss or damage;

C. Collection expense in excess of normal collection cost and made necessary because of such loss or damage;

D. Other expenses, when reasonably incurred by the Insured in re-establishing records of accounts receivable following such loss or damage.

2. THIS INSURING AGREEMENT INSURES AGAINST: All risks of loss of or damage to the Insured's records of accounts receivable, occurring during the period of this Insuring Agreement, except as hereinafter provided.

3. LOCATION AND OCCUPANCY OF PREMISES: See "DECLARATIONS".

4. PROTECTION OF RECORDS OF ACCOUNTS RECEIVABLE: Insurance under this Insuring Agreement shall apply only while records of accounts receivable are contained in the premises described in the "Declarations", it being a condition precedent to any right of recovery hereunder that such records shall be kept in the receptacle(s) described in the "Declarations" at all times when the premises are not open for business, except while such records are in actual use;

5. LIMIT OF INSURANCE: The Company shall not be liable hereunder for an amount to exceed the Limit of Insurance stated in the "Declarations".

EXCLUSIONS

THIS INSURING AGREEMENT DOES NOT APPLY:

(a) to loss due to any fraudulent, dishonest or criminal act by any Insured, a partner therein, or an officer, director or trustee thereof, while working or otherwise and whether acting alone or in collusion with others;

(b) to loss due to bookkeeping, accounting or billing errors or omissions;

(c) to loss, the proof of which as to factual existence, is dependent upon an audit of records or an inventory computation; but this shall not preclude the use of such procedures in support of claim for loss which the Insured can prove, through evidence wholly apart therefrom, is due solely to a risk of loss to records of accounts receivable not otherwise excluded hereunder;

(d) to loss due to alteration, falsification, manipulation, concealment, destruction or disposal of records of accounts receivable committed to conceal the wrongful giving, taking, obtaining or withholding of money, securities or other property but only to the extent of such wrongful giving, taking, obtaining or withholding;

(e) to loss due to electrical or magnetic injury, disturbance or erasure of electronic recordings, except by lightning;

(f) to war risks or nuclear risks as excluded in the Policy to which this Insuring Agreement is attached.

SPECIAL CONDITIONS

1. DEFINITION OF PREMISES: The unqualified word "premises" means the interior of that portion of the building at the location designated in Paragraph 3, "location and occupancy of premises" and described in the "Declarations", which is occupied by the Insured for the business purposes stated therein.

2. PREMIUM: The Insured shall, within twenty days after the end of each fiscal month during the policy period, furnish the Company with a written statement of the total amount of accounts receivable, with deferred payments and charge accounts segregated, as of the last day of each such month.

The premium stated in the "Declarations" is provisional only. Upon each anniversary and upon termination of this Insuring Agreement, the sum of the monthly amounts of accounts receivable for the preceding twelve months shall be averaged and the earned premium shall be computed on such average at the rate stated in this Insuring Agreement, whether or not such average exceeds the applicable limit of Insurance under this Insuring Agreement. If the earned premium thus computed exceeds the provisional premium paid, the Insured shall pay the excess to the Company; if less, the Company shall return to the Insured the unearned portion paid by the Insured, but such premium shall not be less than any minimum premium stated in this Insuring Agreement.

14000 CAG Rev. 6-65   (OVER)

3. **INSPECTION AND AUDIT:** The Company shall be permitted to inspect the premises and the receptacles in which the records of accounts receivable are kept by the Insured, and to examine and audit the Insured's books and records at any time during the period of coverage and any extension thereof and within three years after the final termination of this Insuring Agreement, as far as they relate to the premium basis or the subject matter of this insurance, and to verify the statements of any outstanding record of accounts receivable submitted by the Insured and the amount of recoveries of accounts receivable on which the Company has made any settlement.

4. **RECOVERIES:** After payment of loss all amounts recovered by the Insured on accounts receivable for which the Insured has been indemnified shall belong and be paid to the Company by the Insured up to the total amount of loss paid by the Company; but all recoveries in excess of such amounts shall belong to the Insured.

5. **INSURED'S DUTIES WHEN LOSS OCCURS:** Upon the occurrence of any loss which may result in a claim hereunder, the Insured shall:

    (A) Give notice thereof as soon as practicable to the Company or any of its authorized agents and, if the loss is due to a violation of law, also to the police;

    (B) File detailed proof of loss, duly sworn to, with the Company promptly on expiration of ninety days from the date on which the records of accounts receivable were lost or damaged.

    Upon the Company's request, the Insured shall submit to examination by the Company, subscribe the same, under oath if required, and produce for the Company's examination all pertinent records, all at such reasonable times and places as the Company shall designate, and shall cooperate with the Company in all matters pertaining to loss or claims with respect thereto, including rendering of all possible assistance to effect collection of outstanding accounts receivable.

6. **DETERMINATION OF RECEIVABLES: DEDUCTIONS** — When there is proof that a loss covered by this Insuring Agreement has occurred but the Insured cannot accurately establish the total amount of accounts receivable outstanding as of the date of such loss, such amount shall be based on the Insured's monthly statements and shall be computed as follows:

    (a) determine the amount of all outstanding accounts receivable at the end of the same fiscal month in the year immediately preceding the year in which the loss occurs;

    (b) calculate the percentage of increase or decrease in the average monthly total of accounts receivable for the twelve months immediately preceding the month in which the loss occurs, or such part thereof for which the Insured has furnished monthly statements to the Company, as compared with such average for the same months of the preceding year;

    (c) the amount determined under (a) above, increased or decreased by the percentage calculated under (b) above, shall be the agreed total amount of accounts receivable as of the last day of the fiscal month in which said loss occurs;

    (d) the amount determined under (c) above shall be increased or decreased in conformity with the normal fluctuations in the amount of accounts receivable during the fiscal month involved, due consideration being given to the experience of the business since the last day of the last fiscal month for which statement has been rendered.

    There shall be deducted from the total amount of accounts receivable, however established, the amount of such accounts evidenced by records not lost or damaged, or otherwise established or collected by the Insured, and an amount to allow for probable bad debts which would normally have been uncollectible by the Insured. On deferred payment accounts receivable, unearned interest and service charges shall be deducted.

7. **SETTLEMENT OF CLAIMS; ACTION AGAINST COMPANY:** All adjusted claims shall be paid or made good to the Insured within thirty days after presentation and acceptance of satisfactory proof of interest and loss at the office of the Company. No action shall lie against the Company unless, as a condition precedent thereto, there shall have been full compliance with all the terms of this Insuring Agreement nor at all unless commenced within two years after the discovery by the Insured of the occurrence which gives rise to the loss. If this limitation of time is shorter than that prescribed by any statute controlling the construction of this Insuring Agreement, the shortest permissible statutory limitation in time shall govern and shall supersede the time limitation herein stated.

8. **CHANGES:** Notice to any agent or knowledge possessed by any agent or by any other person shall not effect a waiver or change in any part of this Insuring Agreement, or estop the Company from asserting any right under the terms of this Insuring Agreement, nor shall the terms of this Insuring Agreement be waived or changed, except by endorsement issued to form a part of this Insuring Agreement.

INAPPLICABLE POLICY CONDITIONS

Paragraph 1A, 1F, 1G, 1H, 1I and 1N of General Policy Conditions do not apply to this Insuring Agreement

All other terms and conditions of the Policy not in conflict herewith remain unchanged.

INSURING AGREEMENT No. 6
Business Interruption

1. **SUBJECT OF INSURANCE AND PERILS INSURED:** This Insuring Agreement covers against loss resulting directly from necessary interruption of business as a direct result of all risk of physical loss or damage from any cause (except as hereinafter excluded) to the following property owned, leased, rented or under the control of the Insured:

   A. Data processing systems, computer systems or other electronic control equipment including component parts thereof;

   B. Active data processing media meaning all forms of converted data and/or program and/or instruction vehicles employed in the Insured's data processing or production operation except the following _____

   which the Insured elects not to insure hereunder.

   This Insuring Agreement is extended to include actual loss as covered hereunder when as a direct result of a peril insured against the premises in which the property is located is so damaged as to prevent access to such property.

2. **MEASURE OF RECOVERY:** In the event such loss or damage results in either a total or partial suspension of business then this Company shall be liable:

   A. for the amount stated in the "Declarations" for each working day during the period of such total suspension of business; or

   B. in the event of partial suspension, for such proportion of the amount stated in the "Declarations" for each working day of total production which would have been obtained during the period of partial suspension had no damage occurred;

   commencing with the date of damage or destruction, and not limited by the expiration date of this Insuring Agreement, as would be required through the exercise of due diligence and dispatch to rebuild, repair or replace such described property as has been damaged or destroyed but in no event to exceed the amount of insurance provided.

3. **RESUMPTION OF OPERATIONS:** It is a condition of this insurance that if the Insured could reduce the loss resulting from the interruption of business,

   A. by complete or partial resumption of operation of the property herein described, whether damaged or not, or

   B. by making use of other property at the location(s) described herein or elsewhere, or

   C. by making use of stock at the location(s) described herein or elsewhere, such reduction shall be taken into account in arriving at the amount of loss hereunder.

4. **EXPENSE TO REDUCE LOSS:** This Insuring Agreement also covers such expenses as are necessarily incurred for the purpose of reducing any loss under this Insuring Agreement (except expense incurred to extinguish a fire), but in the absence of prior authorization by this Company or its adjuster, NOT EXCEEDING THE AMOUNT BY WHICH THE LOSS UNDER THIS POLICY IS THEREBY REDUCED.

5. **INTERRUPTION BY CIVIL AUTHORITY:** This Insuring Agreement is extended to include the actual loss as covered hereunder during the period of time, not exceeding two consecutive weeks, when, as a direct result of the peril(s) insured against, access to the premises described is prohibited by order of civil authority.

6. **EXCLUSIONS:** It is a condition of the insurance that the Company shall not be liable for Total or Partial suspension incurred as a result of:

   A. Any local or State ordinance or law regulating construction or repair of buildings;

   B. The suspension, lapse or cancellation of any lease, license, contract or order;

   C. Interference at premises by strikers or other persons with repairing or replacing the property damage or destroyed or with the resumption or continuation of the Insured's occupancy;

   D. Loss or destruction of accounts, bills, evidences of debt, valuable papers, records, abstracts, deeds, manuscripts or other documents except as they may be converted to data processing media form and then only in that form;

   E. Loss of or damage to property rented or leased to others while away from the premises of the Insured;

   F. Error in machine programming or instructions to machine;

   G. Inherent vice, wear, tear, gradual deterioration or depreciation;

   H. Any dishonest, fraudulent or criminal act by any Insured, a partner therein or an officer, director or trustee thereof, whether acting alone or in collusion with others;

   I. Damage due to mechanical failure, faulty construction, error in design unless fire or explosion ensues, and then only for loss, damage, or expense caused by such ensuing fire or explosion;

   J. Short circuit, blow-out, or other electrical disturbance, other than lightning, within electrical apparatus, unless fire or explosion ensues and then only for loss, damage or expense caused by such ensuing fire or explosion;

   K. Delay or loss of market;

   L. War risks or nuclear risks as excluded in the Policy to which this Insuring Agreement is attached.

7. **WORK DAY:** The words "work day", however modified, whenever used in this Insuring Agreement shall be held to cover a period of twenty-four hours and shall mean a day on which the operations of the Insured are usually performed.

8. **DEDUCTIBLE:** Each and every loss occurring hereunder shall be adjusted separately and from the amount of each such loss when so adjusted the amount indicated in the "Declarations" shall be deducted.

All other terms and conditions of the Policy not in conflict herewith remain unchanged.

APPLICATION FOR DATA PROCESSING POLICY

PROPERTY DIVISION

THE ST. PAUL
INSURANCE COMPANIES

Serving you around the world...around the clock

NAME OF APPLICANT (INCLUDE NAMES OF ALL SUBSIDIARIES)

BUSINESS ADDRESS

NATURE OF BUSINESS | EFFECTIVE DATE | TERM

RATING INFORMATION

LOCATION 1						LOCATION 2					
CONTENTS FIRE RATE	COINS. %	E. C. RATE	COINS. %	V. & M.M. RATE	COINS. %	CONTENTS FIRE RATE	COINS. %	E. C. RATE	COINS. %	V. & M.M. RATE	COINS. %

THE APPLICANT HAS THE OPTION of insuring only his data processing equipment, or his data processing media, or his extra expense or business interruption, or he may elect to take any two, three or four of the coverages. If desired, the applicant may also purchase these coverages on a deductible basis subject to a minimum deductible of $500.00.

DATA PROCESSING EQUIPMENT: The applicant has the option of insuring all or only part of the equipment, which may be either owned or leased, on an actual cash value basis or on a retail replacement cost basis.

ACTIVE DATA PROCESSING MEDIA: The applicant has the option of (1) specifically scheduling items or groups by types, establishing per-unit agreed values, or (2) blanketing all or unscheduled items into a total single value.

DATA PROCESSING EQUIPMENT
(Attach schedule or list below under "Additional Information")

LOCATION 1				LOCATION 2			
LIMIT OF LIABILITY	OWNED OR LEASED	ACTUAL CASH VALUE	REPLACEMENT COST	LIMIT OF LIABILITY	OWNED OR LEASED	ACTUAL CASH VALUE	REPLACEMENT COST
$		$	$	$		$	$

VALUATION		COINSURANCE			DEDUCTIBLE	
☐ ACTUAL CASH VALUE	☐ REPLACEMENT COST*	☐ 80%	☐ 90%	☐ 100%	☐ YES ☐ NO	$

*REPLACEMENT COST MUST BE WRITTEN WITH 100% COINSURANCE.

DATA PROCESSING MEDIA

LOCATION 1				LOCATION 2			
LIMIT OF LIABILITY	100% COINS. F.C. RATE	ACTUAL CASH VALUE	REPLACEMENT COST	LIMIT OF LIABILITY	100% COINS F.C. RATE	ACTUAL CASH VALUE	REPLACEMENT COST
$		$	$	$		$	$

LIMIT OF LIABILITY		DEDUCTIBLE	
$ WHILE IN TRANSIT AND WHILE TEMPORARILY WITHIN OTHER PREMISES.	☐ YES ☐ NO	$

EXTRA EXPENSE

AGREED "PERIOD OF RESTORATION"	ESTIMATED EXTRA EXPENSE TO BE INCURRED FOR THAT PERIOD	DEDUCTIBLE	
	$	☐ YES ☐ NO	$

BUSINESS INTERRUPTION

NUMBER OF "OPERATING DAYS"	AMOUNT OF INSURANCE	MEASURE OF RECOVERY	DEDUCTIBLE	
PER WEEK	$	$ PER DAY	☐ YES ☐ NO	$

ADDITIONAL INFORMATION

1495J ADP Rev. 12-64

190

MACHINE CHARACTERISTICS, OPERATION AND EXPOSURES

YES NO

☐☐ ARE ANY MACHINES ENCLOSED IN COMBUSTIBLE MATERIAL OR ARE PANELS LINED WITH COMBUSTIBLE INSULATION OR SOUND DEADENERS?

☐☐ IS THIS INSTALLATION IN A SPECIAL ROOM, HEREINAFTER REFERRED TO AS "THE ROOM"?

☐☐ ARE COMPUTERS EQUIPPED WITH VACUUM TUBES?

☐☐ DOES ANY MACHINE CABLE OR WIRING OUTSIDE OF ROOM PASS THROUGH AREAS CONTAINING COMBUSTIBLE MATERIAL?

☐☐ ARE ALL UNITS INSIDE THE ROOM GOVERNED BY A MASTER SWITCH?

LOCATED: ☐ IN THE ROOM ☐ OUTSIDE THE ROOM

☐☐ ARE MANUFACTURER'S ENGINEERS PERMANENTLY ASSIGNED TO THE ROOM?

☐☐ IS THE ENGINEER'S WORKSHOP INSIDE THE ROOM?

☐☐ HAVE DEFINITE ARRANGEMENTS BEEN MADE FOR THE USE OF SUBSTITUTE FACILITIES ELSEWHERE IN THE EVENT OF A SHUTDOWN?

IS TAPE STORAGE (OTHER THAN TAPE IN USE):

☐ IN VAULT?

☐ IN COMPUTER ROOM?

☐ IN COMBUSTIBLE RACKS?

☐ IN APPROVED METAL CONTAINERS IN A 2-HOUR SAFE?

WHAT KIND OF TAPES ARE USED?

☐ METAL

☐ PLASTIC

☐ PAPER

YES NO

☐☐ IS FLAMMABLE SOLVENT USED FOR TAPE ROLLER OR CAPSTAN CLEANING?

☐☐ IS SOLVENT KEPT IN 6-OZ. CAN WITH SPOUT?

☐☐ IS FLAMMABLE SOLVENT KEPT IN GLASS BOTTLE?

AIR CONDITIONING EQUIPMENT

☐☐ IS ELECTRIC PRECIPITRON PROVIDED IN AIR STREAM TO ROOM?

☐☐ IS ROOM AIR CONDITIONED?

☐☐ ARE DUCT LININGS COMBUSTIBLE?

☐☐ ARE COMBUSTIBLE FILTERS USED?

☐☐ ARE FILTERS OIL-DIPPED?

☐☐ IS COMPRESSOR IN ROOM OR IMMEDIATELY ADJOINING?

☐☐ IS FREON USED AS REFRIGERANT?

IS FRESH OR MAKE-UP AIR INTAKE:

☐☐ WITHIN 10 FT. OF THE GROUND?

☐☐ SCREENED WITH $\frac{1}{4}$ IN. OR HEAVIER GALVANIZED MESH?

☐☐ OVER ADJOINING BUILDINGS OR OVER ANY COMBUSTIBLE MATERIAL OR SUBJECT TO SMOKE FROM NEARBY (150 FT.) STACKS?

☐☐ DOES SYSTEM HAVE CONTROL SWITCH IN ROOM OR ELECTRIC EYE OR OTHER AUTOMATIC SHUTDOWN SWITCH?

☐☐ IS THERE ANY PROVISION FOR DUPLICATION IN EVENT OF SYSTEM SHUTDOWN?

WATER DAMAGE

☐☐ IS ROOM SUBJECT TO ACCUMULATION OF WATER FROM ITS OWN LEVEL?

☐☐ DO WATER LINES OTHER THAN SPRINKLER SYSTEM ENTER OR PASS THROUGH ROOM OR CEILING SPACE?

☐☐ DO STEAM LINES, OTHER THAN RADIATOR BRANCH LINES FOR COMPUTER ROOM, ENTER OR PASS THROUGH ROOM?

☐☐ ARE FLOOR(S) AND ROOF OVER ROOM WATER-TIGHT TO PREVENT ENTRY FROM ABOVE?

☐☐ ARE THERE SPRINKLERED AREAS OVER ROOM?

☐☐ IF ROOM IS SPRINKLERED, ARE COMPUTERS FITTED WITH IN-COMBUSTIBLE CANOPIES TO PREVENT ENTRY OF WATER FROM OVERHEAD?

COLLAPSE

☐☐ ARE THERE UNPROTECTED METAL SUPPORTS (POST OR BEAMS) ABOVE OR BELOW ROOM?

☐☐ ARE COMBUSTIBLE FLOORS ABOVE OR BELOW ROOM (EXCEL. PEDESTAL FLOOR)?

☐☐ ARE THERE SPRINKLERS ABOVE OR BELOW ROOM?

FIRE

☐☐ IS ROOM OF COMBUSTIBLE MATERIAL OR OF ANY MATERIAL ON COMBUSTIBLE STUDS OR SUPPORTS?

☐☐ IS ROOM NEAR OPEN COURTS OR STAIRWAYS OR IN VERTICAL FLUEWAY, OR RECEIVING OR DELIVERY DOCK OR PORT OR ADJACENT TO PASSAGEWAY?

☐☐ DOES ROOM HAVE PEDESTAL FLOOR?

☐☐ IS PEDESTAL FLOOR OF COMBUSTIBLE MATERIAL?

☐☐ DOES ROOM CONTAIN COMBUSTIBLE CURTINS OR DRAPES?

☐☐ IS ROOM CEILING OF COMBUSTIBLE MATERIAL OR ON COMBUSTIBLE SUPPORTS?

☐☐ IS SMOKING PERMITTED IN ROOM OR IN ADJOINING REPAIR SHOP?

☐☐ DO WATCHMAN'S RECORDED ROUNDS TAKE HIM TO ROOM WHEN ROOM IS NOT OPERATING

☐☐ ARE ADEQUATE CARBON DIOXIDE EXTINGUISHERS AVAILABLE IN ROOM?

☐☐ ARE GAS MASKS AVAILABLE FOR ROOM?

IS ANY REPAIR WORK DONE IN ROOM REQUIRING

☐ USE OF FLAME OR FLAMMABLE LIQUIDS

☐ STORAGE OF FLAMMABLE LIQUIDS

☐☐ IS THE ROOM EQUIPPED WITH SMOKE DETECTORS?

☐☐ ARE WINDOWS OF ROOM ON AN OUTSIDE WALL?

IF SO, DO THEY OVERLOOK OR FACE:

☐ A STREET WITHIN 15 FT. OF GROUND LEVEL?

☐ OTHER BUILDINGS, MATERIALS OR STRUCTURES?

EXPOSURE:

☐ NONE

☐ LIGHT

☐ MEDIUM

☐ SEVERE

DUPLICATE PROGRAM TAPES

☐☐ ARE DUPLICATE PROGRAM TAPES MAINTAINED?

☐☐ ARE THEY STORED IN FIREPROOF VAULT OR SAFE?

☐☐ ARE THEY STORED IN A BUILDING RATED AS A SEPARATE FIRE RISK?

AGENCY NAME, CITY AND STATE

_____

APPENDIX 4

BIBLIOGRAPHY

Aaron, William. "Embezzlement—Detection and Control." Speech before National Retail Merchants Association EDP Conference, 1968.

Aaron gives examples of computer misuse, points out security weaknesses in keeping financial records, and gives a check list of controls.

"Accounting System Uses 'Lock and Key' to Prevent Payment Default, Copying." COMPUTERWORLD, May 20, 1970.

Discusses software product that will prevent default of payment and unauthorized copying of software packages.

Adelson, Alan. "Whir, Blink—Jackpot!" THE WALL STREET JOURNAL, April 5, 1968.

Several data processing related crimes are listed.

Allen, Brandt. "Danger Ahead! Safeguard Your Computer," HARVARD BUSINESS REVIEW, November-December 1968.

This is one of the better articles available on general security problems associated with computers.

Babcock, J. D. "A Brief Description of Privacy Measures in the RUSH Time-Sharing System," PROCEEDINGS Spring Joint Computer Conference, 1967.

A brief discussion of some security measures used in a popular time-sharing situation is provided in this paper.

192

Banzhaf, John F. III. "When Your Computer Needs a Lawyer," COMMUNI-
CATIONS OF THE ACM, August, 1968.

Possible liability (for negligence, slander of credit, implied warranty)
and legal complications are explained. Focus is also on troublespots in
contracting for data processing services, in automating record-keeping
operations, and in complying with statutes and regulations relating to
record keeping. Information is given on patents, copyrights, and trade
secret protection for programs.

Baker, H. R., P. B. Leach, C. R. Singleterry, and W. A. Zisman. "Cleaning by
Surface Displacement of Water and Oils," INDUSTRIAL AND ENGI-
NEERING CHEMISTRY, June, 1967.

This report summarizes methods for:
1. Using cleaning emulsions for rapidly removing oily coatings from
   electronic equipment.
2. Using water-displacing compositions that rapidly displace water from
   surfaces of equipment.

———, R. N. Bolster, and P. B. Leach. "Surface Chemical Methods of
Displacing Water and/or Oils and Salvaging Flooded Equipment: Part
6—Field Experience in Removing Seawater Salt Residues from Aircraft
Cockpits and AVIONICS Equipment," NRL Report 6809, Naval
Research Laboratory, Washington, D.C.

This report contains information on salvaging electronic equipment that
has been flooded with saltwater. Some of the information would help
salvage computer equipment that has been flooded because of a fire.

———, R. N. Bolster, and P. B. Leach. "Surface Chemical Methods of
Displacing Water and/or Oils and Salvaging Flooded Equipment: Part
2—Field Experience in Recovering Equipment Damaged By Fire
Aboard USS *Constellation* and Equipment Subjected to Salt-Spray
Acceptance Test," 1961 NRL Report 5680, U.S. Naval Research Lab-
oratory, Washington, D.C.

This report covers the reconditioning of electronic equipment damaged
by water, smoke, and heat during a fire.

Baran, Paul. "On Distributed Communications: IX Security, Secrecy and
Tamper-free Considerations," RM-3765-PR, RAND Corporation, Santa
Monica, Calif., 1964.

A consideration of the security aspects of distributed communication
system. Technical but worth reading. Baran presupposes there are
"spies" and proposes that systems be designed to raise the price of
illegal entry.

Bates, William. "Security of Computer-based Information Systems," DATA-
MATION, May, 1970.

General survey of computer security situation.

Behrens, Carl. "Computer and Security," SCIENCE NEWS, June 3, 1967.

This article summarizes the 1967 SJCC session of computer security.

Berg, Philip J. "The Plane Facts About Data Center Accidents," May, 1970. Available from Applied Data Research, Inc., Princeton, N.J.

Describes the data center disaster of ADR.

Bigelow, Robert P. "Legal Aspects of Proprietary Software," DATAMATION October, 1968.

Bigelow's article gives a complete survey of the proprietary software question. Copyrights, patents, trademarks, trade secrets, and contracts are covered. This is a fast-changing subject so be sure to consult latest sources.

———. "Some Legal Aspects of Commercial Remote Access Computer Services," DATAMATION, August, 1969.

Bigelow discusses legal considerations when using time-sharing services, including contracts, implied warranty security, and government involvement.

Bingham, Harvey W. SECURITY TECHNIQUES FOR EDP OF MULTI-LEVEL CLASSIFIED INFORMATION, RADC-TR-65-415, Rome Air Development Center, Griffiss Air Force Base, New York, 1965.

Contains criteria for hardware and software techniques for security control of on-line users and programming in multiprogramming, multiprocessing EDP systems. For a very complete abstract of this document, see Lance Hoffman's "Computers and Privacy: A Survey."

Binns, James. "Why Man to Man Defense for EDP Audit Control?" DATA MANAGEMENT, October, 1969.

A general discussion of the cooperation needed between the programming and audit departments.

Boni, Gregory M. "Impact of Electronic Data Processing on Auditing," THE JOURNAL OF ACCOUNTANCY, September, 1963.

This is a fairly complete look at the audit question in the pre-time-sharing system.

"Bootleg Bribe Buys Computer Time," COMPUTERWORLD, September 30, 1970.

A U.S. civilian employee reportedly bribed another government employee with a couple of bottles of Canadian liquor to obtain a run on a secret Pentagon computer.

Bride, Edward J. "Audit Trails Lost in Computerization," COMPUTERWORLD, April 29, 1970.

Daytona Beach, Florida, computerized all their record keeping. In the process they destroyed any audit trails and thus were not able to do a complete audit.

———. "DP Center Invaded," COMPUTERWORLD, July 15, 1970.

Scores of welfare recipients invaded the Boston Welfare Department's

computer center, claiming the computer was withholding their checks.

——. "Firms Offer Card, Key Systems for Data Security," COMPUTER-WORLD. August 26, 1970.

The Key reader assembly limits real-time computer access to operators possessing a properly coded plastic key. A second system is designed to limit access to computer centers.

——. "First Program Patent Issued Under New Rule," COMPUTERWORLD, June 24, 1970.

Discusses Bernhart-Fetter program patent.

Buckley, John. "The Future of Computers in Security and Law Enforcement," LAW AND ORDER, September, 1965.

Buckley covers computer security situation, but does not provide much of anything special for law enforcements groups.

"Calculated Computer Errors Manipulate Three Banks' Security; $1 Million Lost," COMPUTERWORLD, March 25, 1970.

Five men used a check-kiting scheme and computer knowledge to unlawfully gain a million dollars.

Carmichael, Dr. D. R. "Fraud in EDP Systems," THE INTERNAL AUDITOR, May-June, 1969.

Good general discussion of EDP fraud from the auditor's point of view.

Carney, P. L. "Police Say Mafia's DP Use Impedes Crime Prevention," COMPUTERWORLD, December 2, 1970.

Carr, Peter F. "Most DP Centers Lax in Arranging Backup Facilities," COMPUTERWORLD, July 15, 1970.

This article discusses the reasons computer centers should have back-up sites available.

Carroll, J. M., and P. M. McLelland. "Fast Infinite Key Privacy Transformation for Resource-sharing Systems." PROCEEDINGS, 1970 Fall Joint Computer Conference.

This paper describes a real-time software system for privacy transformation applicable to the problems of both system and user.

Chu, Albert. "Computer Security: The Corporate Achilles Heel," BUSINESS AUTOMATION, February 1, 1971.

A good survey article on computer security.

Clive de Paula, C. "Problems of Auditing Data: The External Auditor and Computers," THE COMPUTER JOURNAL, No. 3, 1960.

The author outlines a number of measures that can help verify the correctness of computer reports.

Comber, Edward V. "Management of Confidential Information," PROCEEDINGS of Fall Joint Computer Conference. 1969.

Concerned with privacy, but Comber also discusses the subject of intrusion and privacy control by computers. The author is an optimist about being able to guard individual privacy.

"Computer Center Occupied for Bargaining Position," COMPUTERWORLD, April 27, 1970.

This article provides background information leading up to the 1969 Sir George Williams University computer center disaster.

"Computer Bomb Damage Studied," COMPUTERWORLD, September 9, 1970.

Short article on University of Wisconsin Computer Center bombing.

"THE COMPUTER AND INVASION OF PRIVACY," U.S. Government Hearings, House of Representatives. July 26-28, 1966.

Rather lengthy hearings on the proposed U.S. National Data Bank. There is also some information on computer security measures.

"Computer Security," INDUSTRIAL SECURITY, December, 1969.

The complete transcript of a panel of the American Society for Industrial Security. Covers the complete security problem. Very good.

"Computer Takes Rap in Securities Swindle," DATAMATION, August, 1968, 111.

Three employees embezzled half a million dollars while blaming the computer for "computer errors."

"The Considerations of Data Security in a Computer Environment," IBM 520-2169-0.

This IBM pamphlet briefly covers the subject of time-sharing security. A little information is provided for non-time-sharing situations. Well worth reading.

"Cryptographic Package May End 360 Program Thefts," COMPUTER-WORLD, June 24, 1970.

This software package is designed to use cryptographic techniques to scramble the source coding of programs.

Dansiger, Sheldon J. "Proprietary Protection of Computer Programs," COMPUTERS AND AUTOMATION, February 1968.

Dansiger recommends marketing programs through time-sharing or data processing services. He questions the value of nondisclosure agreements.

"Data Lock." Available from Data Lock, 2745 Bernice Road, Lansing, Ill. 60438.

This sales brochure describes a product that locks disks or tapes.

"Data Security in the CDB," EDP ANALYZER, 134 Escondido Ave., Vista, Calif., May, 1970.

This 14-page report covers in some detail the problem of security in

on-line computer systems. Good survey with references.

Davidson, Timothy A. "Computer Information Privacy," THE OFFICE, August, 1969.

This article gives a little background information on the proposed National Data Bank and outlines the general threats to privacy involved. Then Davidson discusses some of the protection measures presented in the 1967 Spring Joint Computer Conference. Good introductory article.

Davis, Morton S. "Service Bureaus Need to Improve Data Security," COMPUTERWORLD, August 26, 1970.

This is one of the few articles on service bureau security. Davis points out the problems from both the customer's and the service bureau's point of view.

DeLair, W. E. "Security Responsibilities of a Time-sharing Service Company," TRANSDATA Corporation, October 25, 1969. Available from TRANSDATA Corp.

This paper discusses the problems and responsibilities of a time-sharing company.

Dennis, Robert L. "Security in the Computer Environment," SP-2440/000/01. System Development Corporation, 2500 Colorado Ave. Santa Monica, Calif. 90406, 1966.

A digest of the presentations made at a conference of the Research Security Administrators. Time-sharing and the destroying of old confidential computer information are discussed. Interesting paper.

Diamond, T. D., and J. C. Krallinger. "Controls and Audit Trails for Real-Time Systems," INTERNAL AUDITOR, November-December, 1968.

Some information provided on auditing of real-time systems. Article for auditors rather than data processing personnel.

"Diners Club Fraud Involved Printout," COMPUTERWORLD, September 18, 1968.

A stolen credit card customer list was used in a million-dollar fraud.

Duggan, Michael A. "Software Protection," DATAMATION, June, 1969.

This is a short summary of some of the questions discussed at the forum sponsored by Growth/Change Seminars in Chicago in March, 1969.

"Electronic Computer Systems 1964," National Fire Protection Association, 60 Batterymarch Street, Boston, Mass. 02110.

This is one of the two best available (See "Fire Protection for Essential Electronic Equipment") pamphlets on computer center fire protection. The price is only 60 cents.

"Employees Accused of Illegal Computer Use," DATAMATION, December, 1967, 78.

The Chicago Board of Education accused five employees of setting up a service bureau, using Board equipment.

Fanwick, Charles. "Maintaining Privacy of Computerized Data," System Development Corporation, 2500 Colorado Ave., Santa Monica, Calif. 90406, report No. SP-2647, 1966.

Charles Fanwick discusses the individual right of privacy, the potential danger of data banks, the law's view, and technology's ability to protect privacy.

"FBI Tracks Wandering Wang," BUSINESS AUTOMATION, April, 1969.

A $2,500 Wang computer was stolen from Argonne National Laboratories.

"File Security Measures," Subcommittee on Privacy and Confidentiality, Draft for California Intergovernmental Board on Automatic Data Processing, 10/18/68.

Brief discussion of proposed file security measures.

"Fire Defenses for Computer Rooms," OCCUPATIONAL HAZARDS, December, 1968.

Gives general fire protective measures for computer rooms.

"Fire Hazards in New Buildings," THE OFFICE, October, 1970.

The article has little on preventing fires, but discusses how to prevent injury or death if caught in an office building during a fire.

"Fire Protection for Essential Electronic Equipment," Federal Fire Council, Washington, D.C. 20405.

Very complete fire protection pamphlet. A must for those interested in fire protection. Available from above address.

"Firebombs Damage a Computer Center," THE OFFICE, August, 1970.

Describes the fire bombing of the Fresno State College Computer Center and lists the new security measures.

"Fortifying Your Business Security," THE OFFICE, August, 1969.

Good readable article on business security.

Freed, Roy N. "Computer Fraud—A Management Trap," BUSINESS HORIZONS, June, 1969.

Roy N. Freed gives several examples of computer-related embezzlements and then points out the legal problems that can involve managers after a computer is misused. Good article.

———. "The Role of Computer Specialists in Contracting for Computers—An Interdisciplinary Effort," PROCEEDINGS, Fall Joint Computer Conference, 1970.

Freed advises the use of computer specialists in the writing of contracts for data processing services. Some information on privacy, security, and service bureau problems included.

Gallati, Robert R. J. "Criminal Justice Systems and the Right to Privacy," PUBLIC AUTOMATION, July, 1967.

Gallati provides a very brief look at computer security.

——. "Security and Privacy Consideration in Criminal History Information Systems," Technical Report 2, July, 1970. Available from Project SEARCH, California Crime Technological Research Foundation, 1108 14th St., Sacramento, Calif. 95814.

This report is designed to serve as a reference on matters of security and privacy for all those individuals who may participate, observe, assess, or otherwise become involved in the demonstration of Project SEARCH or the development of a future system for an interstate exchange of criminal histories.

Garland, Robert F. "Computer Programs–Control and Security," MANAGE-MENT ACCOUNTING, December, 1966.

Garland does a good job of describing methods to protect programs.

"General Information Concerning Patents," Patent Office, U.S. Department of Commerce, Washington, D.C. 20231.

Provides information on general patents, but nothing in particular on computer program patents.

"General Information on Copyright," Copyright Office, Washington D.C. 20540.

Introductory information on obtaining a copyright. If interested in program copyright, also ask for program copyright circular.

Gerhard, William D. NETWORK OF COMPUTERS, National Security Agency, Fort George G. Meade, Maryland 20755.

Contains a 30-page section on computer security, but most of the information is available elsewhere.

Glaser, Edward L. "A Brief Description of Privacy Measures in the Multics Operating System," PROCEEDINGS, Spring Joint Computer Conference, 1967.

The Multics operating system at MIT is very briefly discussed.

Goodman, John V. "Auditing Magnetic Tape Systems," THE COMPUTER JOURNAL, July, 1964.

Goodman discusses methods to protect information on magnetic tapes. While the article has a wide degree of information, most of it is valid only for magnetic tapes.

"Government Offices Lose Things Too," THE OFFICE, August, 1970.

Cursory discussion of office thievery.

Graham, Robert M. "Protection in an Information Processing Utility," COMMUNICATIONS ACM, May 1968.

This paper discusses a solution to access problem by using "rings" of protection. This combination of hardware and software should help control access to shared data and procedures.

Gruenberger, Fred. "Program Testing and Validatting," DATAMATION, July, 1968.

Methods of program testing are given and common mistakes are mentioned.

Guise, Jr., Robert F. "Security and Privacy," CTSS Position Paper, Com-Share Incorporated, Ann Arbor, Mich.

This is a very general discussion of the data bank and privacy problem. Author proposes that industry regulates itself.

"Halting the Electronic Hijacker," MODERN OFFICE PROCEDURES, September, 1968.

Good general article on computer fraud. Includes a good checklist of controls.

"Halting the Electronic Hijacker," MANAGEMENT REVIEW, November, 1968.

A condensation of the article by the same name which appeared in the September 1968 issue of MODERN OFFICE PROCEDURES.

Hanlon, Joseph. "10 Students Convicted in 1969 Computer Center Burning," COMPUTERWORLD, April 29, 1970.

Discusses trial and traces events leading up to the Sir George Williams University Computer disaster. COMPUTERWORLD does the best job of covering the computer security subject.

Harrison, Annette. THE PROBLEM OF PRIVACY IN THE COMPUTER AGE: AN ANNOTATED BIBLIOGRAPHY, The RAND Corporation, Santa Monica, Calif., 1967.

Excellent—contains essay on the problem of privacy in a computer age, alphabetic annotated bibliography, and an index of all entries listed under one of 14 subject categories.

Harrison, William L. "Program Testing," DATA MANAGEMENT, December, 1969.

A special coordinated and supported testing/evaluation group is suggested.

"Has the Mafia Permeated the Computer Community?" COMPUTERWORLD, August 28, 1968, September 11, 1968.

These two articles discuss how organized crime could use data banks.

Hiles, Richard A. "Paper Shredders," MODERN OFFICE PROCEDURES, February, 1963.

A publicity blurb for paper shredders.

Hill, Jr., O. A. "The Role of the Auditor with Respect to Internal Control and Fraud," THE INTERNAL AUDITOR, May-June, 1968.

This is a good article on embezzlement, but does not have much concerning computers.

Hines, Jr., Harold H. Letter to the Editor, HARVARD BUSINESS REVIEW, May-June, 1969.

Discusses insurance protection available for the computer complex.

Hirsch, Phil. "The World's Biggest Data Bank," DATAMATION, May, 1970.

U.S. Census Bureau information is discussed and the author shows how even this supposedly harmless type of information can be used for snooping.

Hoffman, Lance J. "Computers and Privacy: A Survey," COMPUTING SURVEYS, June, 1969.

Covers privacy briefly and then surveys existing and possible proposals for computer security. Some promising research problems are introduced and an annotated bibliography is included. Of technical interest.

———. "The Formulary Model for Access Control and Privacy in Computer Systems," SLAC Report No. 117. May 1970. Stanford Linear Accelerator Center, Stanford, Calif. Available from U.S. Clearinghouse, Department of Commerce, Springfield, Va. 22151.

This thesis presents a model for engineering the user interface for large data base systems in order to maintain flexible access controls over sensitive data. Very knowledgeable author.

———, and W. F. Miller. "Getting a Personal Dossier from a Statistical Data Bank," DATAMATION, May, 1970.

Dr. Hollman and Dr. Miller explain how anyone can obtain personal dossiers from statistical data banks even though no individual identification is allowed. Very good.

Holmes, F. W. "Software Security," American Management Association Briefing Session #6373-60, April 15, 1970.

Nicely written discussion of software security, checkpoint recovery procedures, proprietary programs, documentation, and audit trails.

Holmes, W. S. "Privacy Techniques For Computerized Medical Data Systems," presented at Use of Computers in Clinical Medicine Symposium, School of Medicine, State University of New York at Buffalo, October 2-5, 1969.

Discusses some of the computer privacy problems unique to the medical field and reviews general computer security measures.

"How I Steal Company Secrets," BUSINESS MANAGEMENT, October, 1965.

Supposedly the methods used by a professional industrial spy. Interesting.

"How Safe are Your Business Secrets?" BUSINESS MANAGEMENT, March, 1968.

This article outlines precautions a company must take to protect business secrets. Good article.

"How to Make Sure Nobody Knows Your Business," MODERN OFFICE PROCEDURES, July, 1970.

Survey article on paper shredders.

"How to Protect Against the Million Dollar Racket," MODERN OFFICE PROCEDURES, March, 1968.

Good popular article on embezzlement. This article includes a list of precautions and danger signals.

"How Your Company Can Thwart a Spy," BUSINESS MANAGEMENT, October, 1965.

Good summary of how to stop the professional industrial spy.

"How Vulnerable Is the Computer System?" ADP NEWSLETTER, March 8, 1971.

Four-page computer security article. Has some good checklists.

Huggins, Phyllis. "Programmer Thankful for 'Bug' During Computer Center Bombing," COMPUTERWORLD, May 27, 1970.

Article gives details on Fresno State College Computer Center on bombing.

——. "Computer Plays Big Role in Defrauding Welfare Unit," COMPUTER-WORLD, October 7, 1970.

Los Angeles County discovered a swindle operation in the Data Processing Department of Public Services.

——. "Rebuilt Fresno State DP Center Follows Tight Security," COM-PUTERWORLD, July 8, 1970.

Lists new computer center security measures.

"Human Error," AD-689 365. Available from Clearinghouse, U.S. Department of Commerce, Springfield, Va. 22151.

A 246-page publication on ways to detect and correct input data errors.

"Individual Responsibility," DATA SYSTEMS NEWS, February, 1969.

Over 40,000 paychecks were made out illegally at the New York City Human Resources Administration. Computers were manipulated to make this $2,700,000 fraud one of the largest computer-related frauds thus far discovered.

"INDUSTRIAL SECURITY MANUAL FOR SAFEGUARDING CLASSI-
FIED INFORMATION," DD5220.22-M, Department of Defense, July
1, 1966.

This manual establishes uniform security practices within industrial
plants or educational institutions and all organizations and facilities
having classified information of the Department of Defense. Not much
help in regard to computer security.

"Introduction to CODE," 2/13/69. Available from Economatics, 225 South
Los Robles Avenue, Pasadena, Calif. 91106.

This sales brochere offers a software product which mixes extraneous
data with input/output to yield false information to those not possessing CODE.

Jackson, W. A. "Fire Protection Systems," DATA PROCESSING, March-
April, 1969.

Short article on fire protection system and good 10-point fire protection guide.

Jacobs, Morton C. "Patent Protection of Computer Programs," COMMUNI-
CATIONS OF THE ACM, October, 1964.

This is a good historical article, but much has happened since the article
was written.

Jacobson, Robert V. "Providing Security Protection for Computer Files,"
BEST'S REVIEW, PROPERTY LIABILITY INSURANCE EDITION,
June, 1970.

Lists some of the things which can happen to computer files, uses
examples, and briefly covers a few precautions. This is a shorter version
of the author's AMA speech by the same name.

Jasper, David P. "A Discussion of Checkpoint/Restart," SOFTWARE AGE,
October, 1969.

This is a very good article on checkpoint/restart. Jasper defines
checkpoint, discusses problems encountered in time-sharing situations,
and establishes criteria for determining checkpointing frequency.

John, Richard C., and Thomas J. Nissen. "Evaluating Internal Control in EDP
Audits," THE JOURNAL OF ACCOUNTANCY, February, 1970.

This is a well-documented article that shows the auditor some of the
things which must be checked when evaluating the internal control.

Koefod, Curtis F. "The Handling and Storage of Computer Tape," DATA
PROCESSING MAGAZINE, July, 1969.

Covers the problem of errors on magnetic tapes and a little on fire
protection.

Koller, Herbert R. "Legal Protection Available Now—Patents, Copyrights,"
March, 1970. Available from American Society for Information Science,
1140 Connecticut Ave., N.W. Suite 804, Washington, D.C. 20036.

Covers patents, copyrights and trademarks for software.

Lachter, Lewis E. "Preventing Business-Secret Espionage," ADMINISTRA-TIVE MANAGEMENT, December, 1965.
Very readable article on keeping business secrets.

LAW AND CONTEMPORARY PROBLEMS 31, 2 (Spring 1966).
The entire issue of this journal is devoted to privacy. Not much on the computer security problem, but good material on privacy.

Lawlor, Reed C. "Copyright Aspects of Computer Usage," COMMUNICA-TIONS OF THE ACM. October 1964.
Good introduction to subject of copyright of program, but much has happened since this was written.

Leavitt, Don. "Cipher/1 Designed for Assurance of Total File Privacy," COMPUTERWORLD, June 10, 1970.
Covers a security package that uses cryptographic techniques for file security.

"Light Plane Lights ADR's Fire," DATAMATION, January, 1970.
On November 13, 1969 an out-of-gas plane crashed into Applied Data Research, Inc. In Princeton, N.J. The plane started a fire that caused a great deal of damage to the computer center.

Lunin, Lois. "Protection Against Catastrophe: A Plan for Insuring Continuity of Information Transfer," PROCEEDINGS OF THE AMERICAN SO-CIETY FOR INFORMATION SCIENCE, Vol. 5, 1968.
Describes catastrophe protection system for providing back-up files. Includes cost figures.

Mintz, Harold K. "Safeguarding Computer Information," SOFTWARE AGE, May, 1970.
General survey article on computer security.

Molho, Lee M. "Hardware Aspects of Secure Computing," PROCEEDINGS of the Spring Joint Computer Conference, 1970.
This paper covers hardware failures and modifications which can subvert the security of time-sharing systems.

Moore, William C. "Riot Plan Worked," THE OFFICE, August, 1970.
This letter gives a short description of a riot plan that had been effectively used. Interesting.

Morton, Thomas J. "Bomb Demolishes Army Computer Complex," COM-PUTERWORLD, September 2, 1970.
Covers University of Wisconsin computer center bombing.

——. "DP Centers Dig Out in Hurricane's Wake," COMPUTERWORLD, August 19, 1970.

Corpus Christi, Texas, was hit by a 162-mph hurricane that damaged local computer centers.

———. "DP Centers Feel the Brunt of Hurricane's Fury," COMPUTER-WORLD, August 12, 1970.
Describes several damaged computer centers.

———. "FBI Accuses Youth of Tapping T/S Service, Copying Data Files," COMPUTERWORLD, July 29, 1970.
A Cincinnatti man unlawfully extracted information from a Louisville, Ky., time-sharing computer system.

———. "Firms Sue in Mailing List Theft," COMPUTER WORLD, July 8, 1970.
Three operators of Encylopedia Britannica copied 250,000 names and addresses and sold them to competitors.

———. "Psychologist Views 'Insecurity' at DP Centers," COMPUTERWORLD, July 22, 1970.
A psychologist gives several reasons for the lack of security in computer installations. Interesting.

Mroz, Gene P. "Computer 'Bug' Control," JOURNAL OF DATA MANAGE-MENT, January, 1970.
A strong involvement in the computer area is stressed as necessity for the internal auditor.

Neville, Haig. Letter to the Editor, HARVARD BUSINESS REVIEW, May-June, 1969.
Gives examples of why planned computer back-up sites are usually inadequate.

"Numbers Racket Used Data Cards," COMPUTERWORLD, June 18, 1969.
A data processing operator used 80-column cards in the passing of wagers.

Ottenberg, Miriam. "Electronic Tax Fraud Investigated at IRS," THE EVEN-ING STAR, Washington, D.C., June 24, 1970.
Two IRS computer-related frauds are discussed.

Palmer, R. R., and W. J. Duma. "Auditing with Computers," BANKER'S MONTHLY MAGAZINE, January 15, 1969.
The authors review previous approaches to audits and then propose that both audit with the computer and audit control methods are necessary.

Pauley, Charles. "Audit Responsibilities in the Design of Computerized Systems," THE INTERNAL AUDITOR, July-August 1969.
Pauley demonstrates why it is necessary for auditors to have a say in the design of computer systems. Good audit article.

Peters, Bernard. "Security Considerations in a Multi-programmed Computer System," PROCEEDINGS, Spring Joint Computer Conference, 1967.

Mr. Peters describes the security safeguards provided for a multi-programmed remote-access computer system. One of the earliest and most quoted articles available.

Petersen, H. E., and Rein Turn. "System Implications of Information Privacy," PROCEEDINGS, Spring Joint Computer Conference, 1967.

This paper discusses the technical aspects of security and privacy safeguards for a computer system. This joint paper is used in many other papers and is well worth reading.

"Plan for an Unwanted Reward," BUSINESS AUTOMATION, February, 1967.

This article discusses the disaster protection program of the computer center of the Science Information Exchange of the Smithsonian Institution, Washington, D.C.

Pratt, Lester A. "Embezzlement Controls for Business Enterprises." Order from Lester A. Pratt Company, Washington Building, 15th St. and New York Ave., Washington, D.C. 20005.

Contains fraud exposure, controls for cash receipts, cash disbursements, merchandise, and a check list of internal control procedures.

Presnick, Walter. "Protecting Your Computer's Security," DATA SYSTEMS NEWS, February, 1970.

This is a short interview with Joseph Wasserman of Computer Audits Systems.

"Program Plagiarism Alleged in U.K. Case," DATAMATION, June, 1968, 91.

Involved BOAC reservation system.

"Protection Against Fire," DATA PROCESSING IN NEW ZEALAND, March, 1970.

One-page article briefly describing a fire protection system in Auckland Savings Bank. Article too brief to be of much use.

"Protection of Records 1970," NFPA No. 232, National Fire Protection Association, 60 Batterymarch, Boston, Mass. 02110.

This pamphlet contains complete information on protection of paper-type records.

Queeney, Jack. "Computer Spies: New Worry for Business," CHICAGO'S AMERICAN, January 16, 1969.

This short article describes the computer security measures taken by three Chicago companies.

"Recommended Good Practice for the Protection of Electronic Data Processing and Industrial Automation," Factory Insurance Association, Hartford, Conn.

Provides general recommendations for prevention of fire damage to electronic equipment. Covers location, elimination of combustibles, air conditioning and smoke removal systems, control of ignition sources, fire detection, fire extinguishment, administrative and operating procedures, and standby power.

"Reconditioning of Flooded Equipment," section X of NAVAL SHIPS TECHNICAL MANUAL, Chapter 9190, preservation of Ships in Service, Navaships 0901-190-0002, January, 1970.

Lists chemicals, reconditioning equipment, and procedures for reconditioning flooded equipment.

"Record Retention Timetable," MODERN OFFICE PROCEDURES, April, 1967.

States how long records should be kept before destroying. Useful.

Rich, Theodore, "The Data Processor's Responsibility to Society," speech at the 1968 DPMA International Data Processing Conference and Business Exposition.

The speech contains a great deal about professionalism and a few quotes from articles on computer frauds.

Rofes, William. "Disaster Recovery," PROCEEDINGS OF SHARE XXXI/GUIDE 27, Vol. 2, October 1968.

Outlines protection given to vital computer records. This is a useful article.

"Safeguarding Time-Sharing Privacy—An All-out War on Data Snooping," ELECTRONICS, April 17, 1967.

Mainly a discussion of the 1967 SJCC session on privacy, but a few new facts are added on time-sharing.

Scaletta, Jr., Phillip J. "The Legal Ramifications of the Computer Age," DATA MANAGEMENT, October, 1970.

This is the first of four articles on the legal entanglements involved with computers. Some of the areas covered are: Law suit, for injury over erroneous computer output; computer output as evidence; failure to live up to expectation; patent and copyright laws; the computer and administration of justice; and the computer as a legal aid.

"Scandinavia's First Data Theft Occurs at Service Bureau." COMPUTER-WORLD, November 18, 1970.

Several tapes were copied in Stockholm and sold to customers at a reduced price.

Schiedermayer, Phil. "The Many Aspects of Computer Security," THE POLICE CHIEF, July, 1970.

Covers privacy and security. Cites examples of fraud, and discusses problems of computer security. Rather good article. The author is owner of Security Engineering Company, Lafayette, Calif.

Scoma, Jr., Louis. "Environmental Factors: How Vulnerable Are You?" Data Security Inc., 15 Spinning Wheel Road, Hinsdale, Ill. 60521.

Contains information on protecting a computer center from environmental problems.

——. "Security in the Computer Complex," COMPUTERS AND AUTOMATION, November, 1970.

This is a one-page article that lists several computer center disasters. Scoma gives six basic guidelines for protecting a data processing installation.

SDC MAGAZINE, July-August, 1967.

The whole issue is devoted to privacy and computer security. The privacy problem is traced in some detail, then computer safeguards and programming protection are briefly discussed.

"Security Men Thrive on the Wages of Fear," BUSINESS WEEK, June 20, 1970.

This article discusses the business boom in security due to fear of riots and bombings. Very little on security.

"Security Supplement," COMPUTERWORLD, August 26, 1970.

Eight pages are devoted to security problems: Software security, disaster prevention service bureaus, auditing, frauds, and insurance.

Shannon, C. E. "Communication Theory of Secrecy Systems," BELL SYSTEM TECHNICAL JOURNAL, October 1949.

Shannon develops the mathematical theory of secrecy systems, discusses level of secrecy acquired, and lists desirable qualities of secrecy systems. Mathematical paper. Good original paper.

Skatrud, Ralph O. "A Consideration of the Application of Cryptographic Techniques to Data Processing," PROCEEDINGS, Fall Joint Computer Conference, 1969.

Two digital cryptographic techniques are described: A method of digital substitution analogous to a Vernan double tape system is presented, using a controlled combination of data and the contents of two memories; the second method uses a digital route transposition matrix using a combination of row and column transposition under memory control.

——. "Computer and Cryptography," presented as part of a short course, "Privacy: Legal and Technological Protection in the Computer Age," University of California, Berkeley, October 14, 1970.

A short but complete introduction to modern cryptographic techniques suitable for computers.

Siler, James W. "Data Center Disaster." James W. Siler Business Information Services, 690 Building, The Dow Chemical Company, Midland, Mich.

Describes computer center disaster when war protestors invaded Dow Chemical computer center.

"Sticking Up a Computer," INNOVATION, No. 7, 1969.

A one-page survey of the computer crime problem. Nothing new.

Stiefel, Rudy C. "Proceedings of Carnahan Conference on Electronic Crime Countermeasures," Carnahan House, Kentucky University, Lexington, Ky., April 16-18, 1970, U.S. Department of Commerce, PB 190-589.

The "cash and checkless" society of the future has been given a great deal of discussion and publicity. There is little question that, from a technical point of view, it will become possible to execute, electronically, financial transactions from pennies to billions within fractions of a second over any distance. The key problem, however, is what protection against fraud can be obtained. Credit cards are already causing widespread concern due to fraud even without automatic features to transfer funds. Once credit cards are inserted into cash registers and the amounts deducted electronically from the owner's checking account, opportunities for fraud will multiply and further expansion will be limited until anti-fraud measures can be effected.

Supp, Robert J. "Catastrophe Prevention Management of the Computer Complex," American Management Association Briefing Session, #6373-60, April 13-15, 1970.

Provides information on Varian's disaster protection program for MIS records.

Taylor, Robert L., and Robert S. Feingold. "Computer Data Protection," INDUSTRIAL SECURITY, August, 1970.

General discussion of computer security problem for defense users. Authors predict "that many if not most of the computer data protection problems will be technically solved within the next two to five years."

"Tamperproof Computer," DATAMATION' September, 1969, 173.

Short news article announcing a 2½ year grant by the Defense Department to Edward L. Glaser to develop a fool- and theft-proof computer.

"The Thief Inside," THE OFFICE, August, 1970.

A short, general discussion about embezzlement. Little about computers.

"The Thief Outside," THE OFFICE, August, 1970.

Lists many devices that are available to prevent illegal entry.

Thompson, T. R. "Problems of Auditing Data: Internal Audit," THE COMPUTER JOURNAL, No. 3, 1960.

This is a very short paper discussing some of the auditing problems which are confronting the internal auditor in regard to computers.

Titus, James P. "Security and Privacy," COMMUNICATIONS OF THE ACM, June, 1967.

James Titus provides a good short discussion of the 1967 SJCC session on computer security.

Turn, Rein, and H. E. Petersen. "Security of Computerized Information Systems," "Proceedings of Carnahan Conference on Electronic Crime Countermeasures," Carnahan House, Kentucky University, Lexington, Ky., April 16-18, 1970, U.S. Department of Commerce, PB 190 589.

This paper addresses the vulnerabilities of remotely accessible computerized information systems to electronic crime—penetration of the information system for illicit copying, altering, or survey of the probable threats and applicable countermeasures is presented. Particular emphasis is placed on the use of cryptographic techniques for protecting information in the communication lines and in computer files.

"Twenty Students Take Over DP Center, Promise They Don't Plan Any Damage," COMPUTERWORLD, November 25, 1970.

Students took over the DP facilities of Salem State College in Massachusetts, holding it for ransom for administration acceptance of 42 demands.

Van Tassel, Dennis. "Advanced Cryptographic Techniques for Computers," COMMUNICATIONS OF THE ACM, December, 1969.

The unique characteristics of computer files are presented in regard to their influence on cryptographic techniques.

———. "Computer Crime," PROCEEDINGS, Fall Joint Computer Conference, 1970.

Several examples of computer-related crimes are told.

———. COMPUTER SECURITY MANAGEMENT, Prentice-Hall, Inc., 1972.

This book covers computer security in a complete, readable manner.

———. "Cryptographic Techinques for Computers," PROCEEDINGS, 1969 Spring Joint Computer Conference.

A general survey of cryptographic techniques, many of which are not well suited to computers.

———. "Cryptographic Techniques for Computers: Substitution Methods," INFORMATION AND STORAGE RETRIEVAL, June, 1970.

This paper deals with substitution cryptographic techniques. While some methods can be used with computer files, the use of binary number strings and masking functions is more efficient.

———. "Information Security in a Computer Environment," COMPUTERS AND AUTOMATION, July, 1969.

A general survey of computer security problems. Good for introduction to the subject.

——. "Keeping Confidential Information Condidential," JOURNAL OF SYSTEMS MANAGEMENT, February, 1969.

Elementary survey article of computer security.

Ware, Willis H. "Security and Privacy in Computer Systems," PROCEEDINGS SPRING JOINT COMPUTER CONFERENCE, 1967.

Ware briefly reviews the configuration of time-sharing systems and identifies the major vulnerabilities to penetration and leakage of information.

——. "Security and Privacy: Similarities and Differences," PROCEEDINGS, THE SPRING JOINT COMPUTER CONFERENCE. 1967.

A good discussion of privacy and security differences and similarities.

Wasserman, Joseph J. "Auditing the Computer," MANAGEMENT REVIEW, October, 1968.

This is a condensation of the article "The Vanishing Trail," which was previously published in BELL TELEPHONE MAGAZINE.

——. "Plugging the Leaks in Computer Security," HARVARD BUSINESS REVIEW, September-October, 1969.

An excellent general discussion of computer security situation. Good article for managers and executives.

——. "The Vanishing Trail," BELL TELEPHONE MAGAZINE, July-August, 1968.

This excellent article points out the changes being caused in audit trails by computers. Wasserman outlines Bell Telephone's approach to the problem.

Weiss, Harold. "Reducing the Risk of Destruction," PROCEEDINGS, 1969 International Data Processing Conference and Business Exposition.

The author mentions several types of disasters and recommends preventive measures to reduce most hazards.

——. "The Week the Computers Stopped," DATAMATION, April, 1967.

A very good fictional account showing the vulnerability of typical computer installations.

Weissman, Clark. "Security Controls in the ADEPT-50 Time-sharing System," PROCEEDINGS, FALL JOINT COMPUTER CONFERENCE. 1969.

A time-sharing security system for IBM System 360/50 is described in some detail.

——. "Trade-off Considerations in Security System Design," presented as part of a short course: "Privacy: Legal and Technological Protection in the Computer Age," University of California, Berkeley, October 14, 1970.

This paper discusses security for large-scale time-sharing systems.

Weissman points out that intruders will find it easier to penetrate an information system at its weakest link than by direct assault on hardware or software controls.

Wessel, Milton R. "Computer Services and the Law," BUSINESS AUTO-MATION, November, 1970.

This is the same article that appeared in the September, 1970, issue of COMPUTER AND AUTOMATION.

———. "Problems of Liability for the EDP Service Industry," COMPUTERS AND AUTOMATION, September, 1970.

The 1970's will see a broad expansion of the EDP service industry's liability to the two major groups affected: the public (including governments and competitors), and those with whom the industry has contractual relationships (customers, owners, employees, and suppliers). The companies that fail to recognize this and take protective action may well be among those which do not survive.

———. "Legal Protection of Computer Programs," HARVARD BUSINESS REVIEW, March-April, 1965.

Westin, A. F. PRIVACY AND FREEDOM, Atheneum, 1967, New York.

Very good book on the privacy situation. This well-documented book also contains information concerning computer use.

Whelan, Thomas. "Software Security," American Management Association Session Briefing on Catastrophe Prevention and Security Management of the Computer Complex, November 17-19, 1969.

Discusses testing procedures, environmental protection, program changes, program design, checkpoint recovery routines, and legal protection of computer software.

Witzer, Harold. "Computer Security Bibliography," September, 1970. Available from AVCO Computer Services. 201 Lowell St., Willmington, Mass. 01887.

A good bibliography of computer security articles, including keyword and author indexes, abstracts, case histories of computer disasters, and an index of security products and services.

INDEX

213

DENNIS VAN TASSEL, Computer Center, University of California at Santa Cruz, is an acknowledged expert in the field of computer security. He has published numerous articles on the subject, and with a long and distinguished career in the field is eminently qualified to write this important book.